The

GREAT MOTHER BIBLE

or, I'd rather be gardening....

Also by Mare Cromwell

If I gave you God's phone number....
Searching for Spirituality in America

Messages from Mother.... Earth Mother

The
GREAT MOTHER BIBLE
or, I'd rather be gardening....

MARE CROWELL

to Bernadette .
- you are a beautiful daughter of
the Great Mother !

mare
3/19

PAMOON
PRESS

Pamoon Press
Frederick, Maryland
www.pamoonpress.com

Published by Pamoon Press,
an imprint of Matierra, LLC.

Grateful acknowledgement is made to the following for permission
to reprint previously published material:

Dale Allen, for the prayer "Our Mother". © Dale Allen.
David Spangler, for the "Water Spirit Message". © David Spangler.
Boysen Hodgens, for the poem "The New Macho". © Boysen Hodgens.
Mary J. Getten, for her excerpt from *Communicating with Orcas;*
The Whales' Perspective by Mary J. Getten, © 2006. Reprinted by arrangement
with Mary J. Getten.

ISBN 978-0-9717032-6-1

Library of Congress Control Number: 2014910239

Designed by Octavo Designs/www.8vodesigns.com
Cover Image by Brenda Murphy/www.bdmillustration.com
Author photograph by Marcia Wiley

Pamoon Press
Frederick, Maryland
www.pamoonpress.com

Printed in the United States of America.

1   3   5   7   9   10   8   6   4   2

First Edition

Five percent of the net profits from sales of this book will go toward ecological
restoration/tree planting efforts in the Chesapeake Bioregion and the Amazon.

Dedicated to the memory of
Katherine Carter

and

To all the spiritual teachers, seen and unseen,
who have graced me with
their wisdom and love.

Mother's Thirteen Love Directives & Precepts

Updated from *Messages from Mother.... Earth Mother*

(Pamoon Press, 2012)

1. *I, Earth Mother, gave the planet a song. Come to know you are part of this song as one in the vast web of life, no greater, no less. All that you do affects the song, for better or worse.*

2. *Your thoughts, whether from your higher self or lower self, affect the song as much as your actions, although your Western culture has denied this for a long time.*

3. *Everything has consciousness. The stones, plants, even mountains, rivers and oceans—all join in the song. Know that your thoughts and actions are registered in the song and affect the stones, plants, animals, mountains and waters, in support of the positive universe or not.*

4. *Develop silence of the mind and cultivate thankfulness from this place. Deep gratitude is one of the most positive things you can do for Mother and all others in the song, especially those very sensitive and intelligent ones such as the whales and dolphins who are so closely attuned to the song.*

5. *Fear that comes from your head is an illusion. Fear that comes from your instincts is not. Learning to discern between the two will help still your mind and allow it to be in the moment.*

6. *The song is most harmonious within an energy dance of authenticity, love, compassion, tenderness, patience and cooperation. It is good to learn this dance with all beings with whom you interact, whether two-legged, four-legged, winged, finned or standing ones (trees), or stone people.*

7. *Come to understand your shadow self. Make the act of bringing it to consciousness to heal it part of the dance and celebration.*

8. *It is all just energy—your money, time, job, play, and your love. Choose to make it as positive as possible and lose the illusion of fear within this energy dynamic.*

9. *The foremost energy is Love—a quality of love that transcends what most of you call love. Mother loves you. Creator loves you. You all evolved from Love. Evolution is an act of Love.*

10. *Know that the perception of perfection is an illusion. You as two-leggeds are the most beloved and delightfully flawed beings and that is how it is meant to be. You are perfect in your imperfections, and this makes you all the more lovable.*

11. *Know and honor your Mother as you honor your Creator. And if you want to put an icon of me on an altar, that's fun. But any other graven images are not needed.*

12. *Have fun! Life is a celebration! Life is an adventure!*

13. *The more you celebrate life, the more you help your Mother to heal all over the planet. By celebrating you encourage the whales and dolphins and all others in the song to sing more harmoniously with you!*

And here are my Precepts:

- *Touch me, your Mother, every day. Touch my skin, my earth. Let my healing energy come into you to calm you and heal you. Send your love energy back into me also ... I yearn for you to consciously do this.*

- *Do not gouge my, your Mother's, skin or break into my bones.*

- *Do not create compounds that will last longer than the very short term out in nature.*

- *Honor the forests and replant trees.*

- *Honor the wetlands and restore them.*

- *Do not waste.*

- *Clean up your rooms. Big and small.*

- *Live in community. All are part of the community. Everyone's needs should be taken care of by the community. Share.*

- *Listen with an open heart.*

- *Speak with an open heart.*

- *Be lean of judgment and speech.*

- *Be open to the mystery that lies in people and the world around you.*

- *Be compassionate with yourself.*

CONTENTS

~ *Mother's Thirteen Love Directives & Precepts*

1. Surrender, Listen, and Show Up 15
2. Why *The Great Mother Bible* 25
   – *Who is the Great Mother* 26
3. The Quantum Divine Love of Creation and Earth Mother 33
4. Miracle-Mindedness When You Surrender 39
   – *About Soul Contracts* 43
5. The Universe is the Greatest Recycler 45
6. The Sacred Wise Circle 51
7. Fear and Cultural Conditioning 59
   – *The Multiverse, Nature Spirits and More Here on Earth* 65
8. Aliens on Earth 73
9. The Christ Consciousness 81
10. Soul Woundedness 89
11. On the Catholic Church and God-Woundedness 95
12. Sacred Fire 107
13. Gratitude 115
14. Walking the Beauty Way 121
    – *Listen with an Open Heart* 122
    – *Speak with an Open Heart* 123
    – *Be Lean of Judgment and Speech* 123
    – *Be Open to the Mystery That Lies in People and the
       World Around You* 123
    – *Be Compassionate With Yourself* 124
    – *Have a Generous Spirit* 125
    – *Find Respect for All* 125
    – *Cultivate Silence* 126
15. Sin is an Illusion, Right Action & Wrong Action Are Not 129
16. Nuclear Testing, Toxins and Entropy 133
17. Healing the Sacred Feminine - Divine Masculine Wound 139
18. Love and *Love* 149
19. More Magic and Miracles 153
20. Responses to the *Sincere Apology to the Divine Masculine* 157
21. On the Balance 161
22. To Embody Our Sacred Feminine & Divine Masculine Self 167

23. A Woman's Sacred Belly, Kali & Kuan Yin, & Hugging
    Our Planet...173
24. Messengers, Messiahs & Mary Magdalene.........................181
25. Thoughts, Energy, the Shadow & Technology...................189
26. A Different Take on Extinction...199
27. Earth Mother Communicates with Us—When We
    Pay Attention...201
28. Intentional Suffering is not Prerequisite to Spiritual Growth........209
29. Soup Love and More Love 215
30. Tree Spirits, Ice Storms & Sustainability 217
31. The Miraculous Medal and Virgin Mary.............................233
32. Earth Changes, Rainbow People & Shifting Dimensions.............239
33. The Virgin Mary & Earth Mother.....................................245
34. Earth Mother Never Abandoned Us—We Abandoned Her.........249
35. Food of the Gods 251
36. A Message from Granny..265
37. The Conversation Never Ends 269
38. And Never Ends—But That's Okay, Too! 279

Our Mother who art within us,
Each breath brings us to you.
Thy wisdom come,
Thy will be done,
as we honor your presence within us.
You give us this day all that we need.
Your bounty calls us to give and receive
all that is loving and pleasurable.
You are the courage that moves us to be true to ourselves
and we act with grace and power.
We relax into your cycles of birth,
growth, death and renewal.
Out of the womb, the darkness, the void, comes new life.
For you are the Mother of All Things.
Your body is the Sacred Earth and our bodies.
Your love nurtures us and unites us all.
Now and forever more.

—Dale Allen

1

Surrender, Listen and Show Up

> *If we surrendered to earth's intelligence*
> *we could rise up rooted, like trees.*
> —Rainer Maria Rilke

To start, I'm not certain I'm qualified to be writing a book titled *The Great Mother Bible*. The name was given to me by Mother in mid-November, 2013.

It was 5 AM on a Sunday morning, November 17th of that year. I was woken up by Mother and heard the distinct instructions: "You are not going to move to Washington State. Instead you are to hunker in this winter and write your next book. It will be called *The Great Mother Bible*."

So much for the plans I had to move to the West Coast at the end of December.

This was not the first time I'd been woken up very early in the morning with a message from Mother. This was how my second book, *Messages from Mother.... Earth Mother*, was written in five whirlwind weeks during the summer of 2012—essentially I was repeatedly woken up quite early for some intense listening and writing.

I assumed it was Earth Mother whom I was hearing. Several gifted Native medicine people have confirmed I am closely tuned in with Earth Mother. During this writing process I came to learn it is the Great Mother and Earth Mother who communicate with me.

I'm a *Listener*. Some might say I'm a mystic. I can tune in to the spiritual realms and receive messages. Sitting in a beautiful garden on a sunny day can bliss me out. I'm not alone in having these gifts. I've met a number of people who are *Listeners*, who are far more gifted than I am. Most are guided to be quiet about their listening and follow Spirit's direction in the work they do. I'm supposed to share these messages in my writing.

Let's just say I was stunned by this message in November, 2013 though, and balked. I told Mother I'm not the one to write a book with such an auspicious title. What I heard back was: "Yes, you are. You're the one and you have all you need to do this. Just listen and write. Trust in me." I resisted for several weeks but continued to receive the same message. Along with the message that she loved me very much.

I need to go back a bit further....

Since January of 1997, I have been studying with Native American medicine people. I apprenticed for fourteen years with a gifted Cherokee teacher and then sought teachings from a variety of other medicine people associated with different native traditions: Algonquin, Mohawk, Hawaiian, Okanagon/Cherokee and others.

I also have been an ardent environmentalist since my college days. For most of my life I've known my work here is to serve Earth Mother, though I did not perceive her as an Earth Mother with her own actual consciousness during my environmental career. I'm deeply passionate about helping our society learn how to be more sustainable and come to embrace the sacredness of our beautiful planet Earth.

After leaving an international environmental career in my mid-thirties, I transitioned to writing and professional gardening for seventeen years, along with part-time environmental work. The gardening, along with studies with a Cherokee teacher, opened my senses up to communicating with plants to hear their wisdom. Trees can impart such truth and love. Every individual plant has a consciousness and a specific spiritual/energetic resonance common to its species. There are plant spirit medicine healers who call on the spiritual consciousnesses of plants to heal their clients, and do quite beautiful work.

Over time I've come to be able to tune in to Spirit beyond the plants and this is most humbling. In 2001, I was limping along on year six of writing my first book, *If I gave you God's phone number.... Searching for Spirituality in America*. The murky—and unpaid—writing process had gotten so frustrating I shelved the manuscript and focused on the environmental and gardening work instead.

One evening as I was praying in front of my altar (as taught to me by my Cherokee teacher), a distinct voice came into my head that said: "We have brought you here to this house and it is time now for you to finish the book."

Some might think I'm schizophrenic. But I knew this was a clear message from Spirit. At that point I had been studying with the Cherokee teacher for five years and she conversed with so many spiritual beings it was hard for me to keep track of them. She was constantly chatting with Earth Mother, Creator, people's spirit guides, the birds, squirrels, her cats and dog and more. And they all spoke back to her. This is the way of many a medicine person. So I accepted that Spirit could have some specific messages for someone. Even me.

I took the spiritual message very seriously and right after receiving it I rearranged my life to prioritize the completion of the "God's Phone Number" book. It was published in 2002 and recognized in several national book competitions the following year.

Following the publication of that first book, there were a number of starts and stops on different manuscripts but nothing fully grabbed my attention for the next ten years. Then in late spring of 2011, I was diagnosed with enlarged lymph nodes in my abdominal area. The doctor was not saying "lymphoma" yet but was quite concerned about my health.

To the chagrin of that physician, I was confident I could heal this cancer outside of her domain and outside her colleagues' offices too. Prior to this diagnosis, I had experienced a number of intensely unpleasant past-life memories related to my wombspace, and my instincts told me the lymphoma was blocked energy in my system. I set off on a journey exploring alternative medicine and was guided to homeopathy, herbs, supplements, acupuncture, Chi Gong, and more.

However by early June of 2012, I was not feeling that well. I went back for a new CT scan and it was verified that the lymph nodes were more enlarged. The doctors were definitely stating lymphoma then and I was terrified.

The CT scan was on June 4, 2012. Four days later I was with an Algonquin medicine man I had met the year before, to do a ceremony for Earth Mother in New England. He worked closely with Mother and communicated with her often. Mother had specifically requested he and I do a ceremony that would help "heal her" (her words), just the two of us. I prayed this ceremony might also help me as I drove north to meet him. Cancer is not a fun label to have thrown at you.

The ceremony was held in a beautiful wild park. Before we started, the Algonquin man explained he was going to be bringing Earth Mother's consciousness and energy into my spirit body, yet he was not sure how I would separate from Mother afterwards. I was not concerned though. I knew my life's work was to serve Mother and trusted she would take care of it all. It was just a relief not to be thinking about the lymphoma and to be doing ceremony on a beautiful late spring day in a remote wooded park.

I am guided to not share the details of that afternoon other than there was a palpable shift in my spirit body during it that has never left me.

Several days after the ceremony in New England, I experienced another intense spiritual event. I was in a healing session with a woman who leads music-evoked therapy to help clients work through deep emotional issues. As I listened to the last piece of music in the session, the sound of ocean waves on a beach, I distinctly felt the presence of a powerful dolphin consciousness in the room and heard it call me to the ocean! The healer played the piece again at my request. The second time it was the dolphins and whales calling me to the ocean! I could feel their spiritual presences in the room and hear their specific invitation. This had never happened to me before, but I just knew it was they and Mother at work.

I had to go to the beach. I had just been diagnosed with lymphoma and would follow Mother's guidance anywhere it led if it would help me recover from cancer. I felt deeply scared and deeply surrendered at the same time. Everything inside me told me I didn't need doctors at a medical institution to heal this.

Somehow I understood the path of *Thy Will Be Done* was my best option. Mother was in control of my life at that point. Surely I was not.

I would be lying if I said surrendering to Spirit is easy. It can be a joyous path and a grueling one too. The grueling aspects arise from the ego being unbalanced, fear and resistance. Surrendering is akin to peeling layers off an onion. There have been more and more layers of surrender to test me. And there will be more still, to be sure.

I'm quite good at procrastination and resistance as a rule. Believe me, I'd rather be paid to garden for clients, a rather peaceful and beautiful vocation. And eat bonbons at night. Then the not-so-magical word *cancer* knocked at my door.

I went to various doctors' offices for some obligatory follow-up during that June of 2012. One surgeon was reluctant to biopsy me since it meant invasive surgery. I sought out a new primary care physician open to alternative medicine, and her office computer system went completely down while I was there. This had never happened in her office before. I was guided not to visit her again.

My system is so sensitive I knew the allopathic drugs the doctors would want to give me would knock me out and I'd feel worse. Whenever I tuned in to Mother, she just kept on telling me to steer clear of the doctor's drugs and trust her, and all would be fine. *Surrender, Listen and Show Up*. That became my credo.

Ten days later in late June of 2012, I booked a hotel room in Chincoteague, Virginia, to commune with the Mother Ocean at the wild beaches of Assateague. It was only a three-hour drive from the house I was renting in Western Maryland. Those three days are now a complete blur as I just followed moment-by-moment guidance from Mother.

I did ongoing ceremony on the beach and in the hotel room. My first night, a park ranger actually kicked me off the beach in the dark since they shut their gates at 10 PM. I know he thought I was a bit whacked. I had to finish the ceremony in the hot, sticky car when I got back to the hotel, keeping the mosquitoes at bay with the windows sealed tight.

The spiritual instructions came in very clearly. The first night I was told I needed to put aside another manuscript started that winter (on the Sacred Feminine and my healing journey) and I was to create another book. It was to be called *Messages from Mother…. Earth Mother.* I was given the entire table of contents for the book. I was also given messages from the dolphins and whales, and instructed to keep those private. Then I downloaded the first full message from Mother. That became "Message Twelve – To My Daughters" in the *Messages from Mother* book. I had a basic writing pad (recycled paper—of course) and copiously wrote down all I heard as fast as I could.

I was even woken up at 4 AM on the second night to claim the domain for the book on the Internet. Then I was instructed to go directly to the beach and do a sunrise smudge ceremony[1] right afterwards. It was exhausting and I was in a bit of an altered state by the time I headed home.

Mother told me very clearly during that trip that by surrendering on this level to her, she would take care of me and I would heal from the lymphoma. I just needed to trust her. This arrangement was far more preferable than going the allopathic route of toxic chemotherapy and more.

For the next five weeks I was rousted by Mother very early each morning and instructed on what to write. And believe me, I'm not a morning person so that was quite different for me. The *Messages from Mother…. Earth Mother* manuscript poured out so fast it was completed by early August.

This new-found listening gift overwhelmed me and a big part of me wanted to run away to some far away mountains and hide in a cabin as soon as the manuscript was done. I felt quite insecure about how the whole book was created. Most in our society do not necessarily understand this type of spiritual listening. To Earth Mother, no less. To listen to God, yes. But Earth Mother? Most people don't even believe she exists other than as a hard rock with a biosphere on the outer rim, one that we live within.

---

[1]Smudge ceremony: an ancient spiritual practice still followed by indigenous peoples all over the world involving burning of sacred herbs with prayers to bless oneself and one's physical environment.

But Mother would not allow me to go hide. After all, hadn't I surrendered to her? The instructions were that the book needed to go to print ASAP. Thus I quickly shifted into self-publishing gear, found a graphic designer for the book cover, editors, and printer. The final polished hard copies of the book were delivered to my house by the end of October. That's extremely fast for producing a book.

In July, I also found a new physician who accepted my aversion to Western medicine and my determination to heal outside of it. After seeing the lymph nodes were not getting bigger by early August, he gave me a long rein of six months to come back again for more scans in the winter of 2013. Ah ... let's just say I canceled that appointment as the date approached.

It was only because of a gallbladder attack in late November of 2013—which required a new CT Scan of my entire abdominal area—that it was medically verified my lymph nodes were back to normal. Though I already knew it. When I saw him after the surgery my physician chuckled and told me he considered me the best miraculous healing story.

This is not to say I didn't experience some very uncertain days about my health from the summer of 2012 through fall of 2013. There were days I did not feel that well and contemplated the path that cancer could take in my body. There were many long stares of despair, out the window and into the forest outside the house I was renting, and many long chats with Mother about my condition as well. She repeatedly told me to trust and go up into the mountains near where I lived in Maryland and soak my feet in the shockingly cold mountain streams. And dance more. Plus she continually reminded me to not take everything so personally and learn to cease stuffing my emotions into my wombspace.

The few times I seriously weighed whether to call my doctor back to take the allopathic route, some miraculous healing event would happen to make it unnecessary. One time it was in an impromptu ceremony with another Native American friend that was not meant to be for me but for him. That ceremony sent a tremendous amount of healing energy through me. Other times it was with other healers and ceremonies where beautiful boosts of energy came through. It was all quite humbling and clearly indicated that Mother did not want me to go back to the doctors.

It was shortly before my gallbladder attack that the very clear instructions came from Mother to cancel my moving plans to Washington State and set the winter aside for writing this book. The *Messages from Mother* book had been out for a year and had not taken off as I had hoped and I was searching for the next step in my life. I was surviving off minimal book sales, one small gardening client in Western Maryland, and primarily my savings account.

And then—boom!—Mother gave me the assignment of another book. To be titled a *Bible* no less. Go figure.

When I can get beyond my occasional tsunami of fears, I can see Mother is taking care of me, in amazing ways. I've been so blessed.

Waking Up to the Great Mother

I did not know about the Great Mother as a child. Yes, I was taught about the Virgin Mary, but not the Great Mother as I have come to understand her in recent years. I was raised Catholic in an upper-middle class family in Baltimore, Maryland. The introduction to my first book, *If I gave you God's phone number.... Searching for Spirituality in America*, chronicles some of my journey away from the "Catholic-Great Father" belief system.

When I reflect back, my reason for leaving the Catholic Church at the time was because there was no joy in the services, no sense of connecting to a Divine Love or Spirit. The only thing I experienced were rote prayers and responses to the priest magnified by a sense of spiritual heaviness. I realized in college I was only attending the services to please my parents. It was time to claim my personal spiritual path, away from their expectations and conditioning. That became a multi-year process. Walking away from the Catholic Church was the first step.

Upon graduation from college, equipped with a shiny-new degree in biology and environmental studies, I headed directly out west to work in the National Park Service as a park ranger. First I was stationed at the bottom of the Grand Canyon and then at Denali National Park in Alaska for two summers. I was paid to hike in the wilderness seasonally for some three years, a job I still find remarkable. In retrospect, the wilderness became my church, though I could not have defined it that way at the time.

I'm certain all my years of playing outside as a young child, escaping my parents' arguments by slipping into the nearby woods and fields alone or with siblings, instilled a deep love of nature within me. There was always a sense of wholeness and peacefulness outside in the woods and fields. I've continued to work outside, between desk responsibilities, in some of the more beautiful places on the North American continent, along with stunning gardens—Nature could be considered my spirituality. I would not call Nature-love a religion, however.

There is something about pure wilderness and the spiritual energy of such places, especially Alaska where the days are so long and there is an incredible vitality to the land in those short summers. Everything is so vibrant and bursting with joy with the long sunlight hours. I hiked on my off days with friends and soaked up the pure energies of the land. I never felt so alive and spiritually connected as when I hiked there. Farley Mowat wrote in *Never Cry Wolf* about the sense of childhood joy that can manifest when one spends days in the tundra wilderness. It's true. Glorious exuberance overcame me time and time again.

I do think something deeper has been at play throughout my life though. When I was ten, I named my second cat "Mother Nature" or "Nature" for short. I don't know why I did that. I just felt called ... perhaps Mother was already working on me then, dropping little hints in my ear about how much love she had for me, and I for her. I do know I loved that cat to bits and it tore me apart when I eventually had to put her to sleep nineteen years later.

When I returned back east after the seasonal work in the Park Service out west, I collapsed into a low-grade depression. It was rough culture shock returning to the highly developed East Coast after months in the Alaskan wilderness. I eventually sought out therapy and yoga to calm my troubled mind and heart in the midst of pursuing a career in environmental education—getting a Masters at the University of Michigan and then working internationally. I discovered a large ashram in Western Massachusetts and attended numerous yoga retreats over seven years, even becoming a disciple of a Hindu guru during the last year of studying there. Then the guru was forced out of the ashram for sexual indiscretions.

The guru's departure set me adrift spiritually. Feeling lost, I went spirituality shopping and sampled Unitarian churches, meditation groups and more for two years. At age thirty-seven, thanks to a new friend in Baltimore I met shortly after returning to my hometown, I landed at the doorstep of a Cherokee medicine woman, and everything just fell into place. Her teachings made so much sense and my path on the *Red Road* commenced, though I now term what I was experiencing as the *Great Mother Road*. The Cherokee teacher was the first person I discovered who talked about Earth Mother so intimately. She woke me up to the presence of a very earthy Mother/planetary consciousness who very much exists but has been largely ignored.

I have not looked back since.

The Cherokee teacher healed me of chronic depression in just two sessions the first month I studied with her. Within several months of studies with her, I realized I needed to 'unlearn' so much of what the Western Judeo-Christian culture had taught me. My worldview and understanding of Spirit and spirituality dramatically shifted. I had found a path or a way that opened me up and healed me beyond anything I could have anticipated. This path has helped me cultivate an inner Godspace and connection with the Great Mother in ways I am challenged to put into words other than bliss. I've also come to embrace the Christ Consciousness more deeply through this path. It's been an amazing journey of waking up more and more, though, in truth, I'm still a beginner on the path.

My apprenticeship with the Cherokee teacher extended fourteen years. Essentially, I walked away when our relationship had exhausted itself. I knew it was time to move on. Parting company with her in the early winter of 2010 propelled me to seek out some other native teachers and healers to continue my studies.

The Creatrix

It was a rough transition leaving the Cherokee teacher, akin to a bad divorce. I was very confused and in search of guidance. A good friend referred me to a gifted healer and pipe carrier who lived quite simply in a dilapidated cabin with holes in the porch and water damaged walls in the western mountains of Maryland. (A pipe carrier is someone who has studied for years and is deemed spiritually advanced enough to work directly with Spirit through the sacred pipe to offer prayers and spiritual guidance to others.) The man had spent years studying with Lakota teachers.

During the ceremony, to my surprise and his, Spirit guided him to actually hand the pipe to me so that I could tune directly into Spirit myself. Usually he conveyed the messages from Spirit to the other person. This was one of my first experiences where I realized I could tune in and listen on that level.

At the end of the ceremony, he told me his spirit guides liked me a lot. And, he added, the Great Mother—he called her the Creatrix—was very fond of me also. He shared how powerful she was and that she could be destructive and glorious, and her power was 'hot!' I so wished I had a tape recorder to capture all he shared during that afternoon.

As soon as he referred to the Creatrix as 'hot!', he caught himself and muttered he'd already said too much. Standing across from him in his simple living room, I was stunned, trying to absorb all he said. This was the first time I'd heard anyone refer to a feminine aspect of the Great Mystery/Creator. Up until that moment, I had only been taught about a masculine Father God/Creator as the Great Mystery. Even the Cherokee teacher had implied the Great Mystery was masculine with her teachings about connecting with the masculine Creator and feminine Earth Mother—as a way of connecting with the Divine balance.

The healer also shared that the Creatrix said I have the capacity to become a priestess of hers. I was taken back by that. My initial response was I was highly flattered and humbled by this, but was not sure what being a priestess meant. He encouraged me just to sit with it and see what came up over time. As I drove home late that afternoon, my thoughts spun as to whether I needed to seek out a Priestess School or not . Yet that did not feel right. Again, the wise truism of just *listen and show up* seemed to point out the best path.

Just as I was leaving his cabin, the healer also relayed the Creatrix would like for me to create an altar to her specifically. He reached over to a shelf and removed a small figurine of Kuan Yin, the Buddhist Goddess of compassion and mercy, and handed her to me. "Here take this, maybe you could use her for it," he said.

As I returned home that day with Kuan Yin stuffed into my winter jacket pocket, I pondered the existence of the Creatrix and who she really was. Why would the Great Mother like me so much? I had been feeling like a confused woeful person that winter after leaving that Cherokee teacher. Why would the Creatrix like me?

~

Note to Beloved Reader:

In writing this book, I struggled with the distinction between *Great Mother* and *Earth Mother*. At one point, I connected with *Mother* and asked her specifically for further explanation on the difference between the two of them. I was told: *"While <u>Earth Mother</u> is your planetary caretaker and actual planet, she embodies an archetypal energy that is part of the Great Mother. And, they are both part of the <u>Oneness</u>. <u>Creation</u> is the <u>Great Mystery</u>, as the <u>Great Father</u> and <u>Great Mother</u> merged into <u>Oneness</u>.*

Also, for many, *Creator* carries a more masculine connotation.

Having written all that—the names are actually not important and can quickly morph into dogma, which is farthest from what I am guided to write spiritually. The real *truth* is the Quantum Divine Love that is beyond words that encompasses all of them. *And* that the Sacred Feminine has been ignored for far too long, along with recognizing our Earth as embodying the Sacred Feminine. And it's time for *Balance* and *Harmony*.

Hugs, Big Love to all,
    —mare

2

....

Why *The Great Mother Bible?*

*I am waking up your heart. I am transforming you from the inside out.
I am making permanent changes in you, so that you can never go back to
the pain and suffering of the past. Stay with me.*

—Divine Mother, facilitated by Connie Huebner

Thursday, January 2, 2014
5:10 AM
26° Light snow forecast for the day.

*The spiritual listening and writing within this book started officially on Thursday,
January 2nd, 2014. As was Mother's style, I was woken up very early that winter
morning. The holidays were over and it was time to get started.*

Great Mother: Get up, get up, get up … Mare … yes, I know it's close to 5
AM but it's time for you to get up. I love you so very, very much. I love all
my humans so, so much and all of your collective foibles, your weaknesses
and your great hearts and strengths. I love you all so unconditionally.

Mare, you have been asking me about this book I want you to write.
It's time for us to get started now.

This book, yes, I have asked you to write this with me, and for me.
There is a reason I gave you the title *The Great Mother Bible* in November
and I wish for you to keep this title for the book.

For several thousand years, there has been another book called the *Bible* read by millions. It speaks to a religion or set of religions (Judaism and
Christianity) that offer religious/spiritual direction primarily from a Great
Father perspective. The original *Bible* offers some beautiful spiritual wisdom,
yet it has been written and rewritten from a strongly patriarchal perspective.

It is time for another book to be offered, a book offering spiritual wisdom and guidance that sources from a more maternal lens on spirituality. There have been too many centuries of patriarchal, controlling religious teachings that have created much imbalance on me these days. Frankly things have started to run amok.

This is this book. It could easily be three thousand pages of teachings and guidance, woven with lovely stories. But I can't ask you, Mare, to write a three thousand-page book this year. I'm asking you to set aside this winter and spring and listen to me and get these more important teachings down.

We will chat. You will have questions for me about what I'm nudging you to write. You will even have questions about your personal life and I will try to help you with those as your questions are likely to be the same ones that many other humans grapple with also.

It is time to bring balance back to this most amazing planet. It is time for healing to take place on so many levels and for you, my beloved ones, to remember me and bring me back into your hearts so you can learn to live sourcing from a Divine maternal and paternal love in balance. Things have gotten more than a bit *off* on Earth and this needs to come to an end. A New World is being born these days that will be more balanced. This book, *The Great Mother Bible*, will be one of many tools to help birth this New World.

Oh, and just because this book is called *The Great Mother Bible* is not meant to imply the original *Bible* needs to be replaced completely. This book is to serve as a companion book written from the perspective of the Divine Mother. There is beautiful spiritual wisdom to be found in the original *Bible*. May it still teach and touch those who open it up. And may they also come to understand that book was compiled by a set of religions that did not recognize me, the Great Mother, as they could have. It is time to right that.

And yes, your other book, *Messages from Mother.... Earth Mother*, is a prequel to this book.

Who is the Great Mother?

Very few of you know me, so I need to start by introducing myself. You know of the Great Father/God/Allah/ Creator—choose your term—but not truly about me, the Great Mother. I've been mostly shunted to the side for several thousand years and it's time for me to be recognized as much as the Great Father.

Most of you were not raised with much awareness, if any, of me. I am the feminine aspect of the Great Mystery. Your religions have taught you about God, Allah, Yahweh, etcetera, as the Creator Father but there has been minimal discussion about me, the Great Divine Compassionate Mother, in your places of worship for many, many centuries.

Ah … I am as difficult to define as the Great Mystery or God. I am the *Creatrix*. I am the Great Goddess. I am that beyond description, beyond understanding … beyond religion … beyond dogma.

I am.

Yet that is challenging for you humans to grasp since most of you need something more tangible to help you understand. Perhaps if you perceived me as the greatest Mother figure you've ever experienced, of compassion, gentleness, and love exponential, then you would *begin* to understand. But I am far more than that, as I am beyond your limited human concepts. My energy swirls in every single thing in the universe in dynamic balance with the sacred masculine energies.

I am embodied here on Earth within the powerful consciousness of your Planetary Caretaker, *Earth Mother*. Your planet has a spiritual consciousness and there are those such as you, Mare, who can listen to her.

In balance with the Great Father, I am the procreative force that birthed all of you into existence—including all the four-leggeds, winged ones, finned ones and more—through Earth Mother. The full evolution of stunning biodiversity and energy dances and water cycles and breath-taking flowers and so much more source from my and Creator's love.

I am also embodied in all life on Earth, in all the women and men, stones, insects, trees, all matter on your planet. My energy dances in the very atoms of your cells as part of the Great Mystery and sacredness of life. Your bodies are made up of the sacred minerals, water, nutrients and energies that pulse, cycle and move over Earth Mother's skin. I am there in all.

I am the Great Mother force that can be as gentle as a morning mist, whose capacity for forgiveness, softness and procreativity are huge. Absolutely huge. Or I can rage like a flood-swollen river.

I am the Sacred Feminine force.

I am within the One.

But enough about introducing myself. It feels silly for me to do this yet it's necessary, since few of you have grown up with any real concept of me. But I'm here. I certainly am here. I have been all along.

I yearn for all of you to reach out to accept my love. Reconnect with me since my love is there for you all the time. But most of you have not learned this. I'm here for you, waiting.

The teachings within this book will come from both the Great Mother and Earth Mother. Yet I will be speaking through Earth Mother most of the time. I know you, Mare, can discern between the two of us and our energies, and for this, we love you.

Mare: Mother, it is true I can sense your energy. Or energies. This is new for me. This has been happening since November but I haven't been sure. Part of the time I'm rather certain you are Earth Mother with her sense of humor and grounded, somewhat gritty energy that reminds me of a tough old woman who's been living off the land on some remote mountain for a long time and won't take any shit.

And other times you feel more—this is so hard to put into words— you feel softer, larger, ephemeral yet powerful, and there is a different quality to your wisdom that is timeless, if that makes any sense. It's helpful for me to hear I'm tapping into both of you.

Yet, if this is really who you are, I'm not sure how it is I'm talking with you, the Great Mother, too? Is this really you? The Great Mother? It was enough to think I was communicating with Earth Mother. I mean, I'm just a bumbling two-legged ... really.

When I was writing my second book and receiving the messages from Earth Mother, for some reason that did not feel as daunting as communicating with you, *the* Great Mother.

Then I was woken up so early in November and I thought it was Earth Mother who was yammering at me that morning. I told a good friend you had given me the book title *The Great Mother Bible*, and I joked with that friend about how 'This is No Small Change'. We laughed about that being the subtitle of the book. First, with the word *Bible* in the title. And then the term *Great Mother*.

But you're confirming you're *the* Great Mother as in *the* Great Goddess. Ah, did I really sign up for this level of work?

Mother: I love you, daughter. So much I love you. I think you might already know the answer to that question. Yes, honey, you did. And as I told you then ... you are the one. Just listen and you will be guided.

Mare: Mother ... I love you also. Of course I love you. I can't believe how much love I feel in myself these days, for you, for others. It's so amazing.

And I'm listening. Even though I do have moments of doubt still. It's just I thought I had surrendered to Earth Mother. I guess surrendering to her means surrendering to you, the Great Mother, also? It's been degrees of giving myself over to you, both of you, more and more deeply. Now here I am in bed listening to you on a cold, early Thursday morning in January in Western Maryland. This is very humbling. Very.

Mother: Sweetie, all the years of stillness working in your clients' gardens, studies with the medicine people, and learning to let go of your cultural conditioning have opened you up to the capacity to listen spiritually. You also did that ceremony to me and Earth Mother with the Algonquin medicine man.

There is so much love to tap into when you deeply connect with me and the Great Father. My energy as the Great Mother is more ephemeral, and extends throughout the universe as a sacred vibration in balance with the divine masculine vibration, the other half of Creation. Sometime you humans refer to your mates as your 'better half'. In this case, there is no better or worse. It is balanced and always has been balanced. That is the yin and the yang. It is this balance and dynamic of opposites that is the spark of Creation.

It used to be that all two-leggeds knew and revered me, the Great Mother, as a part of their day-to-day existence. Your archeologists have dug up images of what those earlier humans created as icons of me—the large soft breasts and round belly that could be a female version of the Santa Claus of today.

All were connected with me in a most sacred way. They worshipped me as the giver of all life, all compassion and fertility and kindness. There were temples erected and great ceremonies held to honor me and all of my beautiful beings here on Earth, all sacred life forms. Many of the ceremonies involved Grandmother Moon too.

There used to be such joy, dancing, rituals, honoring the great sacred balance of the masculine and feminine in these ceremonies. And wisdom, yes, such wisdom practiced in those days. Respect for all animals and plants was inherent in all activities and they were seen as infused with my sacred energy also. And women's medicine was honored in equal balance with men's medicine. There was balance, such beautiful balance.

But things started to change several thousand years ago and most of you lost your connection with me. This has made me very sad and I have watched terrible things happen across Earth as things became more and more imbalanced. We will talk more about that later.

I have never left you, my beloved ones. Most of you left me. Your awareness and reverence for me disappeared. Certainly, there are aspects of me that can be found in your mythology and religions, such as Diana—the huntress, Aphrodite—of love and beauty, and more. Within the Gnostic tradition, Sophia is the feminine spirit of wisdom, and in the

Jewish faith, Shekinah is the seat of the feminine power of wisdom. Quan Yin in Buddhism embodies ultimate compassion and kindness.

I am known as Yemoja, the Mother Goddess of the ocean and more, in the Isa or Yoruba religions that originated in West Africa. Kali is the full raging force of destructiveness that I can release to clear out the old ways that are not serving, to allow the new ones in. The Sufis have a very deep understanding of me, the Great Mother, in their divine love-soaked mystical writings and poetry. Pélé, the beautiful goddess energy of the active volcano in Hawai'i is an aspect of me. Then, of course, there is the Virgin Mary in Christianity. There are more goddesses to be found in other spiritual traditions too.

I never disappeared completely but was relegated to a back corner or a side chapel within most of your places of worship, if I was there at all. My presence has always been here but repressed, just as my beloved women have been repressed for so, so long.

Mare: Mother, I'd like to share about a book that leaped off the shelf at me at a friend's house several weeks ago. I suspect you have something to do with that since I've been to this friend's house many times but only this one time was so drawn to her bookshelf. It's called *Rock Your World with the Divine Mother* by Shondra Ray. I tossed it on a chair in the living room when I got home, where it sat for the past few weeks. I guess you wanted me to finally take a look at it last night. I was so tired of working on the computer anyway.

The subtitle of this book is: "Bringing the Sacred Power of the Mother into Our Lives." I didn't even notice the subtitle when I first picked the book up at her house. How interesting, rather coinkidinky. Sondra Ray writes about people she's met whose lives were completely changed by surrendering to the Divine Mother. She goes on to write:

"Since the Goddess has not been an integral party of Western life for the past two thousand years, we as her children are rather maladjusted. The Goddess, or Divine Mother, would lead us in the way of natural law, wisdom, and unconditional love; however, we don't pay enough attention to this aspect of God. That may be because of old beliefs that the Goddess is pagan and heathen. This is most unfortunate, because we then overlook her beneficial, life-enhancing, and regenerative powers and her offer of renewal." [2]

---

[2]Ray, Shondra. *Rock Your World with the Divine Mother* (Novato, California: New World Library: 2007), p. xiii

The sense I get is that it goes back even longer, four to five thousand years. The roots of Judaism dislodged you, Mother, as I understand it.

Shondra Ray also talks about the miracles that manifest when one chooses to connect with you, Mother. I'm only starting to read this book and am eager to learn more since she talks in the introduction about the capacity for these miracles, when one develops "miracle-mindedness". She shares stories in the book about miracles related to being deeply connected with you. AND she states: "If healing happens from reading this book, Glory be to the Divine Mother!"[3]

I guess I already know this outside of reading this book. I've experienced much of your healing in a variety of ways as I connected with you more and more deeply in the past several years to heal my lymphoma.

Mother: Yes, Love. There are many paths to me. That beautiful book is not the only one by any means. I did want you to read it at this time. It is a good affirmation that others have been on this path to rediscovering me and you can add your story to theirs. And there are multiple paths. It is not restricted to any one way so long as people are seeking me out with pure hearts.

Yes, "miracle-mindedness" can be a most wondrous path for living. And I can help manifest healing in ways which you humans might call 'miraculous'. This is part of how I work. Of the sick in the body or heart who go on pilgrimage to Lourdes, Fatima, Medjugorje, the various places where the Virgin Mary has appeared to children, or where Our Lady of Guadalupe was seen in Mexico—many are healed, if they truly want to be healed. They must want to be healed. That is important.

If you really think about it, I—embodied as Earth Mother or Nature—am hard-wired to heal. When Earth Mother is given the chance, she is always healing her damaged ecosystems to bring them back into healthy balance. Within you humans, all illness is a sign of imbalance. My work, as Mother, is to help bring balance back within people when they pray to me, connect with me in a sacred way, and allow me into their lives. I also seek to work on the community and planetary level because things have gotten so out of balance on Earth. And then, of course, I have a great deal of work to do in the rest of the universe but that's outside the realm of this book.

Mare: Sondra Ray also wrote how you, the Great Mother, or Divine Mother as she terms you, are the "very primal force itself". Some refer to you as "the feminine aspect of God, but some call her (You!) the supreme deity, the source of all knowledge, that which is beyond everything" ... that you are "the intelligence behind matter!"[4]

Mother: Yes, my love. Yes ... But truly I am beyond your human comprehension. Now, it's getting on in the morning and you need to go take a break. Your woodstove needs some TLC too. We will continue tomorrow.

---

[4]Ibid

3

The Quantum Divine Love of Creation and Earth Mother

If you knew how much I love you, you'd cry for joy.
—Virgin Mary, Message from Medjugorje

Friday, January 3rd, 2014
5:30 AM
5° Chilling strong winds with snow.

Mare: Mother, it's early and you've woken me up again. I'm writing here in the bed since it's so darned cold in this house right now. Thank goodness for this space heater.

Mother: Yes, it is a good thing you have that space heater. So, here we go. I want to talk about connecting more with me and the Creator. We love you so much. This is just inherent in who and what we are as the primal forces that brought you and everything else in this universe into existence. This love is so powerful, and it is offered to each and every one of you. Yet so many of you have walked away from us, both the Great Father and the Great Mother.

Let me explain this another way. I and the Great Mystery's energy is infused into everything. In you, in the Sun, in the rocks, plants, four-leggeds, mosquitoes, yes—even the mosquitoes. Even the stinkbugs that have gone rampant in your part of North America because some silly human inadvertently brought them over from a region you call Asia.

What I am saying is that the divine energies of the masculine and feminine aspects of the Great Mystery, and you can't get much more divine than that—is infused throughout. What this means is that everything is sacred. You are sacred. The stones are sacred, the trees, the crows, the rats in the cities, the oceans. All of Earth is sacred.

Earth Mother's beloved oceans, they are so sacred. Water, all water across your planet is her sacred blood that flows all over her. Evaporation, transpiration and precipitation (remember those from your science class?) are all sacred acts on her part and that of all the elementals, thunder-beings and others, to keep it all moving, pulsing, shifting, raining, snowing and flowing.

It's such a wondrous dance, sacred dance of energy. Yes, water is energy too. All of you, all of this here on Earth, all of what is in the Universe, is made up of atoms of dancing protons and neutrons and electrons and they are all dancing in the space within these atoms. Everything has these dancing components of atoms. Everything.

Your scientists keep marveling at all the 'emptiness' in those atoms but they need to be gently smacked across the forehead. Gently. Those atoms are not empty. They are filled with the Great Mystery and with my love as well. All of those atoms all over Earth and beyond, are filled with love.

This means all of you humans are filled with love. Along with all the plants and animals. The sun. The moon. The meteorites that flash through the atmosphere. The stars. There is so much more to the Universe that your scientists have not even started to observe. Even the black holes way, way out there. All of these are dancing atoms of divine love and electrons, protons, and neutrons.

And here is the wildest thing. When you beloved humans, with your beautiful (and sometimes troubled) minds and consciousnesses, willingly seek to connect with the Creator and me from the Sacred center of your being, then you tap our quantum divine love to amp up the love energy within all of your atoms. All of your cells, and your energy body or soul-body that extends beyond your physical body get amped up in a most sacred way when you connect more with the Great Mystery and with me. You are tapping into our quantum love field more powerfully and this blesses your energy body. It's a powerful and beautiful relationship to develop.

There are many ways to do this. It can be through deep prayer, meditation, focusing on gratitude that you are alive, calling on us directly and inviting our divine energy into your energy body, grounding into Earth Mother. And more.

The truth is we love you so much. This is inherent in your just being alive. The quantum divine love we have for each and every one of you humans is beyond description. Yet, most of you walk around unconsciously and aren't aware of it, don't tap into it, don't want to tap into it.

I honestly don't get it. All this divine love is there waiting for you all the time. All you need to do is just open the connection between you and us. You can say: "Here I am, your Earth son or Earth daughter," and say your name and how much you love us, the Creator and the Great Mother. In that moment the relationship starts to take off. And that relationship is a sacred energetic connection of love of quantum proportions between you and us.

Do you ever wonder how it is that mystics bliss out in their spiritual trances? Most of you think it's crazy irrational stuff for people to be sitting around in meditation blissing out in the most delicious spiritual joy, doing ecstatic dance. Sufi dervishes dance themselves into a state of utter divine rapture. They create a connection to the divine, and every atom in their body is dancing; all their chakras are aligned and pulsing with the sacred energy they've tapped into. It's just wonderful for me to watch these dancers and experience the beautiful energy they give off in those states. It sure beats the crazy greed energy that comes out of some stock exchanges. By a very, very, very long shot.

And that's not all.

Yes, there is the Creator and myself infused into everything over the universe. Just for the sake of ease you can refer to the both of us as Creation. And then there is Earth Mother, your planetary caretaker, your Earth that you live on, walk on, sleep on, even pee on. Pee is good fertilizer too. Never mind that right now.

So I have said enough. It's time for me to pass this over to Earth Mother now to invite her to speak from here on out. I will be speaking through her also. I love you!

Earth Mother: Yes, I feel like the forgotten one. But I'm here. It's rather hard for me to go away.

It might be helpful for me to share more about me since this was not taught in your schools nor churches. As your planetary caretaker, I am a concentrated mass of spiritual energy and consciousness. All planets have planetary caretakers, but the work is rather mundane for most of them since there is no physical life on them. Bad pun there. Apologies. They do have responsibilities but much of their time is spent in council with other planetary caretakers to strategize about the energies coming into their solar system and other related matters.

Just as important as connecting with the Great Mystery, it's important to connect with me, your Earth Mother, spiritually and energetically. Part of the reason things have gotten so out of balance here on me (and it's a complex set of reasons) is that almost all of you have been directing your prayers and thoughts to some conceived patriarchal Great Being that is off the planet, off of ME. All of this energy, since thoughts and prayers do have energy, oh, indeed they do, has been directed up and out. And a lot of times this energy is directed across too, since you pray for each other and those whom are struggling in another part of me. Which is all good. Don't get me wrong.

But you've forgotten me and your prayers, blessings, whatever need to be grounded back into me for there to be balance. This little known awareness is absolutely huge for healing me, along with you two-leggeds healing your relationship with me. It's gotten a little *off*, this relationship.

Well, more than a little off. All the forests cut, those are my lungs. All the wetlands you've filled or poisoned, those are my liver. They filter out so much beautiful divine detritus and are home to millions and millions of beautiful species, my babies, that feed other babies and move on up or out or across the food web, the sacred web of life that is all over me.

When you remember me and connect with me, guess what? This means that you tap into my love also. I am your Earth Mother and the love I have for you is so incredible, and I'm just waiting for you to reconnect with me. It used to be that all of you were connected with me spiritually and energetically. All of you lived so close to me and honored me and did ceremony all the time, offering blessings to me for good crops and singing to the plants. All of you source from pagan roots many, many generations back. Yes, all of you humans came from peoples who used to know the Old Ways of connecting in a sacred manner with me.

In truth, all you humans at one point had a sacred cord of energy that extended from the bottom of your spine, from your base chakra into me, into the very heart of me. Really. I have a heart. And all of you were so connected to me energetically that this love between the two of us flowed back and forth all the time. You were so tuned into me then. Many of you could hear me as you hear me now, Mare.

I yearn, so yearn for all of you to reconnect with me. It's the same approach as connecting with Creation, in truth. I encourage you to call out to Creation and then call out to me and claim your relationship with me, too.

You can say: "Hey ho, Mother—Earth Mother, this is I, your daughter Mare! I love you, Mother!"

As soon as you express your love to me, the circuitry connects and you and I are in this love dance together even more powerfully. And as the

Great Mother was explaining earlier, this will amp up your atoms and all the divine energy within you, mixed with the Creator's and Great Mother's quantum love. When you keep on doing this, over time it will be amazing what kind of love you can experience and the energy you will feel. Oh, what joy for me to be feeling all this love from you all! It's amazing for me.

You see, I automatically love you as your Earth Mother. Same as with Creation. It's just inherent in being a human here. Or a fish, a tree, a gorilla. We love you so, so much.

But you have *free will*. This is part of the package deal your soul agreed to when it decided to be born on this planet. On me. When you agreed as a soul to come back, to reincarnate again, part of the arrangement is for you to have free will. To live your life as you chose. To buy that car or this one. To marry that person or the other. To take this road or that one.

And we've been waiting, Creator, Great Mother and I, your Earth Mother, for you to remember who you are. There is a spiritual membrane around me that your soul-body passed through to be born into your physical mother's womb. This membrane erased most of your soul memories, to allow you to fully experience your physicality here. And free will was given to you also as part of your accepting a body here on me.

Yet our hope has been that each and every one of you would wake up and begin to remember who you are as ancient souls with a spiritual life that transcends me, your beloved planet. We've been hoping you'd remember the inherent divine love that is showering you all the time from Creator, the Great Mother and me. Remember, and then consciously give your love back to us. We've been waiting for this and watching.

And scratching our heads, and sighing a great deal.

In the interim, things have started to run amok on me. More than amok. My gosh, the holes you've dug in me, my bones. Ouch! Do you know how that hurts to have those huge mines dug into me? Try gouging a friend's arm like that and see how they feel! Then there are mountaintops that have been removed. All the chemicals, the toxins that have gotten into the water and my atmosphere, essentially getting into everything, including your cells, frogs' cells, and more.

Did you know that entropy is another part of the package deal here? Along with gravity? Just as you know that apple is going to fall from the tree, as good ole Newton observed— brilliant man, he was—there is the phenomenon of entropy. By the way, Newton was not the first to notice an apple falling from a tree. Not at all. I, personally, have been noticing for a very long time too.

Entropy is the reality that everything is going to disperse just by sheer dynamics of how energy moves. This means that all of those teeny-weeny chemicals you've created that don't break down on me for a long time, in your sense of time, are going to just keep on spreading and spreading. This explains how Eskimos and polar bears have high levels of toxins in their fat. Those toxins travel through the atmosphere adhering to water particles and then precipitate down in the polar regions because of atmospheric conditions.

Oh, I'm getting all sciencey on you here. And here I was talking about love. But the reality is that your cells, your human cells, the frog cells, whales, dolphins, even grasshoppers, did not evolve in the company of these toxins—these chemicals you keep on producing and spewing forth continue to be taken up by all of you. All of my living beings just keep on absorbing these chemicals. And you wonder why very young children are getting cancer. Many of my babies are getting cancer or other strange diseases. My frog babies are being born with three legs or fish with both male and female reproductive parts. Oy! These actions have to stop!

I'll get back to that later. Just had to vent a little.

Anyway, we have been waiting for you all to remember. To wake up. It is time for you all to remember who you are as sacred beings who can tap into our love. Not just Creator and the Great Mother's love but also my love, your Earth Mother's love.

I'm right here. You stand on me everyday. All it takes is a couple of seconds to start off with, claiming your relationship with Creation and sending your love out to them and then deep into my heart at the center of me. Oh, and the fun we can have! And the quantum love from me you'll tap into is quite amazing—more than magical.

So, that was an earful. Mare, your stomach is starting to grumble and that fire is cold probably. We'll chat more later. Scoot!

4

Miracle-Mindedness When You Surrender

Where there is great love, there are always miracles.

—Anonymous

Saturday, January 4th, 2014
7:10 AM
8° Clear and crisp.

Mare: Mother, I need to ask you about miracles. We were talking about miracle-mindedness two days ago and I'm starting to wonder. For instance why didn't I hear the phone ring last night? Two calls came in and both times I didn't hear them ring. I was just in the other room writing and usually always hear the phone ring. Did you silence those?

And yesterday the song I just happened to catch playing on the radio as I came back from a walk was Patty Griffin's beautiful song about *Mary*—Mother of Jesus, Mother of God. Surely that is a connection to you and what I'm doing this winter with you.

Then last night a friend told me how she went to see a woman who cuts hair out of her house. It so happens this hairdresser has an altar to the Virgin of Guadalupe and Mary in her front hall. Apparently several years ago she had breast cancer and went to see the traveling image of the Virgin of Guadalupe. When she came home and undressed that night, she was shocked to find ancient Hebrew writing on her breast. She had not revealed her breast to anyone while visiting the image. The hairdresser finally found someone to translate the writing and it meant something along the lines of turn to the Mother for love and healing.

39

My friend shared this story with me just after someone sent me a classical piece on YouTube composed for the Blessed Virgin Mary. I knew it was not a coincidence my friend mentioned the Virgin Mary, Madonna and the Virgin of Guadalupe to me then. I really should be recording all of these coinkidinkies. They just keep on rolling in.

I'm certain all of this is not news to you. I suspect you are sending all of these to me, aren't you?

Mother: Sweetie, I love you so much. Yes, of course I've been orchestrating these incidents since I knew you'd notice and see the pattern, and perceive the greater message here. You know how I work. I won't hit you too hard over the head but I'll generally send you subtle messages again and again until you finally understand the message there.

Yes, I silenced those phone calls since you needed to focus on that writing session with me. And that song, and your friend's story about the Virgin Mary and Our Lady of Guadalupé was to remind you of all the manifestations of Mother here on me.

Plus you know I'm sending you messages all the time when I can't get your ear any other way. I send them in my ways, through my four-leggeds, winged ones and more. We'll talk more about that later.

Mare: Mother, when my cat, Marley, was dying three years ago—that was you then too—wasn't it? You were not so subtle that day and that was a good thing.

Mother: Yes, you were so emotional and having such a hard time that I was not sure you'd be able to get your beloved Marley to the vet's that morning to be 'put to sleep' as some of you two-leggeds call it. That's such a strange term and just another way your society does not understand death. But never mind that right now.

Mare: You came into my head like a booming voice that morning and told me to stop "groveling" with grief on the floor next to suffering Marley and to instead focus on celebrating that he was such an amazing and devoted cat. And then you, point-blank, guided me step by step to get the kitty travel box from the basement, and put a towel in it. Then to place Marley in the box and get into the car and drive him to the vet's. I had already made the appointment that morning to have Marley euthanized, and I was a basketcase lying on the floor next to him as he was suffering so much. I don't think I could have done it without you that morning.

Mother: Yes, sweetie. I love you so much, and you were having a very hard time that weekend with Marley's dying. You and Marley were so bonded, and he was a very special kitty in the kitty realms. I knew that morning was not a time to be subtle with you, but to tell you directly what to do to get Marley to the vet. I guided you through the rest of the day. Do you remember how I encouraged you to paint your toenails later that afternoon while you were waiting for your friends to come over for Marley's burial ceremony?

Mare: Yeah, you were definitely helping me see Marley's passing as a beautiful thing and not just the huge loss I would feel. He had been suffering so much with his diabetes. It was important I focus on celebrating his life and love, all the love he gave me. Painting my toenails was a way to bring more joy into that very tough day. I needed it. Before you stepped in that morning, I was paralyzed with grief. He was such an amazingly compassionate presence in my life. And I can be such an emotional mess at times.

Mother: Yes, Marley was a very special cat. I was happy to help you that day. But that is one of the rare times when I've really stepped in to help you. Usually, I'm far more subtle and I let you bumble your way through things, trusting you'll hear me and be guided in the right direction.

But we've gotten a little off-track here. We were talking about Virgin Mary, Blessed Mary and coinkidinkies.

Sweetie, you were raised Catholic. The Virgin Mary is part of your upbringing. You used to have a precious little statue of her encased in clear plastic displayed prominently on a shelf in your childhood bedroom. You received it at your First Communion and liked it a lot.

Mare: That's true. I used to pray to the Virgin Mary all the time as a child. My name was actually Mary but I changed it legally since my parents gave me the exact same name as my mother. I was a 'junior' and it got too confusing.

Several times I called on the Virgin Mary to help protect me in an extreme way. The few times this happened it was late at night while I was lying in bed. I had the distinct feeling something very dark was in my space, long before I started studying with any Native teachers. It was an awful sense and definitely real. It did not happen that often but the few times it did, I prayed intensely to the Virgin Mary. She was the only being I knew to call on at that time. I said the prayer repeatedly:

Hail Mary, Mother of God, pray for our sinners now and...

... Gosh, it's been so many years. I can't even remember the full prayer. All I know is that I prayed it over and over again and the dark energy finally left my bedroom.

Mother: Yes, you were calling on the Virgin Mary. And through her you were calling on me and I came in and protected you in those moments. I've been protecting you all of your life.

Mare: I'm very humbled, Mother, hearing you say that. I'll never forget how in June of 2012, I filled my gas tank up just before leaving for the beach after the dolphins and whales called me to the ocean. I was just starting to hear your messages for *Messages from Mother.... Earth Mother.* And my car gas gauge did not budge from FULL even though I went 110 miles. I thought it was broken at first but then it started to drop as it normally did. I tracked that particular tank by the odometer carefully and by the time the needle was almost at empty, I had gone an extra 110 miles beyond what my car had ever done before on the same amount of fuel. That was rather wild. I knew it was a sign to me that you were taking care of me and that I needed to trust. With the lymphoma diagnosis and the dolphins and whales communicating with me, I was learning to trust.

Mother: Yes, I had to show you that. Even though you felt as if you were going a little crazy and were doing things you were not used to do-ing—such as hearing the dolphins and whales beckon you to the beach, I was taking care of you. I had to show you what you humans would call a miracle, to help you understand that I was supporting you.

Mare: And I got it. I understood you were creating a little 'magic' in my car, my old diesel VW Golf. I knew I was being taken care of by you.

Mother: The sad thing is that magic and miracles surround all of my beloved two-leggeds all the time and 99.99% of you miss it. Only the mys-tics actually sense it, see it, feel it, touch it ... and the rest of my beloved humans are asleep.

About Soul Contracts

My daughter, every one of my human children is special. Yet you made a soul contract before you were born to come into this particular earth-walk to do this work. First you became an environmentalist. That was part of your contract. Then you created the book about calling God directly on the phone. In time, you opened up the capacity to listen to me, Earth Mother (and the Great Mother as well) for your second and third books. I know it's hard for you to access that soul contract right now, but it is all right there.

Mare: Mother, this idea about such a contract makes sense. The Cherokee teacher I was with for fourteen years talked about them also. It's true, I've mostly tried to follow what felt like the right calling for me, by tuning in and listening to some inner voice within me; my instincts, essentially. I suppose those callings are missions I agreed to undertake in my soul contract before I was born. When I graduated from college I was very certain I was not immediately destined for a desk job somewhere and within three weeks I was working at the bottom of the Grand Canyon for the park service.

Several years after that, a cousin made a comment about my not having a 'real job' yet, and in my insecurities, I took her seriously. I quit the seasonal park service work and tried to study pre-school education—and slipped into a deep depression for months. Clearly I had fallen away from my calling. When I finally found my way back to environmental work after two years of trying various jobs, it felt as if I was back in the right groove again. Though to my mostly conservative family, I know it looked as if I moved to the beat of a different drummer.

Mother: There are different aspects to a soul contract. Some of them include men you've met, too. There was that young medical resident from Puerto Rico whom you knew for only a month, but in that short time he really got under your skin and tore your heart open emotionally. That prompted your Cherokee teacher to heal your heart chakra at a level you would not have been ready for before you met him. You and he had been together another lifetime—oh, you two had so much fun in that lifetime!

Mare: That was some years ago. We were so different. It baffled me that we had such a strong connection since he was a true lady's man, such a flirt, and I'm not generally attracted to men like that. Plus he loved living in big cities like Manhattan. We were so incompatible, really.

We spent so little time together, too. Only three dates. I can remember thinking I'd do this man's laundry for him if he wanted me to. It stunned me when that thought passed through my head. I don't even like doing my own laundry. And I've never thought of myself as a woman who would wash her partner's clothes. Yet that's how much I liked him. I guess I had done his laundry in another lifetime and thoroughly enjoyed it.

43

Mother: Yes, you did. And in that lifetime, you had absolutely wild times in the bed too. He was confused about the chemistry between the two of you also. Remember, at the end of that first date, after you talked for hours, he commented how it felt to him you had been together in a past life. You felt that familiar to him.

Mare: I do remember that. But he had absolutely no time for a relationship as well as his work. He was a psychiatric medical resident at one of the hospitals in Baltimore. His hours were crazy long and he was completely exhausted. He commented to me: "so much dysfunction ... so much," referring to his caseload at the hospital.

Mother: He's right. There is so much dysfunction, way too much dysfunction in your society, your world. On me. I am your planetary caretaker and believe me I am completely aware of this dysfunction. And he was witnessing it up front and personal. Poor man. These psychiatrists and psychologists are only treating the dysfunction with band-aid measures since the roots of it are far deeper than anything they can touch in the psych wards or their offices. Far deeper.

Okay, you're starting to fade on me here. Time for you to take a break.

5

The Universe is the Greatest Recycler

A little while, a moment of rest upon the wind,
and another woman shall bear me.

—Khalil Gibran

Monday, January 6, 2014
4:54 AM
6° Very light snow flakes at dawn.

Mare: Okay, Mother, you woke me up at 4:30 AM this morning. What's up?

Mother: Well, I kind of helped you wake up but you've got so much rumbling around in you right now, I did not need to do that much. I love you. Let's talk....

Mare: You're right. I'm definitely in a tizzy. I have a new man in my life. His name is Paul and he's retired. A very kind, sensitive man and he just spent the weekend here and we had so much fun together. It feels as if something quite amazing is going on right now.

Mother: Yes, you are in a tizzy and yes, it will all be good. It may just crack you open, finally, to heal you more completely—and help you learn to trust men more. You are getting ready to be open to a good man. Yes, you are.

Mare: But I'm terrified. This feels as if my whole world is getting the rug pulled out from under it, and my equilibrium is being pushed way off kilter.

Mother: That is what love can feel like between two humans, yes. It has to do with your energy bodies. When someone comes into your life, your energy bodies mix, and of course it will throw you off. Not to mention that your heart is involved, and so all of those fears within you, or un-healed shadow aspects will surface to be healed. It can be like a beautiful path with rose petals scattered all over it, or it can be like a path covered with rose petals mixed with shards of glass. The truth is, all of you have a choice about how many shards of glass and how big and how sharp. It all depends on how much you resist the love and refuse to heal through your old soul wounds.

Mare: Really? I have to think about this. I've never been good at relation-ships at all. You know I have that memory of dying of an abortion from five lifetimes ago. I died in that cart filled with straw ... the memories are not fun to relive. My lover was in an arranged marriage and divorce was not allowed then. The healer I went to for the abortion really messed me up and it was a god-awful way to die. I remember being in such terrible pain and bleeding in that bumpy cart and just so yearning to be held by my lover. We were so in love, and he had no idea I was even pregnant. No idea ... That was definitely not a fun time. And then there were those two very gifted intuitive healers who both shared that I'd been horribly abused, tor-tured, killed, whatever, by man after man after man, in repeated lifetimes.

Mother: Yes, you went through some suffering when that abortion mem-ory surfaced and you had to relive some terrible, terrible agonies. That trauma got embedded into your soul-body. Your reliving it actually helped to heal a good part of it. Paul will help you heal from it even more.

As for the multiple lifetimes of abuse and worse ... let's just say that you, like many women who did not wish to be submissive, have threatened the patriarchal system for many lifetimes. Hundreds of thousands of you were tortured, and died at the hands of men who had lost touch with honoring the Sacred Feminine and the powerful healing gifts of women.

It was so wrong. So very wrong and it went on for centuries and cen-turies. It's still going on in some regions of me now and greatly saddens me.

Mare: I had a session with a gifted past-life-regressionist several years ago and another very clear and horrifying memory came through. I don't know how many lifetimes ago it was but I was trying to hide in the back room of a small, very simple house and these men came to capture me. They broke the doors down, grabbed me out of the back room and hauled me out to the street. The muddy, disgusting street! There they tortured me with a spear. And I know I've been hung. And raped and tortured in other ways.

Mother: Yes, you were and it broke my heart each and every time to see you punished, just because you were trying to speak up for your rights, pushing back against the repressive ways that were shutting down women who were trying to practice the old, healing ways. So many of my gifted healers and priestesses were caught and tortured, sacred women's circles destroyed.

They called you witches. I loved you then and I love you now, offering guidance and help. But some very dark stuff has been playing out for centuries keeping you, my daughters, repressed. This has run deep in your culture for so long that many of you just accept the repressive ways. Many of you continue to repress yourselves even now.

Mare: I guess my soul-body has a very deep distrust of men.

Mother: And understandably so. But men also have suffered terribly under this hierarchical, patriarchal system that has been in play for these thousands of years. It's only a very few of them at the top who have benefitted while the rest of the men are demeaned and degraded—tortured too at times.

Plus you have not always been a woman. Sometimes you've come back as a man. After your death from the abortion, you experienced three lifetimes as a man. It was only in this lifetime that you were finally ready to come back as a woman. As a matter of fact, you already know what you did in your most recent past life.

Mare: Yeah, I was a multi-national industrialist. I know. I was definitely a man and was hugely successful, financially. I had all sorts of industries, coal, timber, etcetera, that raped and pillaged you, Mother. When a gifted intuitive friend told me about this most recent past life, I joked that I'd like to find my heirs from that lifetime and claim some of that inherited wealth! That would be quite something! If I only knew my name from that lifetime.

Mother: Yes, well, that's not exactly allowed. But after you died, your soul was made to know how much destruction you wreaked on me, and you were sent back very fast. Generally, souls will process their past lifetime for about thirty years or so and then reincarnate. But I needed you back here with your new-found awareness of all you did to destroy me. I also needed your other gifts for organizing, communicating, etcetera. You are one of those soul-types with strong organizational gifts, and I needed you here during these times of Great Change. You came back just seven years after you died as a multi-national industrialist.

Look at your career and passion for the environment. For me. There is a reason for this. You knew you needed to make amends for all the destruction the corporations you owned wreaked on me in that most recent lifetime. You ran an international environmental network in your early thirties and then stepped down to become a gardener and writer and student of Native American teachers—initially because of your depression.

I've needed you to take this path less traveled, so very much less traveled in order to facilitate your healing. Essentially I also needed you to learn how to *listen*, and running an organization was not going to help you learn how to listen spiritually.

Mare: Mother, is this why you've had me single all my life? Or practically always single? Other than a few quick romances?

Mother: Yes, my Love. If you had married young and had children, it would have taken you in a very different direction in your life. Plus you have that soul contract in which you agreed to do writing and environmental work. The books have been your children, not to mention all the plants you baby. Your huge gardenia—who you call Oscar—and your orchids are going to have a banner season coming up, because of all the love you are giving them, not to mention proper water and fertilizer too.

Mare: Last year, I became aware of a deep subconscious fear that if I get involved with a man, I'll die or be tortured. It's understandable with these terrible past lives but, wow, it is really hard for me to trust a man, to trust that my heart and my body will be safe in a deeply intimate relationship. Oh, my gosh, just since Paul was here in my house staying in the guest room, my body was starting to seize up and my neck was getting tight. I can feel it now in my lower back—this taut bunching of muscles.

Mother: Honey, this is why I'm encouraging you to trust in the moment and dance. Move that energy. Get it flowing. Don't wallow in your fears, the conscious ones you know about. There are so many layers of subconscious ones too. Keep on dancing.

Mare: Dancing does help me feel better, it's true.

Mother: And also—this is key—give your energy to me. You learned last year about connecting energetically with me, sending your energy down your spine and through your tailbone to the very center of my heart, the center of me, your Earth Mother, and then bringing my energy back up through the arches of your feet and from there up through your whole body, chakra by chakra.

This energy gets stuck in you because you're not connecting enough with me. I invite you to give it to me. No, I implore you to give it to me. You've just recovered from lymphoma which was caused by too much blocked emotional energy in your system. You've been learning to tap into me and work with me energetically in some very beautiful ways in the past few years. Please practice this now, especially now that Paul has stepped into your life.

Mare: I will work on this. I will. Mother, I feel as if Paul is going to be very special. When he walked out the door and left yesterday morning, I knew this was a good man.

Mother: You humans have the expression: "When the student is ready, the teacher appears." You will both be students and teachers to each other. That is how it is meant to be. Oh, I'm actually so thrilled you will experience some love in your life.

Sweetie, there is another side to this though. Just as you have experienced so much trauma with men, you also have *been* a man who treated women terribly. The ball is not only in their court. When you all reincarnate, which you do countless times, you come back wearing many, many hats. Both as men and women. You currently don't have memories of those lifetimes when you were the abuser, but it did happen.

And then there is the truth about you being born into soul clusters and how you come back together in different variations of relationships to work your woundedness out. You could be a parent in one lifetime, a lover, or a child, all sorts of variations. This is playing out all the time.

But in knowing that you have also been the abuser and the abused is important. It helps you learn how to forgive on a far deeper level. And forgiveness is the only way forward, truly. At some point you need to let go of the thorns still in your heart, heal your mistrust, and forgive these men. Most of them are good people trying to find their own way forward into healing and love. Very good men.

6

·····················

The Sacred Wise Circle

The Circle has healing power. In the Circle, we are all equal. When in the circle, no one is in front of you. No one is behind you. No one is above you. No one is below you. The Sacred Circle is designed to create unity. The Hoop of Life is also a circle. On this hoop there is a place for every species, every race, every tree and every plant. It is this completeness of Life that must be respected in order to bring about health on this planet.

—Dave Chief, Oglala Lakota

Tuesday, January 7, 2014
8 AM
0°F Very cold and clear.

Mare: Mother it is 0°F outside right now. This is really cold for Maryland. The Polar Vortex that has swooped down has brought sub-freezing temperatures to just about all of the USA other than the very southern part of California and Florida.

Mother: And Hawaii. Don't forget Hawaii.

Mare: You're funny … right, Hawaii too. They're not freezing. Other than on top of Mauna Loa.

Mother: Yes, it's been a bit of time, in your little human ways of looking at things, since this type of weather pattern has taken place on your continent. Your weather forecasters are saying some twenty years. Believe me, it's gotten colder other times. When those glaciers covered huge chunks of North America and Europe and other parts of me, it was much colder then.

Mare: Well, I'm grateful you let me sleep in this morning; at least I was able to stay bundled in my bed a little longer this time. It's freezing in this house. Well, not cold enough for the water in the glass in my bedroom to freeze, but still really cold.

Mother: I can be kind. But you are so stubborn about not turning the thermostat up. At least you turned on the space heater and pulled it close to the bed where you are writing. I'm proud of you for that. I know you're trying to be climate neutral and not contribute any more carbon dioxide to the atmosphere than necessary but you don't have to suffer. But I also know you like the adventures of heating by woodstove. Sometime soon we'll talk about Sacred Fire but we'll save that for another day.

I'd like to talk with you about *Sacred Circles* and *Sacred Webs* and more today instead.

Your culture created a worldview about me and the way things work on me that is a bit *off*. Unfortunately this worldview has become very prevalent and has led to many disastrous events, ones that continue to play out. We could call this your cultural conditioning since most of you have absorbed this way of seeing the world as a *truth* when it is not one at all. Part of this Western worldview is based on the malinformed hierarchical thinking that humans are at the top. The truth is that you two-leggeds are only part of a huge web of life that includes all the other species, the four-leggeds, six-leggeds, standing ones or trees, finned ones and more.

This hierarchical thinking also includes overly simplistic, linear ways of understanding things. This flawed straight-line thinking ignores the greater system of webs of connections and causes and effects, and this has led to many serious accidents and more.

For instance, if you deforest a steep slope on a mountain and then high rains come which completely saturate the ground, odds are good there will be a landslide. There would be no more tree roots stabilizing that soil and all that moisture and soil would then follow the way of gravity. It's inevitable. But a forestry company that is lacking in understanding about how everything is connected and only considers the profits involved in timber sales from clear-cutting a steep slope will not think about all the longer-term effects. And believe me, there are many of them.

My native peoples have lived for thousands of years with the concept of *All My Relations*. The Lakota say in their language *Mitakuye Oyasin*. It is challenging for me to define this fully in English since your English language is a technical one which does not convey a sacred energy as you speak it, compared with native tongues.

But I will try.

All My Relations may sound like a holiday gathering to many people. But it's far more. Although, if more of you celebrated your existence here on me instead of fighting, worrying, holding resentment, etcetera, it could be like a continual holiday gathering, I suppose.

Mitakuye Oyasin means all are related. All are interconnected. It is inclusive of all the four-leggeds, winged ones, finned ones, standing ones, stone people, six-leggeds—the creepy crawlies, worms and all of the creatures here on Earth, on me. You are only one species out of millions and millions. You are two-leggeds. There are far more four-leggeds, finned ones and more.

This concept of *All My Relations* also connects you to the mineral kingdom, the weather, and the elements. All forces here on Earth. Nothing exists in isolation. There is not only the actual physical cycling of minerals that go from your body at death, for instance, to break down into the soil, but there are energy webs that link all living beings and weather patterns together.

All My Relations. To truly understand it means living it. It means living humbly, honoring the wisdom of all the other creatures and knowing it's not about hierarchy with humans on top. It's about understanding the sacred web of life, one in which humans are only a small part. Your whole species is one piece of a web of great complexity, woven with golden strands of Divine Love, Earth Mother Love, along with the actual physical predator-prey connections, and resource cycling taught in ecology classes.

This web of life is spiritual, sacred, physical—emotional even! We can start with the scientific, ecological angle, since many two-leggeds never took an ecology class, hence the lack of any understanding of the ecological systems in your corporate and governmental decision-making. And hence the consequent havoc wreaked on my beautiful, beautiful ecosystem to its farthest corners all over the planet.

The CIRCLE is the overriding principle here. It's such a brilliant design. The Creator and Great Mother came up with such an amazing concept when they created the circle. It represents so much intelligence, and more.

For instance, everything is cycled in the web of life. I, as your Earth Mother, know no waste. Creation does not understand the concept of waste either. I did not evolve everything here with Creation with a rubbish bin on the side for disposal of waste. All waste from one being is food for another.

This is the foundation of the vast web of life. Animal poop in a tropical rainforest is decomposed in all of two hours. The biodiversity and efficiency of the decomposers in those parts of me is rather impressive.

Not to toot my own horn too much, because it's not about me. It's about the spiritual intelligence here on Earth that is part of the universal intelligence.

So everything is cycled again and again all over me. All the minerals, the nutrients, the water, all of it. Each of you has had a water molecule pass through you that also passed through Jesus Christ.

All the calcium in your bones, the magnesium, the oxygen bouncing around in your blood vessels, has been here for several billion years. Your body is yours for this Earth-walk but then it goes back to me through the decomposers and it's a beautiful dance. And this is true for all life here on me. All are cycled and are part of this beautiful dance.

This includes your souls. They are cycled too and this is called reincarnation. We've already been talking about your numerous past lives. But this is just another example of how the Creator is the greatest recycler. Some humans might return as animals or pets even.

Your friend's beloved kitty, Maximilian, was an example of what some of you two-leggeds call 'cross migration'. She called him Max, but she and the Cherokee teacher with whom she worked knew who he was. He was *the* Maximilian, Prince Maximilian, from the Hapsburg Empire who tried to rule Mexico in a flawed attempt that ended quite tragically for him. He had been set up by some European powers to try to control Mexico in the mid-1800's. This soul was also the same conqueror Maximilian a thousand years before.

Maximilian chose to come back as a cat for a number of lifetimes since he had extreme power issues. He went through a series of nine lifetimes and still had not healed his soul's inclination to want to be a conqueror, so he came back another two. Your friend had him in his 11th lifetime, the one in which he finally worked through his soul tendency to need to control vast quantities of land and people.

When the Cherokee teacher was away and could not lead Max's burial ceremony, an Algonquin medicine man happened to be in town that weekend and led it in full honor and love. You were there for that ceremony, Mare. You could see how he was communicating with Max in the spirit after Max was 'put to sleep' that morning. Max was a very devoted guardian cat for your friend, yet he died much younger, at age 11, than most cats since he knew his work with your friend was done. His guardian kitty work and the great compassionate presence he offered her while he lived with her were completed. He was always with her when she went outside. He would wait for her outside nearby neighbors' homes when she would go visit. He joined her for walks in the woods across the street. He was watching out for her and would alert her spirit guides and her Cherokee teacher if she confronted any problems the Cherokee teacher needed to know about. He took his work very seriously, and I love him for this.

And you remember what the Algonquin medicine man said about Max. Apparently Max shared with him that he was very torn since he was 'so fond' of your friend and wanted to come back and be with her again as a cat. But he also knew on a soul level that it was time for him to return back to me, Earth Mother, as a two-legged since I could use his good leadership skills again, without his ego-driven conquering tendencies.

Many times, highly evolved souls are with us as animal companions. This is one of the many reasons it breaks my heart to witness how many animals are mistreated in your society. But my more spiritually committed humans—many of you have been gifted with a four-legged companion-guardian to help you with your spiritual healing and work. Some of you are aware of this and some of you aren't. That's okay.

Some of you even recognize when your beloved kitty or dog who passed several years ago has come back again as another wondrous four-legged pet in your life. Just a different body in another incarnation to help you even further along and love you. Their work is very real and beautiful and I love them so much for all they do for you.

Getting back to this recycling idea though—what's been missing from your ecology classes is that all of these minerals, gases such as oxygen, even when you pass gas (which you have been doing a lot of in the past few days, sweetie, you need to balance your GI system a bit), all of them are infused with sacred energy. Even farts are sacred too.

Mare: Mother! You are going to give away all of my secrets here. It is true I've been farting a lot and I think it's partly because of the gallbladder surgery—my system is just not the same. I would like to figure out how to stop them.

Speaking of "sacred farts" though, there is a video up on YouTube of the Dalai Lama from his 2013 *Beyond Religion* tour in Australia.[5] In the midst of talking about warm-heartedness and humility, he starts to talk about how he needs to fart sometimes on a plane. He even acts out how he checks to see who might be noticing him and pretends to lean to one side to pass the gas. He's just giggling and laughing as he's talking about it. The man is so hilariously humble and huggable. I just want to go find him and give him a huge bear hug when I watch his videos.

Mother: Oh, I love my Dalai Lama. Such a delightful, delightful soul. So

---

[5]https://www.youtube.com/watch?v=IUEkDc_LfKQ

humble and so wise. You see, the Tibetan Buddhists understand the circle as it relates to reincarnation. This current Dalai Lama was discovered at a very young age because of his spiritual gifts and the signs given to the Lamas seeking him out. The young boy was born quite enlightened and the Lamas could tell he was the reincarnation of the previous Dalai Lama.

The Tibetan Buddhists also are intimately aware of the sacredness of all. Yet they don't talk about me, Earth Mother, that much. I wish they would. But the White Tara is a beautiful Goddess of compassion and kindness that comes out of their tradition. And to tune into her wondrous energies is a deeply healing experience for those who pray to her. Truth be told though, the Buddhists could have more feminine balance in their teachings, but that is for them to come to in time.

Getting back to what we were talking about before, there is a deliciously complex web of life that is a dance of life AND energy, sacred energy all over me. As I mentioned before, all of you two-leggeds, four-leggeds, six-leggeds, winged ones, finned ones, standing ones—all are infused with sacred energy that sources from the Sacred love that created you, from the Great Mystery and myself.

So when my indigenous ones talk about *All My Relations*, they are talking about a beautiful dance of Sacred Love that connects all of you two-leggeds with all the other beautiful sacred beings here in a way that honors and bows in humility to all of it, all the Great Mystery of it. All the beyond brilliant intelligence from the universe of it. How humbling and wonderful it is to be part of this glorious, wonderful community here on me.

My native peoples have as their intention always to serve *All My Relations*. They ask me, how can their actions, their words, their thoughts, serve me, their current generation and all the creatures around them, from now into the next seven generations?

This is quite powerful. And this way of thinking is starting to come back. I am most, most excited about this!

Life is a great *circle*. Many of my native peoples teach about how life begins in the East, as you are born, where the sun rises and a new day comes in. Then they turn to the South where there are the energies of the youth, of playfulness, dancing, vitality and more. From there they move to the West, the place of adulthood, shedding the youthful ways to coming into maturity. Then they shift to the North, the place of the elders and wisdom. And the circle starts over again from there. It has neither beginning nor end.

At the very center of the Sacred Circle is Creation or the Great Mystery. All beings have a place on the edge of the Sacred Circle of existence.

Two-leggeds are only one out of many, many beings on the rim of the circle. You are not the center of the circle but only one of many, all equidistant from the center.

Perhaps I need to say that one more time. *You are not the center of the circle but only one of many, many wondrous species on me.* All the other species are your brothers and sisters here on me, your Mother. This is the *Hoop of Life.*

It is important for you humans to come to a place of humility and understanding that you are equidistant alongside these other species and beings such as the trees, the rocks, birds, flowers and more. This will help my planet come back into balance and harmony.

The circle is also the shape of me, Earth Mother. Grandmother Moon is a circle. Grandmother Moon moves in a circle around me, as we both also rotate around the Sun, also a circle. When a stone is tossed in pond, there are circles of ripples that move out across the water. The Sacred Circle is the seat of profound wisdom.

It used to be that human councils met on me in circles for decision-making. Within these councils were men and women, elders and even some young, all balanced in numbers. It was non-hierarchical and a beautiful way that honored the collective wisdom that came forth from the council. These councils also honored the presence of the Creator in the center and grounded their decisions into the implications for future generations. It was a most wise way of decision-making.

There is so much more I could teach about circles. Atoms, sub-atomic particles, the vortexes of hurricanes and more. Some of it is touched on in your teachings about Sacred Geometry. There are books and books about the brilliance of circles in a celestial library accessed by beings from all over the universe. Don't you think there is a reason UFO's are round? To teach about all of that here in this *Bible* would take hundreds if not thousands of pages. But I don't think we have the time for this, this winter. Your physicists are only starting to scratch the surface of the brilliance of the circle in their work.

Okay, now I can hear your stomach grumbling and I sense the bathroom is calling you. Go and we'll talk more tomorrow.

7

Fear and Cultural Conditioning

Love is what we were born with.
Fear is what we learned here.

—Marianne Williamson

Wednesday, January 8, 2014
7:33 AM
10°F Gray, still and cold.

Mare: Okay, Mother. I'm here. Out of bed. Finally. I've peed. Got the woodstove cranking again. Didn't need to use any matches even. There were some nice coals from last night. I'm tucked back into bed, writing. The space heater in my bedroom is quietly chugging along which is a good thing though my fingers are already starting to get pretty chilled just typing this so far. It's rather frigid in the rest of the house.

Mother, I know you want me to trust and most times it's relatively easy for me to trust you. But there are moments when it's hard. Take this house I've been living in, the one you guided me to rent two years ago. This house is going to auction today. You did not want me to move to Virginia to live at that intentional community at that time. You guided me here and I've loved living in this house.

Yet the reality of this home is that my friend lost it to the bank several years ago because of financial challenges. And by sheer grace and some forms she learned to submit to the bank (and lots of prayers) the bank had not foreclosed on her during that interim.

So I've been here for two years now by sheer grace too. But, Mother, this house is finally being foreclosed on and going to auction this afternoon. I will need to move soon and it's all quite uncertain when and where. You keep on telling me to trust and I will have all the time I need to write this book. And you will guide me to the next place just as you guided me here.

This does rather feel like you're hanging my butt out over the cliff a little precariously. I know I'm not down to my very last penny in my savings account. But still—it is dwindling more and more each month.

I'm really trying to trust. When I truly think about it, you've taken care of me in so many ways. Every way, really.

Mother: Yes, I have. I do love you so much. I love all my beautiful humans so much. And I am taking care of you. Don't worry. There is a plan afoot for you to be in the house as long as you need to, to finish the book and get some other projects going. You will negotiate with whoever buys this house at auction, this cozy tree house of a home with the woodstove you love. Then I will guide you to the next place where you will be.

Mare: Please can it be the home where I can garden also, and grow lots of veggies and maybe have chickens and where I won't be living by myself? Kinda community-ish with good neighbors? But, Mother, how will I be able to afford all that?

Mother: See, there you go again with all of your fears. You need to just stay focused in the moment and let me take care of it. There is an expression that many of you say: "Let go, let God." Well, you can create a mantra in your head that is: "Let go, let Mother," too. I am that Mother. Trust me. Love me, listen to me … keep on writing and sharing these teachings with the world. It will all work out.

You are one of my daughters who has learned how to really listen. I love you so much. I love all my daughters equally, it's not about favorites. It's just that some of you are tuning in to me so beautifully again, more and more. And you, you are an author. You help me get the teachings out so much farther and wider. It is needed these days.

Mare: Okay, okay … It still feels as if you're hanging my butt way over the cliff though. But I guess perhaps I'm learning how to turn off gravity and just float there. That is what this is about, yes? No *fear*. Just be. Absolutely be in the moment and trust your love. Pure Love.

Mother: Yes, love, it is. It is. Pure Divine Love.

Sweetie, I know you go through your anxieties. I'd like to talk about these, and about fear in general. You are not alone by any means. Truly, the amount of fear rampant in your culture is off the charts. All of those in the spiritual realms who work on me are just stunned at how much fear there is here on me, your Mother. Much of this fear is because most of you have lost your connection and capacity to trust me and the Creation. And your media continues to stir up so much fear. The stories they focus on are mostly ones about terror and violence.

It was never meant to be like this. But look at your society. Your economic system is based on fear. You have empty homes in many places and people living on the streets in other places. You have people huddled by a furnace that is barely working, or people being evicted from their homes and forced to live in the streets. Meanwhile you have other people a few blocks away with absolutely huge houses who could accommodate an army. I could go on and on.

The people living in the big houses live in fear that someone will take their stuff. Yet the people on the street or huddled around their gas stove could benefit from more stuff just to meet their essential needs. And everyone is afraid.

Well, almost everyone. Some of you have learned to trust. TRUST. You hear me say that to you a great deal, Mare, and you're finally getting it. The house where you're living is going to auction today because your friend lost it to the bank.

This house has been a perfect place for you to heal and write—the woodstove, the deck high up in the trees. You have loved living there and it has been a most positive, fruitful space for you. You have a lease that is good for another six months and that will be more than enough time for you to finish this book. I will guide you to your next home. I am taking care of you.

It's true some bank now owns the house though the banks have shuffled the papers around like they're all playing some big card game similar to that game you call Monopoly.

Oy ... Monopoly. You even played that game as a child and thought nothing of it. Most of you were taught to play games like that where the idea is for the winner to collect all the stuff and for everyone else to walk away with little or nothing. Few of you even wonder about these games and what they've taught you about collecting wealth with little regard for those who lose out. You've absorbed this cultural conditioning without question. Most of you. And now just about all of you are sitting in this place of deep fear. The cultural conditioning is so, so deep.

What do you call it? Capitalism? Greed? There are those in power in totalitarian, communist or other corrupt governments that are also supporting such inequality. How I wish I could take a huge eraser out and just delete this mindset from all of your brains.

I'd replace it with *Community* and *Compassion* and the awareness that if any of you possess more than ten percent beyond what you need, really need for your personal survival and simple comforts, then you have too much.

It's even lopsided across me. The people in the northern part of me are the ones obsessed with wealth and a lifestyle that sanctions greed, while the ones in the southern part of me are being pressured to adopt these systems as well. Frankly, there is not enough of me, including all my trees, minerals, fossil fuels—as you call them, etcetera, to support this runamok way of living across all of me. Just not enough at all.

There would need to be about four or five planets just like me, to keep all of you across all of me in a modern home with all the technology that a comfortable smallish home in the USA has. No being would be able to live on those other planets since their "resources" would be used to support all of you humans on me.

Ain't happening.

Just can't happen. More than anything, it's not supposed to happen. I'm tempted to go more into greed here. I spoke about that in the other set of messages, the other book you put out before this one, Mare: *Messages from Mother.... Earth Mother.*[6] About how I wanted to put some special chemical, an environmentally friendly one, of course, in all the water systems, especially in the northern parts of the world to eradicate greed.

People would drink it and, poof, any tendency toward greed would just leave them. Waft away into the wind. Maybe I'd send all that loose greed out to the moon. Some of my native peoples such as the Shoshone do focus on sending darker or heavier energies out to the moon. I would not want those energies sticking around here anyway. The greed energy might stick to someone else.

Think about it though. Manhattan would be such a different place without greed. Maybe I would start there. Or London. Or Hong Kong. Just think of all the places where we could start to eradicate greed!

The beautiful thing is that by getting rid of greed, we would help solve hunger and poverty issues automatically. People who have acquired more than they need would simply donate their monies to those in need. Job trainings would be better funded, hunger programs established more broadly. No one would go hungry.

---

[6] http://messagesfrommother.org

Several things have been missing on me for these last several thousand years as more patriarchal, hierarchical thinking has taken root and evolved to this *Time of Great Fear*. First, is the understanding there is enough for everyone if all of you truly knew how to live in community, if you prioritized the community's needs over your own individualistic needs. The second is greater compassion. The third is how everything is infused with sacred energy. The list is long, actually.

Getting back to how there is enough for everyone, this is true. Yet there are an awful lot of you here on me these days. We have not spoken about aliens before but they do exist. The reason some of these aliens are coming to me these days is to try to figure out what is going on here since too many souls are being born here. Some of these souls are supposed to be born on other planets instead of here. But you are essentially hogging them. These aliens are going back to their home planets with some interesting reports about how dysfunctional things have gotten here on me.

Mare: Whoa, Mother, are you talking about extra-terrestrials again? I know they exist and even saw a space ship once. It was when I was a child and it was hovering over a nearby field behind our house. And the father of a friend of mine, a rather conservative man, said he also saw one which was a huge confession for him. He was definitely not the type of person who would be talking about spaceships unless he truly saw one.

Mother: Oh, they most certainly exist and have been visiting me for hundreds of thousands of years, long before you two-leggeds evolved into being here on me. I'll talk more about them later.

How I long for a time when things will be back in balance on me again. We'll get there, but we have a long way to go.

But getting back to this discussion about energy—what has also been missing in your cultural conditioning—is the awareness that money is just energy. Some of you know that and have been working on prayer, and manifesting abundance, and holding good intentions and all sorts of other positive ways to move energy for a variety of purposes.

We've talked about energy somewhat before. Your thoughts have energy. Your prayers can have powerful energy. Your words are potent emanations of energy. It is important to be careful with where and how you direct your thoughts and words to have them be as affirming as possible.

Mare: Mother, a native Hawai'ian elder I know taught me they have a way of ending their prayers/chants with singing *ua lele kapule*, which means "the prayer has flown." He explained it meant the prayer has gone to the heavens to be heard by *ke Akua*, their word for the Creator.

Mother: Yes, prayers do fly. That is the way of energy, especially when you two-leggeds pray from your hearts and from your love of the Creator and for me. Just by saying that, the Hawai'ians give an energetic boost to their prayers to carry them more powerfully. And we do hear these prayers. We do.

When the book *The Secret* came out along with the film, they included some lovely truths in it. Yet they were missing a big piece, the *Community* piece. *The Secret* was created by humans who played Monopoly, and all those other games as children. As young ones, they never questioned your economic system, or asked if it's a system that really serves the highest good of all, for now, and into the next seven generations, or if it has rather been doing the opposite.

So many of these humans took the spiritual principles of prayer, intention and manifesting and have focused on accumulating more stuff. Many have been successful at accumulating stuff. Certainly some have been using those principles of prayer and manifesting to serve the highest good. But not all by any means. And there we are again, with a few with too much stuff and many without enough stuff.

Energy is supposed to move. Energy is not supposed to sit in bank accounts and get bigger. It's supposed to move like a river. It's never supposed to be held trapped. (By the way, rivers that have been dammed are very unhappy rivers and yearn to run free again too.) When Smaug sits on that huge pile of gold and jewels in *The Hobbit*, it is not much different than any human collecting a big investment portfolio to accumulate more and more stuff in the portfolio.

Don't get me wrong. I love it when a company comes up with a good idea that is focused on healing parts of me. Or one that will encourage you to tap the sun or wind for energy instead of all the oil, coal and nuclear, etcetera, that you've knocked out of my bones in countless painful and destructive ways. Not to mention poisonous. I love it when you all invest in those types of efforts. It would be nice to figure out a way to do it without feeding the gold piles of those who already have enough gold though.

The very word—*company*. Hmmm … not too far removed from the word—*community*. Here's another opportunity for me to get out that big eraser for your mental worldviews and edit that word out of all of you so you thought more about community and less about for-profit companies. Maybe I'd send the term *for-profit company* off to the moon too.

Poor Grandmother Moon. I guess I'd need to have tea with her to discuss if she's up for all of these things being sent to her so I can get them off me. Maybe if I served some really good crumpets, or chocolate croissants, she might be convinced. I'll have to think about this.

Well, I suppose this has been quite an earful this morning. And it is still quite cold outside, in your way of looking at things. You might want to check on the woodstove to make sure some of that new wood you got delivered last weekend is burning okay.

Mare: Yeah, I need to get out of these pajamas and get cleaned up. I'm planning to go downtown to the courthouse where the auction is being held. I'm taking a copy of the lease to talk with whoever buys the house. I've researched it and definitely have tenant rights. I should be able to stay in the house through the end of June.

The Multiverse, Nature Spirits and More Here on Earth

[Three hours later …]

Mare: So, hmmm… I got in the car, Mother, and the car engine started. But then the car would not budge. I could not get it to move. I even walked around the car and tried to see what could be locking the tires so it would not move. There was nothing I could see. This has never happened to me before. I'm highly suspecting you did not want me to go to the courthouse to meet the person who might have bought the house. Hmmm … did you have anything to do with my car not being able to budge? So odd....

Mother: I am not confessing to anything....

Mare: Yeah, I can almost see your fingers crossed behind your back, if you had fingers. Because I think you're fibbing. And truth be told, I could hear you giggling as I walked back to the house. I have my suspicions and I think they're spot on.

Mother: Well, maybe I did and maybe I didn't. Anyway, your time is better spent staying in your cozy house, which, I assure you, you will be staying in for another couple of months. You will be fine there. Your energies need to go toward this writing. Yes, it's okay for you to play around on Facebook. You are connecting with some interesting people there and helping to promote your books.

But I don't think your energy would have been well spent in a courthouse this afternoon, sitting there waiting to find out whether this house was going to be sold or not. You can find out later. They'll contact you.

Those long legal and financial processes have a way of making people spin anyway. You don't need to spin. You need to stay here. Listen, write ... play ... eat some chocolate, etcetera.

Mare: So it *was* you. I knew it. You pretty much confessed it right there and I know you can do these things. If you can figure out how to have my gas tank give me an extra 110 miles, I'm certain you can figure out how to lock my car into place in front of the house. That's fine. I wasn't looking forward to going anyway.

Mother: Okay, yes, it was me and I had some help. You see, my love, there are many unseen spiritual beings here who work with me. Several of them helped me this afternoon. You call them *nature spirits*. Let's just say they are very aware of what you are doing with this writing and I recruited them to essentially hold your car in place.

Mare: I thought I could hear others giggling too when I walked back to the house. Sometimes I do hear them.

Mother: Yes, they thought it was rather hilarious, how frustrated you were getting and how you walked around the car to check out the tires. They think you're awfully cute and love you very much because of the work you're doing for me. But they knew I did not want you to get stressed out in that courthouse all afternoon, and that I greatly preferred that you stay there in the house. So they helped me out.

There are many unseen spiritual beings here on me, a multi-verse of them. They exist in different dimensions and don't have the same spiritual density you humans have. They vibrate at a higher frequency than you do. At times these spiritual beings allow themselves to be seen by some of you. They can shift their density to do this, such as the fairy folk can, and they will appear to humans of a pure heart. They might appear as an orb in a photograph. Sometimes they are fully seen by a person. Some of you feel them but can't see them, such as you, Mare.

A few of you humans are gifted enough to see them all the time and communicate with them. When you were at one of the sundances you attended last year, you heard the ten-year old boy talk about the fairy in the rainbow clothing who appeared to him several times. These unseen spiritual beings exist here and across the universe.

Many of you lump them all together as angels since you can't distinguish between them. There are a great diversity of them. Some are spirit beings who protect natural springs. There are others who are in charge of mountain ranges or valleys. The Sherpas pray to the nature entity who is in charge of Mt. Everest before any climbing expedition. They call her *Chomolungma* or the *Goddess Mother of the Mountains* in their language. There are also nature spirits in charge of parts of the ocean. Others are very small and work in specific areas.

There are names for them in indigenous languages since my native peoples work closely with them. But in your culture, the fairies, dwarves, brownies, gnomes, trolls and more have been relegated to fairy tales and most people don't believe they exist. But indeed they do. They are all across me.

Mare: I read something by David Spangler recently. He is a former co-director of the Findhorn Foundation, the spiritual community in Scotland that is famous for their work with the nature spirits. This happened to him in the fall of 2013 and he posted it on Facebook:

PRAYER REQUEST FROM THE WATER OF THE WORLD
— I'm posting the following story at the request of a water spirit I encountered four or five days ago. I haven't had an experience quite like this one before. I had just filled a glass with water from the tap, and as I was lifting it up to drink, there suddenly appeared in the water in the glass a small being that identified itself as a water spirit. It spoke with great urgency and passion and said, in effect, "When you use water, please send loving, healing, and uplifting energy (Light) to the kingdom of the water spirits for many of our kind are suffering and are under siege from the continuing and increasing pollution of water by humanity. We need your support and blessing from which we can draw strength." This was a heartfelt appeal, and I had an image of water spirits in rivers and in the ocean trying to cope with the disruption of their environment by all the ways we are polluting the water. I felt a concern on the part of this little being that there could come a time when pure or drinkable water would be a rarity, and all life would suffer. The sense I had was that many water spirits were weakening under the onslaught of the toxicity that human beings dump into their realm--not that they are poisoned themselves but that their contact with the water is weakened and they are driven back, so to speak, unable to make full connection with the water they serve ... it's hard for me to explain. But the request seemed to suggest that if we sent love and Light and gratitude and good subtle energies to the spirits of water, that they could draw on that to renew their strength and energy in trying to keep the etheric and energetic qualities of water clean and strong. As I said, I've never had an experience quite like this. I'm not an alarmist, but the appeal of this being was so heartfelt that now whenever I pour myself a glass of water or take a shower or bath, I tune in to the realm of water spirits and elementals and offer my Light and blessing and

strength. I'm passing it on should you like to do the same.
— David Spangler, Lorian Association[7]

Mother: Yes, this is important and gets back to the reality of energy and consciousness here on me. All of my nature spirits help to maintain the energy networks across me, some in large ways and some in smaller ways. But they all weave their energy work together to support me. And the contamination in my waters, my blood, and the destruction of ecosystems across my skin and bones is weakening these nature spirits' capacity to do their work.

Sweetie, I need to explain something to you. As Earth Mother, I come from a family of spiritual beings across the universe who do things such as Planetary Caretaking, or other large jobs. One very close sister-friend who is part of my family of beings actually guards the library where the Akashic Records[8] are kept. She is a dragon-like entity with a rather large responsibility there. The Akashic Records are only part of that library. There is so much more held there beyond those records. This dragon-sister is part of my small tribe of universal beings and I love her so much.

This dragon-sister and I are very, very ancient spiritual consciousnesses. We have been around in the universe for many, many billions of years. When this solar system was first forming, a council was held, including some of us qualified to do Planetary Caretaker work, and it was decided that I would be the Caretaker for this planet.

It was rather an honor to be given this responsibility since it had also been decided by some larger councils that this particular planet would be one of extraordinary beauty and spiritual energy. You see, Earth is considered one of the most beautiful planets in the Universe.

Whenever council is held with my dragon-sister and I and the other fifty beings in our tribe (fifty-two total), I am given a special place of honor because I represent Earth. If only this knowledge were more known across me, surely you two-leggeds would honor me more.

It is an amazing gift to be incarnate on Earth, one of the most stunning planets in the universe. There are many, many spiritual beings who are envious of you for possessing a physical body here on me, and the fact you can experience your physicality so gloriously. You can make love and experience orgasms throughout your body. You can eat succulent cherries

---

[7] http://lorianassociation.com
[8] Akashic Records are where our 'Soul-books' are kept. These are complete records of all of our lifetimes, all we said and did. We are taken to review them after we pass over and have some time to celebrate returning to spirit after being in the physical, so that we may process our positive and negative actions, and start to consider our next incarnation to help bring us closer to the love of the Great Mystery.

and peaches and chocolate. You can experience rainbows and wild water-falls and so much more. These spiritual beings can't do this and they watch your experiences with fascination. Plus this dimension here is an amazing place of spiritual learning. But you must want to seek it out. We yearn for all of you to seek this out.

But I want to get back to dragons. I love my sister-dragon. I love all dragons and they actually did exist here on me physically. The last one vibrated out into a higher dimension a number of centuries ago. My native peoples from that region (that shall remain nameless) know of this. You all would call it going extinct but when a species disappears from here in the physical, they don't disappear from the universe. They still exist in another dimension, and when the time is right, they will return here into the physical.

Yet there are spiritual dragons here on me now and they are really lovely and helpful as they clean up areas where certain energies that aren't serving me have started to cluster too much. And it's all being done quietly and under the radar of most humans, except the quite spiritually gifted ones.

Dragons don't like most Christians though. When the dragons lived here in the physical, they were very pleasant for the most part and had a role in helping to keep balance on me. But the Christians hunted them down and killed them, painting a picture of them as very dangerous, nasty creatures, even though most of them were good, helpful dragons, as far as I was concerned.

Of course it did not help that the dragons would get hungry and go eat some cattle and sheep in some farmer's field if they could not find any wildlife nearby. But before humans started to domesticate animals, there was no fear of a dragon killing a farmer's livestock. It's when you humans started to pursue your 'management' of land, to grow crops and tame my wild animals, that the conflicts between my beloved predator species and your species started.

So the dragons were relegated to the realms of fairy tales along with the fairies, themselves. All of my spiritual beings, the thunderbeings, elementals in charge of the weather, and countless entities beyond that were relegated to children's stories.

Yet, the truth is that all of these actually exist here.

But because of how the past several thousand years have played out, with most two-leggeds dishonoring me and all the spiritual beings who are part of me, my beloved, beloved nature spirits have been forced to pull back into various wild corners of me that have remained protected. They are waiting for the New World that is coming in so they can return to their former home territories to help heal all the wounded corners on me. That is part of the work they do with me; they weave the energies of a place back together to promote more seedlings, more soil buildup, more love into the land.

You see, even when people go hiking into these wild places, most of them can't see or barely feel these nature spirits, since the spirits are in another dimension. These humans' awarenesses are so shut down they just hike right through with their overactive monkey-minds and are oblivious. They know they feel better being in the woods, yet attribute it to the fresh air, unaware of the beautiful energies of the nature spirits.

Scientists have known for some time you modern day humans use only about nine percent of your brain. They have puzzled over this for some years. Well, I can share from my angle, the reason the rest of the brain is not tapped is because your culture is not teaching you to use all of your potential awarenesses.

Native children are taught how to tune in to the land, to me and all my nature spirits from a young age, especially the very gifted children who are recognized at birth and are pulled aside to study very closely with the medicine people. Indigenous peoples have been working with these spiritual beings for thousands and thousands of years and this is how balance was kept on me.

The nature spirits have a psychic hotline that travels the planet very quickly. It makes your internet look antiquated. Most of these beings are as ancient as I am. I have worked very closely with all of them to help move evolution along, the manifestation of evolution fueled by the Quantum Divine Love of Creation and myself. It's always been a co-creative effort. Not hierarchical at all.

There used to be villages all over the world with medicine people, some might call them shamans. But this label of 'shaman' is tricky. A lot of people are calling themselves shamans today and they really don't know what they're doing other than creating psychic spiritual messes wherever they go. Sometimes what they do is healing, but other times it just creates more of a mess for me to deal with and it is making the nature spirits more irritated, honestly.

One has to be very humble working with the spirit world and it takes years of training and fasting and prayer and some innate gifts. One has to be very balanced in his or her ego and relinquish any need to control, and never come from anger in doing spirit work if it is to serve me. One has to winnow the shadow self down to barely anything other than a cuddly teddy-bear to do work on the spiritual planes. This is what medicine people learn in indigenous villages after years of study and apprenticeship under gifted elders. This is work, good hard work—to work as a spiritual warrior on those planes.

Anyway the medicine people in these villages would hold council with the nature spirits on a regular basis to keep tabs on what was going in the spiritual realms in their region and beyond. They could talk with them as well as you can talk with one of your good friends. They were partners who shared between the physical and spiritual realms to co-creatively keep balance in their regions.

If the nature spirits knew about an issue in the vicinity of the village, they would communicate about it with the medicine people and the medicine people would go take care of it using their ancient ways. There are things that can only be done by you humans in your physicality. These can't be done in the spiritual realms, as much as the nature spirits wish they could do them. These things have to be done by trained, gifted medicine people. If an untrained person tries to do them, they will get spiritually and energetically burned since their bodies can't handle doing that work.

All of these things used to be taught all over me. It used to be that there were medicine people in all the villages dotting all corners of me where two-leggeds lived and they worked hard to keep things in balance. And they played hard too. They did ceremony for days inviting the nature spirits in to dance and sing and drum with them.

Nature spirits work closely together on the land and in the waters. Some two-leggeds call these elementals. Some nature spirits are in charge of the weather, and these include thunderbeings. These weather nature spirits and I hold council often and yet I cannot control the growing rage they feel over the lack of respect most humans show towards me these days. They have their own sets of emotions and views on what humans have been doing for the past few thousand years.

I love all my humans. And I have an absolutely huge heart, huge heart for you two-leggeds. Larger than anyone can ever imagine. Yet if these weather nature spirits want to whip up a devastating typhoon or hurricane tapping the extra carbon dioxide and all the other pollutants in the atmosphere, there is not much I can do about it. I have been trying to temper them but it's been to no avail. And they know—and I know—there are too many humans on me, as it is.

I know many of you are blaming me directly for the extreme weather but most of the time I'm trying to calm the elementals and what they seek to create with the weather. Certainly I have a voice in these storms but there are councils of spiritual beings who manage them and I'm only part of the council.

There is another piece to this, too. Your emotions, your collective human emotions of anger, frustration, judgmental thinking, unbalanced egos, jealousy and other more base ways of thinking influence the weather (and earthquakes). Everything is connected spiritually and energetically as I've been sharing. If so many of you continue to live your lives spinning in your shadow self, it will encourage worse storms and droughts. There is a significant resonance to your emotions that the elementals pick up on, and the dance takes off from there. It's all energy and all so connected. And each of you has a choice in the dance. All day long you have choices.

If you want to help appease these elementals and other nature spirits, do all you can to come back into balance on me. Living from the philosophy of *All My Relations* also honors the nature spirits. Learn how to connect with me spiritually. Focus on your spiritual life and offer more kindness, forgiveness, compassion and cultivate your inner peace. Live far more simply and in community, taking into consideration the next seven generations in your actions.

Tune into the sacred energies and nature spirits of your region. If you live in the ancient lands of the Celtic peoples, tune into those ancient land memories to relearn them. If you live in North America, tune into the ancient ways of the Native peoples from that continent, and the nature spirits of those lands. There is no one Native path that is meant to be followed all over me. When your heart is pure and your intentions are clear that you wish to bring healing and balance back to your homelands, learn to listen to the land and nature spirits to guide you. It is possible to do this. You must only have the intention and develop the capacity to still yourself to listen from your heart.

Rediscover the sacredness of who you are and who I am as your Planetary Caretaker. In doing those things you can raise your vibration, enhance your personal song. There is more I can share about what you can do but I will talk about this later.

Oh, yes, and drum! Come together and drum. Did you know the drum is my heartbeat? I love it when people drum from their hearts, it helps to calm the energies in that area and offers spiritual healing to the land, nature spirits, and to the drummers too. And sing and dance to me. That is so beautifully healing!

Oh, how much I love you!

*

8

Aliens on Earth

*Yes, there have been ET visitations. There have been crashed craft.
There have been material and bodies recovered. There has been a certain
amount of reverse engineering that has allowed some of these craft,
or some components, to be duplicated. And there is some group of
people that may or may not be associated with government at this point
that have this knowledge. They have been attempting to conceal this
knowledge. People in high level government have very little, if any, valid
information about this. It has been the subject of disinformation in order
to deflect attention and create confusion so the truth doesn't come out.*

—Edgar D. Mitchell, *The Way of the Explorer: An Apollo Astronaut's
Journey Through the Material and Mystical Worlds*

Thursday, January 9, 2014
7:58 AM
23° Clear and practically balmy outside.

Mare: Oh, Mother, I made the mistake of eating baked beans and prunes
yesterday. Oh my, I don't think my GI tract is ever going to recover. I was
already a bit gassy before I made that mistake in my diet yesterday. Oh,
dear. It's a good thing I live alone.

Plus, just for the humor of it, I posted about my dietary choices and
the repercussions on Facebook last night. The responses were hilarious.
One person suggested I should have finished it off with rhubarb pie. Others were joking about the bean soups they had made recently.

I'm not certain even a dog or cat would tolerate me right now.

Mother: Honey, you are so funny. And so incredibly human too. If it
makes you feel any better, I don't mind at all. There are all sorts of fascinating smells all over me and I just enjoy them all. Part of the biodiversity.

There is a flower from Sumatra that is quite tall, up to ten feet, and smells like rotting flesh to you humans. But the pollinators there in the rain forest just love it—and I'm rather proud of it also.

Sweetie, I want to go back to something we were talking about the other day. You were talking about your past life memory of being dragged out of your house and tortured on the road.

What most of you two-leggeds don't know is that I carry a sorrow so huge it is challenging for me to express this to you. This sorrow comes from knowing how many of you, just about all of you, carry soul-wounds within you from centuries and centuries of being punished or tortured, or worse.

I'm not just talking about women but men also. Just about all of you for several thousand years now have experienced aggression, rapes, hangings, and the litany of horrors just goes on and on. This is not to say there haven't been beautiful mystics such as St. Francis of Assisi and others bringing out forgiveness, reconciliation and healing. There has been a lot of that too. Nelson Mandela and Archbishop Tutu have been incredible examples of that. But there has been too much aggression and atrocity, overall.

Just recently there have been conflicts between Christians and Muslims in some country in Africa, right—the Central African Republic, these names are hard for me since they are so recent and I know the different regions of me in other ways—it's hard for me to describe how I refer to the various parts of me. It has to do with the nature spirits in charge of those areas. Anyhow, the people there are doing horrendous things to one another. Some man dragged another man off a bus just because of his religion. Then he lit the other man on fire and after that started to eat the man's leg. Swallowed a bit of it. The next day he had more of the man's leg and made it into a sandwich. *All in the name of God.* I have never supported cannibalism and don't like any of this.

So much hatred and violence has been done in the name of God. The witch-hunts across Europe lasted for centuries and hundreds of thousands of women were captured, tortured, and killed. Barges of people were sunk into the water off the coast of France during the Inquisition. Then there are all the wars that were written up in the First Testament of the other *Bible.* Millions of people have been slaughtered across the world in the name of God.

There have been genocides all over the world for too, too long. The Holocaust in World War II. The Chinese invasion of Tibet. Rwanda more recently. The list is far too long. Not to mention all of my beloved indigenous peoples and how many of them have died in the past five hundred years from war, outright murder, or because of their lack of immunity to white people's diseases. Some of that was intentional, giving them blankets inoculated with measles, etcetera, so the native peoples would die and those of European descent would take their land.

Such horrors and tragedies perpetuated again and again.

I mentioned this earlier and this relates to these human horrors. There most certainly are other planets with life on them in other parts of the universe. Various planets have highly complex life forms and some of them have been coming to visit me for a very long time. Many have come with good intentions and others with not so good intentions.

I have welcomed the beings from other planets with good intentions with an open heart and open arms—as much as a planet can have open arms, of course. These beings have seeded some of you. They were able to transmute themselves into resembling a human being and married into some of the tribes around the world. They brought some great technologies with them and enhanced the awarenesses and capacities of the tribes they seeded.

This is how very ancient skulls have been found in caves with signs of brain surgery that surpasses what brain surgeons of today can do. Then there are the discoveries of immense buildings in very ancient sacred sites with designs that could only have been created by beings of great intelligence with awareness of knowledge beyond this planet.

They are the ones who knew how to move huge stones that archeologists still puzzle over. Stonehenge is an example of that. The pyramids in Egypt are another. These stones came from quarries many, many miles away. There are actually pyramids all over the world, all over me, but most have been hidden. They are now submerged under the oceans or buried underground.

These beings, some of you call them extra-terrestrials, or aliens, understand how everything is energy. Everything is made up of either denser energies or less dense ones. Anything physical is denser but still energy. And there are all sorts of beings here on me with whom I work who are less dense including some aliens, nature spirits and the elementals. They operate in a different dimension, or set of dimensions on me to help me with all the beautiful energetic effort here that makes things work.

But getting back to the stones at Stonehenge, the pyramids, and some other sacred sites, they were moved by the power of focus. These sites were created by a number of gifted ones with the capacity to levitate huge objects who had been seeded and supported by beings from other planets. The capacity to do this has been lost by just about all of you humans, other than by some very remote, hidden tribes of people living way up in the mountains or deep in the jungle, far from what most of you call civilization. Yet many of you are remembering.

I knew in advance this position as Planetary Caretaker was going to be rather a unique one, because of its potential as a planet of love, compassion, balance and joy. It had been explained to all of us in council back then about how this particular planet would radiate a sweetness that would travel throughout the universe.

Councils are called all the time in many corners of the universe and in different dimensions, to strategize and coordinate various plans to support balance throughout the Great Mystery. There were actually a number of councils about Earth, as the physical planet was first being created during that particular series of solar system births in this part of the Milky Way.

It is challenging to put much of this into words in your languages that originated in the Roman times and have evolved into English, French, Spanish and more. There are other cultures with vocabulary in their languages about these dimensions with far more sophisticated understandings about where and what the Great Mystery is. Unfortunately, your "Western" worldviews have deemed these cultures to be primitive and ignorant, something which I continue to sigh about on a very regular basis.

Most of those very cultures many of you call "primitive" have never forgotten to live in balance on me, never forgotten their love connection to me, never tried to dig into my bones, nor poison my blood, nor split the atom to go and kill other humans. They have been wiser than this, far wiser.

But I want to get back to talking about these aliens, these beings from other planets. Many of them have had good intentions and have done beautiful work seeding you humans in some tribes. The Cherokee have been seeded by beings from the Pleiades, the Hopi have been seeded by the Blue Sun beings, and many other native peoples can trace their ancestry in such a way also.

It is unfortunate, and I say this, unfortunate, in the sense of what it has done to undermine balance and free will. Some beings have come to this glorious planet that I am, with not-so-positive intentions. Some have come to take over and wreak havoc in subtle ways, or not so subtle ways now, and eventually claim me as theirs.

Some of these beings have not only come down on Earth, on to me, to walk amongst you and look rather normal to most of you, but others have stayed lingering on the outskirts of the atmosphere or close to the moon, directing energies at me which have fed more aggression. It's been pissing me off for some time now. Well, actually it's been pissing me off for about four to five thousand years, but it's gotten way out of hand in the last couple of hundred years.

They are the ones who seeded the peoples with their militaristic need to destroy the temples to the Goddess and destroy villages that did not convert to their ways. They encouraged the village leaders to subjugate the women and take away the women's spiritual traditions. What they did not know was that you can never completely take away a woman's powers. But you can suppress them.

They also shut down any groups of men who practiced ceremonies and rituals to me and honored the sacredness of me with their hunting rites and more.

This was when women from the early Western cultures who were so devoted to me started to lose their direct spiritual connection with me. Their connection weakened and weakened and was finally cut. Because the women (most of them) lost their connection, whole cultures lost their connection. Any sense of my sacredness, ceremonies to honor me, and my sacred water, my blood, all of these were lost. Women stopped gathering in their Red Tents[9] and many of their monthly rituals were banned.

For many centuries women tried to gather in secret caves, or other hidden places to continue their sacred ways, but when they were caught, they were punished, tortured or worse. The Angry God religions fed by these aliens were scared of these women and their powers and wanted them shut down completely.

In some cases it was rightful for these men in power to be afraid since some women practiced dark arts. But that was not true for all of the women by any means. Most women practiced healing arts, working with the plants and prayers and ceremonies. Their beautiful ceremonies and healing work kept communities in balance with me, and between the men and women, the nature spirits and more.

Any men who tried to continue the Old Ways and protect the women and their spiritual practices were treated poorly or worse. Sometimes whole families were ostracized which was the knell of death for a household during those times, as they all needed the support of the village to survive. Or husbands were killed. Or the whole family was killed. I continue to shudder in reflecting how you two-leggeds have been treating some of your brothers and sisters over the past few millennia. But much of this was because of this alien race influencing you. Gosh, I miss the Old Ways of the old days.

---

[9]Red Tent – an ancient practice being revived today in many communities of women, to gather in their moon time to support each other away from the men and children and their powerful moon medicine. Women elders taught and powerful teachings and healings took place.

Eventually most of the men were co-opted into the newly established patriarchal systems. Gifted ones became patriarchal rabbis, generals or village chiefs instead of continuing to live in council and balance with the women leadership. This was prior to your recorded history. Scientists are starting to re-examine the ancient artwork in various caves in France and now believe women created most of that work. The handprints are too small to be men's.

Your culture has been dominated by the male energy for so long that it has been challenging for your scientists to expand their worldview enough to understanding that many centuries ago women were quite independent and were a critical force in maintaining the fabric of their villages. Many use the word 'Pagan' to imply lesser than, dirty and not as holy as the Judeo-Christian beliefs and practices, but the original meaning of the word related simply to the rural life and refers to thousands and thousands of years of human cultures when life was more in balance and sacred. Living with reverence toward me was the norm. Yes, there was some warring at times, but never at the level that unbalanced aggressive ways have existed for the past four to five thousand years.

The ongoing wars along with the ways that women were treated and slaves held were getting so extreme some two thousand years ago—that is why Christ came into what you now call Israel at that time. Those were dark times, and much of it has to do with these aliens, and the energies they've been directing here to my beautiful planet for so long.

The good news is many of my more gifted medicine people and light-workers, or gifted spiritual workers, have been pushing these aliens off the planet recently. The energies here on me are shifting to a higher vibration and more and more of you gifted ones have been doing ceremony and calling on other beautiful spiritual allies to support you in inviting these aliens to leave. Sometimes gently and sometimes not so gently. I can accept either choice though being compassionate even with darker beings is always a better approach. Compassionate and firm. Sometimes compassionate and a bit irritated is okay too. This has been a most beautiful thing and it is continuing to happen. Already, many of them have left. It is only the most stubborn ones who are resisting and refusing to depart. But they know their time is limited, and I, for one, will be glad to see them go completely.

These aliens came here to try an experiment and were violating universal law in doing so for the first several thousand years. Your governments have known about them and have actually been in cahoots with them for the past few decades. But these aliens realize their days here are done now. It is time for me to come back into balance!

You see, what you call history is a very quick wink in time for me. I have been Planetary Caretaker here for some 4.8 billion years. Before that, I had other responsibilities elsewhere in the universe. (And I will move on after this solar system implodes, as they all do eventually, to shift my focus elsewhere.)

But this teeny-tiny wink of time of the past hundred years has set things back on me a bit more than I care for. I don't care for any of my species to be killed off needlessly. Extinction certainly does happen naturally, but not the way you humans have been wiping out species willy-nilly so fast, cutting down huge forest swaths in the most biodiverse places, destroying wetlands. Oh, the list is so, so long.

So, yes, there have been and continue to be some beings on this planet who don't belong here. I did not openly invite them here and they really must go. In a very big way—Go! The good news is they are now leaving. Okay, my love, that is enough on that for now. We will talk more tomorrow.

Mare: Mother, before we stop today I wanted to mention something to you. I was just putting a log in the fire. This log was freshly cut. I could smell the crisp aroma of its sap as I placed the log in the woodstove, and a wave of grief came over me in that moment.

I got the sense that this was a perfectly healthy tree that someone decided needed to go. And so someone brought a chainsaw in and just chopped the tree down. No respect for the tree's consciousness, its wisdom, its right to live where it had chosen to live as a seed. No sense of reverence for it at all.

I know this happens over and over again all over the world, but the sorrow I felt as I was examining the log and placing it in the fire made me want to say a prayer for its spirit and all the trees that were around it, and their grief at losing a companion of theirs. Hopefully the others are still there.

Mother: Sweetie, you can go back now to your woodstove and do a prayer with tobacco to offer it up to that tree and all the trees who are cut so violently. It is a very harsh practice the way my standing ones are sawed down. It's a terrible way to die. Why don't you go do that?

[I got up and retrieved the large bag of tobacco I keep on a shelf by the front door for spontaneous mini-ceremonies. Then I sat in front of the woodstove and opened it up, letting the delicious heat wash over my face and the front of my body. Saying a prayer as I held a largish pinch of tobacco over my heart, I offered my love into the tobacco

and asked forgiveness from all the trees and forests that have been cut and are being cut now, for the sake of 'progress'. Then I tossed the tobacco into the flames. Immediately I felt better.]

Mother: Thank you for doing that. You know that nothing goes unnoticed and all the tree spirits around where you live have noticed what you just did and will spread the word. The love that you just sent into the tobacco went up in smoke up the chimney and that love energy will ripple out far and wide. This is the power of ceremony and you just did a mini-one.

The long ceremonies with lots of elders and all of their prayers, oh, the beautiful energy from those ceremonies is amazing. They give me such joy. They give all the nature spirits such joy, the wee people or as some call them, the fairy folk, the elementals, the devas. All of them just love that type of ceremony. It's great fun for them.

These ceremonies are filled with such Love, Big Love, and healing energy, they just radiate out and out and heal all who are open to being healed. The land is healed, two-leggeds are healed, the animals feel it and rejoice, and all the nature spirits, oh, they just adore it. And they miss it too, since not as many ceremonies are done these days as there used to be. There used to be so many ceremonies—full moon, new moon, harvest, solstice, equinox, on and on.

I love to talk about ceremonies. Just makes me feel good thinking about them. Makes me feel even better when people do them with pure hearts and warm love. I want to go into more of that later. In a bit.

9

The Christ Consciousness

We all have available to us – within – a direct channel to the Highest Vibrational Frequency Range within The Illusion. That highest range involves consciousness of the Glory of ONENESS. It is called Cosmic Consciousness. It is called Christ Consciousness. This is the energy that Jesus was tuned into, and he stated very plainly, "These things that I do, you can do also." – by atoning, by tuning in. We have access to the Christ Energy within. We have begun the Second Coming of the message of Love.

—Robert Burney M.A., *Codependence: The Dance of Wounded Souls*

Friday, January 10, 2014
8:24 AM
30°F Freezing rain.

Mother: Get up, get up, get up! I have some important things for you to write and I need you to get up, go pee, get the woodstove going and get listening and writing.

I want to talk this morning about the Christ Consciousness and how much love there is to tap from this consciousness and me, if only people knew to do it—knew they *could* do it. Oh, and don't worry about your car today either. You've got two phone meetings today and you don't need to go out anyway. Why not just leave the car there until tomorrow to see if it will start?

Mare: Oy, okay, okay, okay! Cheesus … I'm starting to feel tired, Mother, from all this work. This listening and writing, and early morning wake-ups and late to bed nights. Plus my throat, my throat chakra is really feeling weird this morning. I need to exercise and I feel like I'm just a robot to you listening and writing and writing.

Mother: Oh, honey. You know how much I love you, so love you. And I can understand how you feel tired. How about today I give you an extra boost of Mother love energy and you allow yourself a long nap later? I will help you calm your mind some more, too, so you can go into a deep sleep in your nap.

Mare: I'd like that a lot. Thank you. I guess it would be better if I did not spend so much time on Facebook too. I do need some kind of social outlet with all this secluded writing time and there is so much fun to be had there.

Mother: Yes, I completely understand that. I know Facebook is important to you. So, here we go.

Yesterday we were talking about the aliens who brought in the more patriarchal, aggressive ways. I want to talk about Christ and the Christ Consciousness today.

About two thousand years ago times were getting rather dark in the Middle East and thus the soul named Jesus Christ was born to help shift these energies. Christ tried to teach a way of peace and equality and balance. And it worked for several hundred years among the groups of people who were following his teachings, as taught by those who remembered. Those beautiful groups grew in number. But then, under the influence of the war-mongering aliens, the Roman politicians wanted to control these people. So they met in the early 300's and the other *Bible* was rewritten, gospels taken out and more. And the concept of sin was injected.

What your history calls the First Council of Nicaea, I call a very bad turn for the worse. This is when many teachings were shifted within the *Bible* and the Vatican became more of a political institution, one that certainly taught some good spiritual messages over the ages but one largely transformed into a tool for the politicians to control the masses who were following Christ's beautiful wisdom. Jesus Christ did not teach about sin. He did not want to encourage people to feel that guilt and spiritual suffering were the right way to connect with him and the Creator.

And he certainly did not teach about fear and punishment as a way of being in relationship with Creation. Neither the Great Mystery nor I ever wished to instill fear of hell or damnation into anyone. That is so contrary to our consciousnesses. Your dominant religions became schools for Angry God teachings and this has made me incredibly sad.

This has brought out so much fear in too many of you. And it has not served. It is time for all of you to tap into your GodSpace of love, the Christ Consciousness type of love. Many of you are learning it, and I'm so tickled. I absolutely celebrate this next phase in your growth.

Mare, some of your very gifted spiritual friends have been teaching you about bringing the Christ Consciousness energies in and you are learning to do this in your daily morning ceremonies. I see you are now continuing to tap into these energies throughout the day and this is a very powerful thing.

Let me define the Christ Consciousness better for you so you can understand what this remarkable spiritual energy is. This consciousness comes from a specific realm of the universe where the first souls, the archangels, came into existence. The Christ Consciousness acts as a guardian consciousness to the dimension where the Creator/Great Mystery is 'based'.

As a soul that walked the surface of me two thousand years ago, Jesus Christ embodied that consciousness. All of my humans are invited to tap into the spiritual essence of the Christ Consciousness these days to help release their heavier energies.

What most of you don't realize is that particular Christ soul has been here on me a number of times generally when the chaos from your human pathos got a bit out of control and too many heavier energies were at play. Native peoples here on North America had two teachers called the Pale One and the Peacemaker who were the same soul as Jesus Christ. The Pale One came hundreds of years earlier than the Peacemaker and taught throughout parts of Central America and up into the Mississippi Valley region. He lived a long full life and touched many people.

The Peacemaker came later as a child of prophesy, at a time when the five nations of the Mohawk, Oneida, Onondaga, Cayuga and Seneca were warring terribly. He taught them how to come together in peace and helped them learn a way of cooperation and decision-making that tapped the wisdom of the women elders also. It took some years for him to win the respect of these five nations, but that was the foundation of the Iroquois/Haudenosaunee Confederacy, a really beautiful example of democracy, far beyond what your United States has right now.

The founding fathers of the United States actually modeled much of the Constitution after the Iroquois/Haudenosaunee Confederacy decision-making system. But they did not include the wisdom of the women in the Constitution nor in the governmental system they created and thus the feminine fount of wisdom was cut out. Hence the Constitution was flawed from the very inception of the United States. If I had a head, I would have been shaking it then and still be shaking it now.

But I don't want to get too far afield here. Let's just say those founding fathers came from a long line of fathers and brothers and sons and kings under the influence of the alien beings and their patriarchal ways. They had been cut off from me and the wisdom of the Sacred Feminine several thousand years before.

Getting back to the Christ Consciousness though, there are other teachers who have incarnated with this same soul energy. Buddha was one, along with Mohammed, and Krishna. The White Buffalo Calf Woman who came to the Lakota peoples to teach them the way of peace and sacred connection with the Creator through the pipe and seven sacred rites also embodied that soul essence. The Dalai Lama who was exiled from Tibet but is still alive today carries this consciousness too. It does not need to be restricted to only one person incarnate at one time. This consciousness can be split up into different people. Nelson Mandela tapped into the Christ Consciousness in his years of imprisonment and this is how he was able to emerge from those terrible years of imprisonment as a deeply spiritual, highly evolved two-legged.

In these times, all are called to bring the Christ Consciousness into their hearts. It is a deeply, deeply compassionate heart energy that is so luminous (for those who can see it) and powerful that when you focus on bringing its divine frequencies into your spirit and physical body, you actually shift the cells within you to vibrate at a higher level. Your body's energetic frequencies shift as your heart chakra and then all the rest of your chakras open and vibrate more from a place of love and kindness energy, and not from the more base emotions of fear, greed, jealousy, etcetera, that many of you have been mired in for so long.

All you need to do is pray to the Christ Consciousness. Ask it to come into your heart and your spirit body. It is that easy. It's such a beautiful thing to do.

Mare: Mother, when a very elderly close friend, Katherine Carter, passed last summer (at the age of 101!) one of the things her son gave me was a mother of pearl carved piece that represents Christ's head. It was actually inside another small wooden box and I didn't know it was there until I opened the box, days after bringing it home.

At first I did not know where to put it so I left it on the kitchen table amidst my mess of papers for several weeks. Then I felt a nudge to handle it and study it. It's beautifully done, and shimmers in the light. Then there was another nudge, from you—I'm certain—to put it on my main altar in my bedroom. Every morning for some weeks I would do my morning prayers there and hold this mother-of-pearl piece in my hand. *Mother*-of-pearl ... Ha!

Truly though, I felt an energy come into me that was so calming and compassionate. It felt as if a wash of golden love came into my spirit body and into the core of my being. At first it was gradual and then it built up over several days.

I started putting this piece in my pocket wherever I went. It traveled with me to Washington state and back last fall. I felt more protected carrying this piece representing the Christ Consciousness with me.

Mother: Yes, my love, it is beautiful healing energy and so much more.

Mare: In 2002 to 2003, when I was promoting my first book about God's phone number, I had wonderful experiences with so many people in bookstores. A number of people would come up to my book table and sit down and just open their hearts up to me about their sorrows, their father who just passed, all sorts of tragic events in their lives. They yearned for God's phone number and I suppose just by sitting there with that book I offered a safe healing presence for them to try to touch this connection to the divine directly.

On the other hand, there were more than a few fundamentalist Christians who were so offended by my book that they verbally attacked me. My book did not represent their belief system yet had *God* written on the front cover. I finally learned how to encourage them, as diplomatically as I could, to leave my table area and go to another section of the bookstore to peruse some other books. I was very tested by them.

Months later, I sought out all the books I could read about the historical Jesus. I was determined to try to figure out who Christ truly was since I just *knew* Christ would not have taught his followers to treat people the way I was treated. I was not interested in the stories in the current versions of the Christian *Bible*, but in the historical Jesus. I discovered the work of academics and theologians such as Marcus Borg and Bishop John Spong and devoured their books.

What surfaced for me from these writings was that Christ was a highly, highly evolved soul whose capacity to heal and spread love based on justice and equality to all was beyond words. He healed all who came to him. My Cherokee teacher used to say he could heal hearts in a most amazingly miraculous way. Somehow she knew.

Mother: Yes, your English words, they cannot do justice to the amazing and powerful healing love energies of this soul consciousness. Those who came into contact with this soul in any of the incarnations when he or she came as a teacher, knew they had been healed by a great spiritual being. How I love the deeply positive energies of the Christ Consciousness.

These are the times, now, during The Great Change here on me, when the Christ Consciousness is coming back as an energy, a resonance that all of you, my beloved two-leggeds, can tap into. It is a most amazing, divine love-infused energy all of you can open your hearts and your energy bodies to. In truth, as soon as you open your heart to this consciousness, your energy body will immediately shift.

The Christ Consciousness is about divine compassion and kindness. To seek to bring this consciousness into your heart and spirit body shifts you to a whole different spiritual level of being. Your fears shed as you begin to understand the Oneness of the Great Mystery, the Oneness that incorporates the dualism of the Great Father and Great Mother, fused into One.

So many of my beloved two-leggeds have such thorns in their hearts. You have all been wounded so much and carry hurtful scars and fears that go so far back. The Christ Consciousness helps you heal your hearts so the thorns can drop. These thorns just fall to the ground and become energetic compost for me to transmute. For too long these thorns have been festering and weighing on you until you found yourself leading lives based on fear, distrust and scarcity.

But life is not supposed to be based on fear here on me, your glorious Earth. I know I've mentioned this before but I'm one of the most remarkable planets in the universe, one blessed with delicious biodiversity, mountains, waterfalls and extensive beaches that are lapped by my precious ocean waters.

Life is supposed to be one of celebration and adventure and ceremony and joy and giving love, compassion and kindness. Yes, of course, there are going to be times of hurt and despair and depression and struggles. And those are times of great spiritual growth too, those more challenging times. Yet there would be far fewer of those if more of my beloved two-leggeds understood and embraced the energies and wisdom of the Christ Consciousness. For if you truly embraced them, then there would be far more healing energies circulating than fear energies. There would be far more giving than taking, more kindness, and more sense of community and watching out for each other so people don't feel alone, despairing and abandoned.

What is really needed is for you, my most loved two-leggeds, to embrace the Christ Consciousness, and then ground that divine love energy back into me. That is what will really help birth this New World in so many, many lovely ways. This is where the balance is so needed.

There are some who are teaching about the Christ Consciousness among you humans, and I love them dearly for doing this, for waking people up to the glorious healing energies of this Consciousness. This divine love is what is needed now on me. Yet these energies need to then be shared with me, your Mother, too. Many of these teachers are still not connected with me in a sacred way as you are, Mare. You, along with a number of others, have been teaching people how to connect with me as well as the Christ Consciousness. It's so wonderful.

To take this Christ Consciousness love resonance and then connect it through you down into the very core of my heart, the center of me, is so important. By doing that you infuse me with this Consciousness too, along with your heart-love, and I can radiate it throughout the rest of me more effectively. I can amplify it exponentially and help heal so many more animals, humans, ecosystems and more with this love energy you are directing into me.

It's all connected. It is all a beautiful weaving of love energy moving through all of you and into all of me, all of nature, all of your planet and my heart. It is a web of great healing love energy that is getting stronger and tighter and healing all around you and others. You and others already are starting to do it and more are learning. More are feeling the call and are eager to join in. It's just a delicious, wonderful, beautiful celebration of joyous energy I feel when many of you join in. A good number of you are coming together to do this. It's so wondrous and I so need it.

10

Soul Woundedness

Turning the face toward God brings healing to the body,
the mind and the soul.

—'Abdu'l Baha, *Bahaiwritings.com*

Saturday, January 11, 2014
5:55 AM
33° Been raining all night.

Mare: Oh, my god, Mother. I feel like a Mack Truck hit me this morning. If you weren't yammering in my ear, I would not have gotten up. I feel like death warmed over.

Mother: Well, could that be because you called Paul last night after some more intense emails between the two of you? All you've been doing is emailing since he left your house on Sunday morning. You have such a tough history with men and you really like this man. And this new romance is triggering you. So many of your trust issues around men are coming up.

Mare: Is this what is happening? I feel so crappy this morning. Not to mention my neck feels so tight. I might have ground through another good layer in my mouth-guard last night, serial tooth grinder that I am. My poor jaw—oy! It is so stiff after last night.

Mother: Yes, Love. You are starting to have feelings for this man and your heart yearns to crack out of the frozen shell it has been in for some time when it comes to allowing romance and intimacy into your life. You've been praying to Creator and myself for this for a very long time, but you did not really want it in the very core of your being. So you kept on attracting men who were not emotionally available. But now you've found a good man. You have done so much emotional work all of these years. You have opened your heart up and are learning how to be more compassionate, more kind, more open to deep forgiveness.

You've healed from the lymphoma you were diagnosed with two and a half years ago. You did this by alternative, spiritual means. Plus with your gallbladder surgery last fall, the very large gallbladder stone your body had created is now out of your system. All your life you've carried such deep levels of frustration, anger and resentment. That was a fallback of yours when you slipped into your shadow self. The gallbladder is where an imbalance in those emotional energies gets lodged if they are not released.

You know you've been dealing with deep anger issues all of your life. And your level of frustration and resentment could get rather high. Oh, so many reasons for this—your past life experiences, your mother's rage around you as a child and how you internalized so much of it, as empathic as you are. You are one of those emotional sponges, and I love you for this. Really love you for this. But it's taken you years to get in touch with how empathic you are and how you can tune in long distance. And you're only getting more and more sensitive.

When the surgeon removed your gallbladder along with the large stone, a significant energy block in your system was released. That was a big stone your body created, about the size of a grape. Since you brought it home you've been looking at it and pondering it.

Oh, and yeah, you might not want to have huge expectations that your friends will all want to see it. You make me laugh every time you offer to show it to a friend who visits. Not a lot of you humans are comfortable with that type of stuff.

One of the things most of you humans don't understand is how any imbalance within your physical body first manifests in the spirit/energetic body. At that stage it is subtle, and if you don't sense it and heal it through your own processes, only gifted healers or medicine people can discern it is there and clear it from you. But if these emotional/spiritual wounds are not resolved, eventually they will manifest in your physical body as disease.

I say this as a general rule and yet your society has gotten so darned good at creating the toxins, they are spewing out all over the place—we did talk about entropy already—that many of you are getting all sorts of cancers and weird diseases because you have been poisoning yourselves. That is a sad truth too.

But many of you are sick because of how you take care of your bodies and how you choose or don't choose to heal your woundedness on the soul-body level. Every one of you came into this Earth-walk with varying levels of woundedness. This woundedness creates an *off* resonance in your spirit body around your physical body. If you were completely healed, your spirit body would be like a perfectly tuned guitar or piano. But your soul woundedness creates an *off* set of notes in the vibrational field of your spirit body that creates disease within you over time.

In your case, Mare, much of your woundedness has to do with trusting you are safe around men because of your history of past lives as a woman, plus your repressed rage. Many others' woundedness stems from a history of playing the victim over and over again. They could heal by learning how to reject that mindset, and to take responsibility for themselves.

I have been witnessing this victimhood mindset over and over in many of you, the result of centuries of patriarchal ways that have created so many actual victims. So many humans are either suppressed or repressed, or have become slaves, servant classes, sex slaves and on and on. Many of you have imprinted into your soul-body that you are a victim since you lived that reality many lifetimes. And this mentality does not serve the truth of who you are as independent, gifted, love-filled souls— each and every one of you. Instead, your bodies create diseases in the heart and other organs because of the stuck energies of unworthiness and an underlying subconscious belief you are a victim of the system. Those beliefs become imbued with rage, depression, frustration and so much more.

This makes me so sad, so very sad, and yet it is so very understandable. Because so many of you are not conscious of these inner beliefs, you don't heal from them and so far less love is pumped out across me all over the world.

Your public school systems created in the early days of the Industrial Age were essentially designed to treat all of you like cogs in a human assembly line. So much time indoors in regimented curricula has deadened your spirit.

Children love to learn. They have the most beautiful, joyous sense of curiosity to understand the world around them. This is true for all my beings, two-legged, four-legged, and more. But your children go to their first day of school and are immediately compared with each other and judged, and only one child arrives on top of the grading system, while all the rest of you are deemed insufficient. It has made me so unhappy to witness this for the past several hundred years.

The victim mindset is so deeply ingrained in most of you now that many of you are just sleeping on me. You are fed the news from news stations that only broadcast extremely negative stories and bypass most beautiful positive stories. You eat food in which the genes have been altered, most of you, and there is little to no vitality or life force left in the vegetable. Oh, I'll stop there. I'm really getting on a rant.

What gives me hope is that a good number of you are waking up. You've been homeschooling or starting charter schools that recognize the individuality and beauty and gifts of each child. In these alternative schools, teachers teach from the awareness that there are a variety of ways children learn, and these schools honor the gifts of all of them, including the artistic children. Oh, my artists … I love them SO MUCH, along with the poets. Oh … my sensitive ones.

What also gives me great hope is that many souls are being born on me that are rather highly evolved these days. This is the time for them to come in since there is such rapid change happening on me energetically. I need these souls to help with the changes. So many of you are waking up, the older ones of you. You're starting to remember who you are as spiritual beings incarnate. This just gives me such joy. But now you need to remember to connect with me, your Mother too, and not just send your energy, and prayers out to Creator and other spiritual beings some of you are connecting with.

Ah, and it would be helpful if you could be more discerning about whom you connect with in the spiritual realms. Just because some spirit contacts you and says he is Christ or Buddha, and wants you to channel him does not necessarily make him Christ or Buddha. He could easily be some Joe Schmoe spirit who wants to take advantage of you and all the people who come around to hear Joe Schmoe speak through you. And everyone thinks they are listening to Buddha. But that's not the case at all.

If there was a way I could teach people to check ID's at the door, so to speak, when they start channeling, or automatic writing, or listening to Spirit. The only thing I can say is to spend some time with some gifted indigenous elders and learn from them. Ask them to check on that spirit who calls himself Buddha or Christ. It takes some very discerning, gifted people to sort this out. It's true these very gifted ones are hard to find. Most of them hide very well. There is a reason they hide themselves too. It is wise for them to do this. But if you truly seek one out, you will find one.

Which is not to say that some of you are not tuning into highly evolved, very positive beings that are seeking to help in the changes taking place on me. Some of you are, and this is beautiful. I, as your planet, need a great deal of help these days and there are beings from other parts of the universe such as the Pleiades and Sirius coming in to help me birth this New World being birthed right now. All sorts of very highly evolved beings are supporting this huge Shift in both physical and spiritual ways and I'm loving this particular party on the planet because they are some of the midwives for this birthing process. Along with many of you. There is a reason why you, my dear reader, are reading this book as you are among those chosen on a very deep soul level to be a mid-wife too.

Now, you must go get your breakfast, sweetie. I've been going on and on here for a couple hours. Go and we'll talk later. Love you SO MUCH!

11

On the Catholic Church and God-Woundedness

It's okay to doubt what you've been taught.

—Anonymous

Sunday, January 12, 2014
8:55 AM
40's Gray, not raining.

Mare: Mother, my car still won't move. I tried to move it yesterday and got the engine started again but it still won't budge. I guess you don't want me to go anywhere yet. It's a good thing I stocked up on lots of veggies and other staples the last time I went to the store, but that was about ten days ago! I'm actually starting to find food at the back of the refrigerator I forgot was there. I guess that's a bonus with this situation.

Mother: Yes, my love, I know your food supplies are in good stead. You really don't need to go anywhere yet. It's good for you to stay in this sacred space of listening and writing with me. There are many things to discuss.

Mare: Mother, there is something I have wanted to ask you about. It's related to a conversation we were having early on with all these coinkidin-kies about the Virgin Mary and Our Lady of Guadalupe. I'm sure you are not implying I need to return to the Catholic Church since you know that is not happening. I loved the Virgin Mary, still love her. But I'm *certain* what we were taught about her in Sunday School and in Mass is not all the truth about her. I can't go back to the patriarchal and repressive ways of

95

the Catholic Church after all the sacredness and joy I've felt from Spirit and from you in my studies with these Native medicine people.

The Catholic Church still won't allow women as priests. And a good chunk of the history of the Vatican is so sordid—the Inquisition, the labeling of women healers as witches and then torturing them. The list extends from there. It became more about politics and controlling the masses than about discovering God and the beautiful original teachings of Jesus Christ.

On the other hand, I do like this new Pope Francis and how progressive he is. If he can actually get the Vatican to approve women as … wow … I was going to write 'women as *priests*' but then 'women as *popes*' typed itself out—that is your voice, isn't it, Mother? You dropped in *popes*. That's a trip.

Mother: Yes, my love, I did.

Mare: Well, I guess if the Vatican was going to allow women to be Popes and run the Vatican, or better yet, drop the hierarchy and create a council of elders balanced between men and women, this would really encourage me to consider rejoining the Catholic Church.

But then it would not be a Church anymore, would it? Certainly not "the one and only Apostolic Catholic Church" as we used to recite in Mass. The Vatican would essentially be disbanded, all the assets sold and given to the poor and the woman who was Pope would reinstate ceremonies to honor the Sacred Feminine, Grandmother Moon, and more. Along with ceremonies for the Divine Masculine, of course. This is very radical thinking.

When I was grappling with the lymphoma, I wrote an essay two years ago as part of another manuscript about the Sacred Feminine and my healing journey. This is the book project you told me to put aside in June, 2012 so I could write the *Messages from Mother…. Earth Mother* book with you. That essay just poured out of me in one afternoon—just as quickly as this writing is happening … hmmm … I suspect you were at play there too!

I was far angrier then too, admittedly.

In this story, a group of women gathered in St. Peter's Square at the Vatican in Rome. It was in the warmer months. First it was a very small group and then it got larger and larger. Somehow in the midst of their group they had wheeled a cannon under cover into the center of St. Peter's Square next to the phallic obelisk originally from Egypt. And at one point they aimed the cannon, whisked the blanket off of it, and BOOM!

BOOM! They demolished the Vatican section by section. As the final part of the huge set of structures fell, women started to pour in from the far corners of the square and streets outside. Women with babies, older women, younger women, thousands of women ran in. Some hobbled in, skipped in, did somersaults in … the excitement in the air was amazing.

They danced. They drummed and sang and celebrated. It was wild! A few men were in the square and watched with shock at what was manifesting. They witnessed what was playing out and the glorious joy the women were experiencing and decided the most positive thing to do was to support the celebration.

The men ran back outside of the square and brought back food vendors, paying for all of it so the women could eat for free. They organized all sorts of food booths to feed the women dancing and laughing and frolicking in the square. A number of women set up a huge drum circle too.

The men also stepped forward to take care of the babies so the mothers could dance and drum. They could see that the best way to be there in that moment was to serve the women as the women celebrated the demolition of the enclave of buildings housing a religion in Western Society that has perpetuated the repression of women for so, so long. The celebration went all day into the evening.

As dusk fell, a council of women elders met in the center near the cannon at the foot of the obelisk—thirteen of them. It was a clear night and some stars flickered down on them through the city lights. As was only fitting, there was a full moon that night. Of course the auspicious activities of that day had been scheduled on the full moon.

The women elders met deep into the night as all the other women slept on the cobblestones (the men brought in blankets and sleeping bags, all they could retrieve). And in the morning after a good breakfast was served by the men, a loudspeaker was brought out and one chosen Elder woman started to speak about *Peace*—and the New World being birthed. It was eloquent and touched the hearts of all there, including the men.

Some Elder men had gathered on the side also, and a chosen one came forth after the Elder woman had finished and asked permission to speak also. He spoke of seeking forgiveness from the women for what men have done to women for so long. And of how they, the men also, had suffered terribly from the patriarchal, hierarchical ways they had all been living in for so many centuries. He wished to apologize for all men who have hurt, oppressed, abused, tortured and killed women.

He also promised that he and some other men were going to take down the Egyptian obelisk towering above him in the coming weeks.

They had already decided they were going to replace it with a statue representing the balance of the Sacred Feminine and Divine Masculine energies in Creation. They wanted to create a committee with an even number of men and women to help find the most gifted sculptor in Europe to design and construct this statue.

It was a beautiful, heartfelt speech the man gave. When he was finished, he turned to the Elder woman to give her the loudspeaker and she stepped forward and hugged him so deeply. It was as if the healing energy from that hug emanated out into the whole Plaza, and women were clapping, crying and hugging the other men who had been cooking and babysitting, providing blankets and more. It was a truly remarkable healing experience, this vision—this story.

Mother: Yes, Daughter … in some ways it would be a wonderful thing to see such healing between men and women happen so spontaneously like this. There are centuries and centuries of woundedness on the part of both women and men because you humans have lost the balance between the masculine and the feminine. This was lost when you lost your sacred connection with me. Almost all of you. And the patriarchal ways have caused such suffering for too, too long.

But it would *NOT* be good to demolish the Vatican like that. Too many lives would be lost. I'm not about killing. Plus there are so many valuables in the Vatican that could be sold to help the poor, and they would be lost, as well, not to mention all the significant books in the Vatican library. There are many well-kept secrets in that library and those books would be helpful to keep to better understand your culture's history.

When you wrote that, as you admit, you still had so much anger in you. That was two years ago and there was so much more repressed rage then, but you're in a different place now. That's part of what led your body to develop the lymphoma, all of the bottled-up rage that you carried in your system for most of your life. Many lives actually. Plus that gallbladder stone. Not to mention all the Catholic and wounded inner child guilt.

But let's get to that in a second. I never responded with that large question you posed to me when we started this morning. No, I'm not encouraging you to return to the Catholic Church. There are a multitude of reasons you should not go back there. The biggest one of which is that it's not your soul path in this Earth-walk.

It was where you were meant to be as a young girl so you could have that experience and then leave it and follow all your questioning and searching to eventually study with Native American medicine people and deeply tap into their wisdom and worldview of sacredness. The gifts within you were waiting to be woken up. You needed to find some good healers and teachers to heal you and activate your gifts. You are continuing to develop them each and every day. This is a beautiful thing. But, no, the Catholic Church is deeply entrenched in its patriarchal ways and you've long outgrown that.

Mare: Mother, I had a conversation with a good friend in the past few weeks. She was raised Catholic also and still attends church. She's been to Medjugorje where the Virgin Mary continues to appear in apparitions to give messages to several people there. This friend had a mystical experience outside the church there that was deeply healing. She had been struggling with terrible depression and received a very direct message from the Virgin Mary about how much she was loved by God and the Divine Mother. She had been wavering about her spirituality but that experience brought her back to the Catholic Church.

Mother: Yes, that is one of the great many miracles that have occurred through the love of the Great Mother—and the Great Father too. We have talked about miracle-mindedness before and all the healings of the heart and body at these shrines where the Virgin Mary has appeared to the children. I have played a part in this too in partnership with the Great Mother and all the nature spirits and other spiritual beings there. Though just about all the people who go to those places are oblivious to me and the nature spirits. They just know the spiritual energy there feels very good.

Sweetie, your path is outside of Christianity and recognized religion. Your path and work now is to wake people up to me, Earth Mother, as your sacred Planetary Caretaker and the source of all life here, and how much love I have for all of you. And to wake more people up to the Great Mother, most definitely, also—how I work so closely with the Great Mother.

Yes, I would like to see all women heal and find their voices and their womb-wisdom along with their feminine power based in the very center of their being. I would like to see all men heal from the repressed ways they've been taught and heal their wounded hearts. I would like to see all religions and belief systems speak to the balance between the Sacred Feminine and Divine Masculine.

All of you are supposed to be living in joy celebrating life here on me. You have forgotten but you will start to remember. It will happen in time. These are part of the changes happening on me now. It's inevitable and so beautiful. I so welcome these changes.

There are many women and men who won't or can't leave their more patriarchal religions, and I do love them. I love them just as much as I love my two-leggeds who have left their religion of birth to find spiritual community in more open, all-embracing churches or other groups. Many have turned to Buddhism, yoga, or meditation groups. Or other alternatives.

So many of my human children are God-wounded. It's so sad and it's not because the Great Mystery wounded them. It certainly wasn't I that wounded them either, because they were not learning much about me in their churches or synagogues or mosques. It's the version of God they learned about while young, and how that God was described to them that wounded their hearts and their spirit.

They were taught to fear God—*God* would punish them. Yet this is so far from the truth. But again, these have been teachings influenced by those alien beings who are leaving me now. And it is such a relief to see their energies departing. It is time to heal these ways of perceiving the Great Mystery, since the Creator has never been about fear.

The Creator and I have been about divine love from the very inception of life, a beautiful, unconditional divine love for all of you!

Mare: Yes, I do feel this love often. It is so powerful and fills my heart up with so much warmth. My God/Goddess space of Divine Love overflows within me so often. Such bliss. Such a gift.

Mother, I need to talk about something that happened on Facebook several weeks ago. I've wanted to talk about this with you for a while. I still have some areas of thin skin when it comes to patriarchal religions and how women are treated, I guess, and got quite triggered.

I posted this quote from Jimmy Carter on my homepage:

The truth is that male religious leaders have had—and still have—an option to interpret holy teachings either to exalt or subjugate women. They have, for their own selfish ends, overwhelmingly chosen the latter. Their continuing choice provides the foundation or justification for much of the pervasive persecution and abuse of women throughout the world.
    —Jimmy Carter

My community on Facebook is rather progressive and if they are not, they usually choose to ignore the postings I share. But yesterday this total stranger, a very Catholic British woman, who is a "friend" of a "friend", vehemently disagreed with this quote from Jimmy Carter. I suppose I'm so naïve it stunned me that a woman would disagree with this. I can imagine a man disagreeing, but not a woman.

This British woman then drew me into a bit of a religious debate, and it was my mistake for even getting involved. The gist of it is she is convinced that women are not subjugated by the Catholic Church at all. Her perception of the Catholic Church shocked me. I tried to be respectful and yet disagree. It was my posting and my page as it was. I just did not want to avoid any response for fear of conflict. So I pointed out how the Catholic Church and the Vatican have encouraged the torture and murder of hundreds of thousands of women (and men) through the centuries, gifted, spiritual women who were herbalists, healers and more. And the Catholic Church still does not allow women to be priests.

One of the things that floored me though was this woman stating that:

> ... *All Christians - men and women alike - are baptized Prophet, Priest and King, yet men and women approach the relationship with Christ very differently. Men tend to see their relationship with him as filial whereas women are more able to grasp the spousal quality of the relationship between Christ and his Church, an image that Jesus himself gave to us. It is that filial quality that* **makes men better able to function as ordained priests since they have to act "in persona Christi"** *[Mare's emphasis] when they are using priestly faculties. And finally, Jesus himself instituted the ordained priesthood, and the Church belongs not to us, but to him.*

I guess like many active Catholics, this woman might not realize how the ordained priesthood and the way the church structure and policies were created is largely the work of men born long after Christ died, influenced by the politics of that time.

There was no way I could convince her that perhaps her view of the Catholic Church is flawed. I don't even know why I tried. A waste of my emotional energy, for sure. She was pissing me off, honestly. Her complete submission to the doctrine and dogma of the Catholic hierarchy was downright scary. Honestly, how could only men *"act 'in persona Christi'"*? Women have just as much right and capacity to do that as any male priest.

She really made me see red when she wrote in a further comment: *"... I don't mean you any disrespect either, but being a lapsed Catholic seemingly caught up in New Age pantheism does not mean that you understand the richness of Catholic teaching..."*

Just rereading her judgmental take on me is making my blood boil even now as I'm typing this. *"New Age pantheism?"* Since when is studying with Native American teachers *New Age pantheism?* Native traditions far outdate even Christianity. I mean—cheesh!

I had to back away from the computer and Facebook at that point to try to calm down. When I finally went back on, I started a whole other post about this dialogue between myself and this woman and wrote:

Interesting ... having a chat with a woman here on FB about whether the patriarchal religions have been suppressing women for centuries. She doesn't think the Catholic Church has been repressing women. This rather floors me. This chat is in response to a Jimmy Carter quote. Her stance (and that of the Catholic Church) is that only men should be called to be priests since only men can act "in persona Christi" and not women.

So long as some people (and religious institutions) believe that women can't act "in persona Christi", women will still be repressed and worse. It's as simple as that. All of us, men and women, can act "in persona Christi". We all can embody the Christ Consciousness equally and this is what we are being called to do in these Changing Times. Allow the amazing love and compassion energies of the Christ Consciousness in to heal our woundedness so that we can embody the values and spiritual energies that Christ embodied. All of us are invited. We can all be priests and priestesses, if we so choose.... We can live this and our Earth needs us to wake up spiritually to live this for the changes the planet is going through.

Okay, I need to go back to writing "The Great Mother Bible" so this book can come out sooner rather than later. The chat this woman and I are having is only more of a reminder of how this book needs to come out.

Then one of my friends, a deeply spiritual and astute man, responded with the following:

Well, think of it this way, Mare: There's no Catholic woman more thoroughly suppressed than the one who has internalized the voice of the suppressor so fully that he no longer even needs to monitor her thoughts and behaviors.

His statement was so brilliantly accurate it took my breath away. Figuratively, of course.

One of my biggest realizations from that dialogue with that Catholic woman (beyond how she triggered me) was how sad and disappointed I was that *another woman* could not see how repressed she is by the Catholic Church. A deep grief came over me for the rest of that morning. That British woman chooses to continue to be blind and swallow the archaic dogma. I truly think she, and women like her, are betraying the rest of us who are working so hard to bring balance back and help heal society from all these centuries of god-awful treatment of women (and I mean that pun).

So long as some women continue to support the patriarchal dogma and societal structures they will hinder the awakening of those close to them. And they will continue to lash out at total strangers like me to try to prove their blind sense of *religious rightness* that is so flawed.

Mother: Sweetie, sweetie, if you can let me step in here. I know you were very upset by that woman and shocked by her insistence that she's not repressed and that no women are repressed by the Catholic Church. And yes, she is wrong and has been so indoctrinated with the Catholic teachings that it may take her some lifetimes to fully extricate herself.

I don't think the Catholic Church will continue to exist as it has for many more decades. The energies coming in for the Great Change will not support those types of religious structures much longer. Certainly, the name of the church may stay but it will be forced to operate far differently. Look at this current pope, Pope Benedict, and how radical he is already. He's rattling quite a few people, ah—men—in his actions and decisions there in the Vatican. And this is a very good thing. It is so needed. That very huge religion still has patriarchal tentacles out all over me.

And yes, that woman was condescending and a bit smug and, quite frankly, she was triggered by you too. She was fuming on her end and you could feel her empathically, and it was setting you off even more. At least you were being more respectful toward her than she was to you.

But do you remember how you were taught as a young girl that the Catholic Church is at the apex of all religions and belief systems? You had to let go of that conditioning of arrogance and did so willingly once you began your search for a spiritual path that offered more balance and wisdom than what the Catholic Church offers. It was hard at first, but slowly you came to find wisdom regarding living here in balance on me, with me, honoring me.

That woman has never questioned the Church. It's important to be compassionate toward her with her blindness. She is most certainly among those getting a little triggered by Pope Benedict's actions. She is choosing to hang on to the ways that are breaking apart in front of her eyes and she is afraid. Deep down, she is afraid of these changes coming in. She may not feel them that consciously but subconsciously she is feeling them.

She is not alone. There are so many people who are very afraid these days. They know that the old world is cracking at the seams and yet are at a loss as to how to deal with it. Your governments have only made it harder to adapt to the changes—they've been so influenced by a corporate world mired in the unbalanced patriarchal ways. We've already been talking about much of this. Let's just say the options for alternative energy and more compassionate, community-oriented solutions have been bypassed again and again.

For every woman who has stayed within the patriarchal folds of the Catholic Church there are dozens who have walked away from it (along with men). That woman is in the great minority and she along with her church community are frustrated by the mass exodus but are really not sure what to do. That was part of the reason the woman was so forceful about her religious perceptions. She's been defensive for a long time about staying within the Catholic Church. It would be nice if she and all the women and men throughout the Catholic world would wake up a little. It's true. Many are. More need to. I do like this current pope though.

For you though, sweetie, this is another opportunity to look at and heal your trigger points. You know already you've had lifetimes of being persecuted by religious zealots. This rage you harbor inside you still needs to be healed though. It's not serving you and you need to learn more compassion toward people who trigger you, like this woman. You need to be careful with your assumptions that all will agree with you all the time and learn to slough it off when someone does not see your exact spiritual worldview. Your anger is not serving you and is part of your challenges with lymphoma.

You are healing and learning and evolving, and listening to me, and weighing all of this. I know you are. I love you so much. You are aware of dogma and are trying to steer clear of it with what you teach and share. And your attempts to be humble—you could work on this a little more, but you are getting better and better.

Mare: Sigh. I'm trying here, Mother. I'm such a work in progress. And I feel your love. I do. Such teachings, again and again. It's all good. It's all grist for the mill.

This has been a bit of a writing stretch. And learning stretch. I'm trying, Mother, you know I'm trying.

By the way, total change of topic here but I've drafted up some observations late last night. I'm calling them: "Notes from surviving the Arctic Freeze". Thought I'd share them with you.

— *Writing from the bed really is the best place to write. Period.*
— *Taking phone calls from the bed and taking notes is not so easy, but I'm learning new skills here.*

— *All authors and very committed writers need a chef, butler, housekeeper and woodpile stacker. You see, writing is very time consuming work and there is no time for these extraneous tasks.*

— *The squirrels in the storage space above my bathroom have parties sometimes and have been rather loud during the Arctic Freeze. I think they are the ones who stole my favorite hot chocolate mix and were sipping hot chocolate while I was suffering down below them with only my dark chocolate Hershey's kisses.*

— *Having one huge Arctic block of a woodpile congealed from frozen rain and snow blocking the parking pad to the front door, along with a car that won't move means:*

* *No one is allowed in the house unless they bring a sled to go down the other part of the steep yard, and,*

* *No one is allowed to leave the house. Unless it is a squirrel trying to get more hot chocolate mix from the neighbors and if that is the case, then I am waiting for them with my peashooter.*

Mother: You are so cute. And you know those squirrels love living up-stairs in the attic crawl space where they find a warm place to nest with these frigid temperatures. Now, you need to go take a break.

12

Sacred Fire

Gie me ae spark o' Nature's fire,
That's a'the learning I desire.

—Robert Burns

Monday, January 13, 2014
8:34 AM
24° Serious frost on the pumpkin, if there were any pumpkins outside.

Mare: Oh, Mother, I fell asleep in my clothes last night and woke up with the lights still on and my back is sore. This working out of the bed is not really so great for my posture. I needed to do some good yoga stretches this morning and am trying to figure out a way to be all warm and cozy working in the bed with the space heater next to me. I've got to prop these pillows up better or something.

Plus it was really cold in the house. My father used to have this expression about frost on the pumpkin. That lovely pattern of frost on a late October morning. Well, let's just say that any pumpkin outside in this part of Maryland is completely frozen over right now. A round pumpkin brick.

On top of the bitter cold, the congealed mass of logs frozen together on the parking pad is turning out to be a royal pain. It's all green wood and the pieces I can kick out of the edge of the pile don't burn that well. I have to really work at the fire, with more than the usual kindling, paper and blowing on it to get the big logs to catch. It's a real hassle. So much for the really warm roaring fires I enjoyed with the seasoned wood I had in December. Those logs burned so well, I barely had to do anything other than poke them a little and blow on them. Oy, I guess I'm just going to have to surrender to staying warm in bed, and work from here.

Mother: Yes, my love, it's Monday morning, isn't it?

Mare: Yes, it is. On the plus side, I do still have enough dark chocolate kisses and Planters peanuts to last me a few more days. And kefir too. My food supply is not out completely.

But, Mother, Paul has yet to call me since Thursday evening when I called him. I'm actually doing okay with this but still—this is hard. I do really like this man and there is this connection between the two of us. He's fun, very intelligent, so caring, sensitive and he likes hugging a lot. Plus he's a beekeeper.

We had been emailing everyday until I called him on Thursday evening. It's been silence since then. This was triggering my abandonment issues by Saturday midday. But then by Saturday night I realized I was enjoying my solitude, and experienced a moment of knowing I did not need to hear from him to have a sense of well-being in my life. Still, I'm not sure where he is with me, and this is a test.

I did send him a link to a Patty Griffin song last night in an email, just the link and a happy face in the subject. It's a beautiful song called *Heavenly Day*. The lyrics talk about how there are no clouds in the sky and embracing the heavenly joy in the moment.

I was not sure if it was okay to send him that email even with a link to a song. Men like their man cave space and are like rubber-bands and need to pull back, I guess. They need to figure things out when they're not sure, and—oh, I don't know what's really going on with him other than silence.

Sigh, I'm just jabbering.

Plus, Mother, there is my car. I still have not been able to get it to move. I was going to call a tow truck this morning but don't want to have to pay for that and the mechanic's bill to fix whatever is going on. Those are not really in the budget.

Mother: Yes, silence from a man can be hard for you, can't it, Love. As for your car, why don't you hold off on calling the tow truck until later this afternoon? See if your car will move then.

Mare: Okay, I can wait another few hours. Getting back to that *Heavenly Day* song, I'm going to check on the lyrics. It's really a beautiful song.

[I go to my email wondering if that is a wise move since there may be an email or two that might distract me from writing. And there is an email from Paul! Holy crap! I was not sure when I'd hear from him. This is what he wrote:

Sweet, Mare. Thanks. Been thinking about you, wondering how Mother was treating you, but thought to be quiet lest I interrupt. If this song is the evidence of your state, I'm glad. And I'm glad to be with you, too, on this heavenly day. I am finding a score of those myself. Pretty magic, as this engineer can come up with absolutely no reason it is happening this way. Doing my best to accept what is and marvel with it.

The bees were flying today. That was sweet to see.

- Paul]

Oh my god, Mother! There is an email from Paul and it turns out he was giving me space so I could write! Here I was, going through all these contortions in my brain about him and what was or was *not* happening. I feel like a teenager with all my ups and downs with this man.

Plus I just tried to listen to Patty Griffith's *Mary* song again and it would not play again for me on YouTube. Just would not play, though I tried several times.

Thanks, Mom. Guess you don't want me getting too distracted here, do you?

This reminds me of when I went to the beach, when you and the dolphins and the whales called me there in June of 2012. And you pushed me out of bed at 4 AM that second morning, to claim the domain for the book on that blogging site.[10] When I tried to continue setting up all the configurations to create the look of the website, the website froze on me.

You told me to go to the beach then. *"No more playing on the computer,"* was your message. *"You need to do more ceremony at the beach."* You can be kind of a slave-driver at times. I love you but you do work me a bit. I like that *Mary* song from Patty Griffin but you didn't want it to put me in a blessed out, mystical state again. That happens sometimes when I listen to it.

Mother: Sweetie, yes, I do want to keep you focused as you can start to get distracted by some music or Facebook. As for this past weekend, I watched as you started to lapse into your abandonment issues, your fears from so very far back. I did not want to step in and be too loud about the

---

[10] http://messagesfrommother.org

fact that all is fine with Paul and you. You needed to go through all of your emotional gyrations so you could finally realize on your own how some of your woundedness about men can now be released.

And this abandonment piece, this particular aspect of your woundedness, well, many times in your life you actually pushed men away because subconsciously you did not want them close to you. You thought you were being abandoned while what was actually happening was you were encouraging them to walk away by your subconscious actions and words. You were operating from those deep, deep wounds.

These are all good and wonderful learnings for you. You are starting to deeply heal some of these and I'm ecstatic you are getting the lessons.

Mare: Mother, I have a question for you. It has to do with Paul. And the fire in the woodstove. Several times now when I poke at the logs to get them a little closer to each other so they can burn better, I hear you telling me this is what you want Paul and me to be doing, to be closer together physically. Can you explain more?

Mother: Honey, there are so many lessons from a *Sacred Fire.* Yes, I am whispering in your ear there and sometimes it is the fire speaking with you also. You can learn how to communicate with the fire also. Some people have that gift. You are that sensitive and you can develop the capacity to tune in, too. You think I'm speaking but you may be connecting with the sacred consciousness of the fire as well. Fires are just as conscious as you or the crows that sit outside your house sometimes.

I will answer your question though. My love, it has been so long since you've been touched and held by a man. The messages you are receiving there in front of the woodstove are nudges to encourage you to get close to Paul. To hold him. Allow him to hold you. He needs it also. Be like the logs that nestle next to each other with a small amount of space between them. Hug each other. Be close.

There is more to this teaching about the fire. A fire needs oxygen to burn and thus having the logs piled on top of each other with little to no space for air to move will not work that well. Just as a fire needs spaces, you humans need space for a healthy relationship too. There is a powerful kinetic energy that can exist between two lovers. Many have experienced this. The beautiful passion shared between two people in love gives me such joy.

It can get too extreme though. If you try to be together all the time, giving each other little space to be yourselves as individuals, your fire will eventually get smothered since there is not enough air, not enough opportunity for you to kindle your own inner fire that will then feed the sacred heart fire kindled between the two of you.

I'm not trying to say your relationships need to be all fiery though. I could be talking about water and stones in a river and the spaces between stones that are needed for life to grow on those stones, and yet the stones have a relationship between each other, too. Very few people in your modern culture understand this, but stones are chatting back and forth and can be lovers over time. They have stone parties too.

A long stonewall created by a farmer some generations back is a party. Same with a stone house. The stones form bonds between them and share secrets only stones can possess. Oh, and they prefer to be called *stones* and not *rocks*. It feels more respectful to them.

Ancient mountains next to each other are lovers too. Of course they can't move really close to each other for hugs but the space between them is sacred. Their love relationship is sacred.

Maybe I'm getting far afield. But everything does have consciousness. And you know people who can chat with the stones and have gathered some good wisdom. Maybe talking about stones that can't hug each other or even smother each other is not the best metaphor, but you get my drift. But you are here in your cozy home, tending a sacred fire, so using the fire as a teacher for you and Paul is easy.

Paul is so sensitive to your need for space with me that he is giving you what he thinks you need, perhaps more than you cared for this weekend, with the silence from his end. Plus he actually needed the space too. He understands this lesson from the fire. Allowing space between two beautiful hearts who are learning to intertwine, even hearts that have been together for a very long time, is a beautiful way of being in balance, allowing each person to grow.

It's all about energy, divine energy, soul energy, growing more in sacred relationship with each other.

Sacred fires are rather powerful. When a person prays into their fire and offers blessings such as tobacco, the sacred energy in the fire grows and grows. When there are ceremonies, it is the sacred fire that burns throughout it that holds the sacred energetic space of the ceremony. Even a candle can suffice to do this in a small ceremony. The initial flame struck to light a sacred pipe is very powerful.

Nothing is to go into the fire other than prayers and more wood. One must be careful what words are spoken into the fire because those words are carried up into the heavens as prayers too.

Where there are gifted medicine people tending the fire, the sacred energies will be amplified and great healing can take place around these fires. It is the sacred fire that heats up the grandfathers, or the stones, for sweat lodges. When there are vision quests, a sacred fire is kept burning for the four days the person is "out on the hill." The medicine person or the vision questers themselves tend the fire along with others sending prayers out to Spirit that the person on the quest receives the vision they are seeking for spiritual direction in their life. It can be quite powerful.

Fire is part of the magic of being here alive on me, your Earth Mother. It is an alchemical dance of energy between the Creator and myself that transforms everything. Sometimes this is a destructive transformation from the eyes of you two-leggeds, if forests or homes are lost or lives are destroyed. I do grieve with you when lives are lost so needlessly.

Yet various parts of me have evolved dependent on fire. In some ecosystems, certain seeds can germinate only by being scarred by fire. Fire is a beautiful aspect of living on me. You humans would not be able to survive without it.

When you light a candle at a table to sit down and eat, many of you don't realize you are blessing the table and food. It can be subtle but if you do it with prayers also, it makes it more beautiful, more powerful. If you have an altar where you pray and you light a candle there, it activates the altar and sacred energy radiates out from there in a lovely way for as long as the candle is burning, and some time beyond.

Fire is one of the gifts from Creation to you all. It would be so amazing if all of my beloved two-leggeds remembered the sacred aspect of it.

Mare: Mother, I learned a Lakota term recently. It is: *peta-owihankeshni*. It means: "Sacred fire without end." I love the concept of that.

Mother: Yes, to develop that concept of your heart carrying a *sacred fire* connection to the Great Father, Great Mother and myself is to live a beautiful spiritual life. It is an honoring of your inherent sacredness and how your life journey can be a most beautiful one of serving Spirit. It means committing your every step to being a prayer of giving and serving the highest good. A most powerful and humbling journey for any of you humans to commit to. The truth is that all of you are called to do this. Whether you listen to it and follow the call or not is up to you.

Now you need to make some phone calls. Plus that firewood outside. It would be good for you to stack some of it at least. Maybe later in the afternoon you can figure out what's going on with your car that is sitting outside your home and won't move.

I love you so much! If all of you humans knew how much I loved you, oh, it would be the most amazing planet, ah, me! It would help you to remember divine love between all of you, and all of the four-leggeds, winged ones, finned ones, six-leggeds, all of my species-babies—all of them. Love you!

Mare: [Several hours later] You're funny, Mother. I got in the car after stacking some firewood. It had warmed up enough that I could loosen most of the pieces to stack. Well, the car engine started. I put it in gear and, lo and behold, I was able to drive it around the block as if it had been fine all along. No reason for it to be seized in place. Except, perhaps, your reasons for me to stay put the past six days.

Mother: Yes, my love. We have had quite the lovely quality space together here. You had enough food in your refrigerator. You did not need to leave, and it has been a good rich session of listening and writing.

Mare: Okay. I surrender. I trust you. Thank you for taking care of me. And I'm quite grateful for the fact I did not need to get a tow truck or have to pay a mechanic's bill. Thank you, Mother. This does make me wonder what else you have up your sleeve. But I'm not even going to ask, or guess, at this point.

13

Gratitude

It is not joy that makes us grateful;
it is gratitude that makes us joyful.

—Brother David Steindl-Rast

Tuesday, January 14, 2014
5:20 AM
30° Was raining last night. Supposed to rain all day.

Mare: Ouch, Mother, you really wanted me up early this winter. Note to self—go to sleep much earlier. I turned the light off close to 1 AM, reading more of Sondra Ray's fascinating book, *Rock Your World with the Divine Mother.* And you wake me up this early chanting: "The Great Mother, The Great Mother, The Great Mother …" in my ear.
   I'm literally shaking myself to wake up enough to write.

Mother: Sweetie, you did make that New Year's Resolution not to roll over to go back to sleep. I'm not trying to be a slave driver here. We do have lots of work to do, though, and you are on a timeline to get this book done sooner rather than later. We've got tracks to make and you really might want to get to sleep earlier.
   I want to talk about gratitude this morning. You met that very kind Apache man last fall at a Native American Festival. He was a Sundancer and had that beautiful calm energy around him. I know you remember how he talked about waking up each morning and saying *Thank you* one hundred times to start the day. That made a big impression on you.

If every person in your very busy culture woke up each morning and took several minutes to sit still in front of a candle or some altar that helped you touch your spiritual center, and said *Thank you* one hundred times, that would make a huge difference in the energy you'd carry within you for the rest of the day.

Gratitude.

Just thinking it during the day is a healing, calming experience that shifts your vibration, your song.

Sending gratitude to me, your Mother, would be healing for me too, in ways that are hard to explain but very true. When you two-leggeds express your gratitude and love to me, not only does it help to heal you, but it sends that calming healing energy down into me. When several of you gather together and focus your gratitude and love toward me—oh, it's amazing.

When you learn to do ceremony and call on Creator and myself together, have sacred fires, and offer prayers of gratitude and love, this is so, so beautiful and powerful. It's like the old commercials for *Lucky Charms* cereal that many of you in your country watched on television where the elves would say: "It's magically delicious!" For me and all of my beloved beings, it's quite "magically delicious." It really is!

Gratitude is very powerful. We have been talking about energy for some time now and gratitude brings out such beautiful, healing positive energy. To sit in that place shifts the energy in your body to allow for a spiritual expansiveness, an openness, giving energy out to all around you, and allowing more abundance to come in to refill your gratitude bowl. It's a beautiful dance of gratitude and abundance.

Whenever any one of you, my beloveds, starts to feel a sense of lack or depression, taking out a piece of paper and writing down all you are grateful for is a beautiful exercise. Then to state out loud what is on your list makes it even more powerful. This spiritual exercise will help to shift your mood and your day to a more beautiful experience of joy, happiness, and calmness. It will also make your song—the song you are giving off that day from your energy body—more beautiful.

Each of your souls has a distinct song that resonates your soul energy and purpose here on me. Some of my indigenous peoples know how to tune into a baby when it is still in a mother's womb to listen to the baby's soul song. Several of the village women will do ceremony with the mother out in the wilderness to hear the song of this unborn child. This song is sung back to the baby when born and at different significant transitions in the child's life. It is also sung to them if they violate the village code to help them remember the pure song of their sacred being when they've been led astray.

Your society never recognized you on this level. This has made me very sad. There is so little singing altogether. Instead, your society has taught you that abundance means a great quantity of material things. A bigger house. Fancier car. And more. And if you achieve that, it is wonderful, especially if your house is environmentally friendly and your car is too. Yet striving for an abundance of spirit and of positive energy are more important goals while incarnate here in the physical, on me, your planet. That is the real abundance. Gratitude feeds this spiritual abundance.

Your beautiful spirit body emanating all this gratitude ripples out from you to touch all around you. Your plants feel it, your animals feel it, the trees outside absorb it, the walls of your house also take this energy in. This is true.

When you specifically direct this gratitude toward your plants and thank them, they all feel it even more strongly. Or toward your cat or dog or the tree outside, even the mountain across the valley. Your beautiful energy feeds them as they feel more love and connection with you. This is part of the dance of living *All My Relations*. You can include the nature spirits in there too. Offer them gratitude also. There are so, so many spiritual/energetic layers to this dance that are so beautiful and healing for me, your Earth Mother, and all my relations on me. It is a very good thing to think, feel and speak your gratitude each and every day. An especially powerful way to wake up in the morning. It is also even more powerful to be able to tune into your soul song and live from that place of your sacredness here on me.

Mare: Mother, I've learned that even petting tomato plants helps them grow better, especially from a place of love. They love to be touched and caressed. And my big, beautiful gardenia plant, Oscar, he adores being in the center of attention wherever I live. When I tune into him and ask him where he'd like to be when I bring him in for the winter, he always chooses the place where I'll interact with him the most, where I'll give him the most love.

This winter he's been living in the rather large kitchen here since that's where he wanted to be. I touch him every day and talk with him, give him love, and he is just flourishing there, even though the kitchen is far darker than the office where my other plants are for the winter.

Mother: Yes, my love, you and Oscar have a deep bond. You've had him since you propagated the cutting from his mother gardenia plant, Isabelle. And he's been the happiest gardenia plant with all the love and gratitude

117

you send him for his blossoms too. A lucky plant to be living with you. And he is continuing to send you so much loving, healing energy too.

Mare: I'm just starting to realize how much Oscar has been helping me. He sent me a distinct wave of love energy last week when I was talking with him. I was amazed when I felt it—subtle and yet palpable. He's been sending love energy to me all along but I was not tuned in enough to notice until recently. I am just in awe of this gardenia plant and our bond.

It's tough being a plant communicator and loving them so much when I walk into any plant nursery or greenhouse though. When I open up intuitively to those greenhouse plants, they all want to come home with me. I can't exactly afford that. Nor do I have the space for them. So I'll rescue one of the saddest plants in the greenhouse and bring it home to baby. It's so much fun to see them bounce back. I wish I could rescue all of them though.

You know, I wrote something up a few years ago. I'd like to share this with you. It's called: *"An Alternative Currency of Kindness and Gratitude."*

I wish that instead of greenbacks, our currency were kindness and gratitude. Banks would be set up to take deposits and offer loans in generosity and thank you's.

Interest would be paid in the form of flowers and vegetables and tree seedlings. Vegetables and tree seedlings in the warmer months and orchids and amaryllis in the winter months. Free bags of manure and pouches of orchid fertilizer would be available in the parking lot.

There would be no penalties if someone did not make a payment, the amount due would simply come from another person's account that was surplus in giving thanks or being kind.

On special holidays, vouchers for forgiveness would be mailed out to all the bank customers, and blessings of chocolate would be available at each bank branch.

If a customer left without a smile and a lighter step, there would be serious evaluations within that bank and federal deposits of the highest positive order would be issued to that branch. Those would be quantified in heart-gilded blessings and be made available to every member of that bank instantly.

If one bank customer had a spare room in their house, they would offer it into the 'roof over your head' exchange program where a person recently out of a job and on the verge of homelessness would be matched with them to use the room, with payments of dishwashing and window cleaning agreed to on a monthly basis.

The bank would have a vegetable garden growing around its periphery and solar panels and composting toilets included in its construction. Plants would grow on the roof. Employees would be given days off for royal bad moods and really lousy mornings and other volunteers who were feeling particularly good that morning would fill in for them.

And the sun would shine. The plants would grow. People would feel like people instead of like mini-cogs. And children's joy would soar higher than our current national debt.

Mother: Sweetie, that essay speaks to how living in positive community would feel. Deep compassionate Love is a currency far greater than money. Love and trust and community and hope and so much more. I'm so excited about this New World coming in, founded on these values. It will be so, so beautiful. I love you so much. So very much.

You need to go take a break. I can tell more fanny fatigue is setting in. Go get some breakfast. I can hear your stomach growling. Ah, the song of your stomach is getting louder! Love you! Be back soon!

14

....

Walking the Beauty Way

In beauty may I walk.
All day long may I walk.
Through the returning seasons may I walk.
On the trail marked with pollen may I walk.
With grasshoppers about my feet may I walk.
With dew about my feet may I walk.
With beauty may I walk.
With beauty before me, may I walk.
With beauty behind me, may I walk.
With beauty above me, may I walk.
With beauty below me, may I walk.
With beauty all around me, may I walk.
In old age wandering on a trail of beauty, lively, may I walk.
In old age wandering on a trail of beauty, living again, may I walk.
It is finished in beauty.
It is finished in beauty.

—Navajo Blessingway

Wednesday, January 15, 2014
5:35 AM
27° - Cold but not Polar Vortex.

Mare: Ugh, another early morning wake-up. I think you've got me making up for all those other mornings during the rest of my life when I did sleep in, Mother. I guess I've slept in so much I must have deposited enough of those morning roll-overs hours of extra sleep. It's time to withdraw from that bank of sleep deposits.

Plus, I keep hearing the lyrics to Patty Griffin's beautiful song about the Virgin Mary. I just started playing it again this morning. I know this

is distracting me from writing but I'm feeling so called. It's as if I'm connecting with another aspect of you, the Great Divine Mother, by tuning
into this song and the energy within it from Patty Griffin. Patty must have
such lovely energy, a pure heart, connected with you, Mother. She wrote
the lyrics to the song and I can just feel her connection with you in this
particular song.

Mother: They are very beautiful lyrics, it's true. I do love how the song
makes you feel too. It does put you in a deeply sacred place. Very sweet.

Mare: Yeah, I think I could bliss out on that song for a good part of the day.

Mother: Well, I might need to rein you in here. We have some writing to
do. I love you so much and love the energy within that song, but I'd like
to share some things now.

My daughter, we have been talking about numerous topics here.
About energy and how everything has consciousness, stones, trees and
more. About how much love Creation and I, as Earth Mother, have for
you. How the very essence of your atoms is sacred love dancing. We've
also talked about gratitude. Lovely amazing gratitude.

I would like to bring up other ways of being that will bring out greater
wisdom and balance in your lives. These are included in my *Precepts* listed with my *Thirteen Love Directives*. Some of my native peoples of North
America talk of *Walking in Beauty*. This is a way of being in which your
every step can be a prayer and an honoring of the Creation and myself,
your Mother. You are all beings of light and you have the capacity to learn
how to walk in a way that brings forth your beautiful light.

Listen with an Open Heart

To be in good relationship with another is to be a good listener. If you
can still your mind to listen deeply to the sacred truth of another, then you
will be able to honor their truth. If both of you can listen from a deep well of
stillness within, you may well find your sacred truths evolving and you might
meet each other in the same place. Even if you might not meet in the same
place, you have learned to hear each other's truth deeply.

Listening deeply comes from putting your own opinions aside—as hard
as that might be since those can be your unbalanced ego at work—to be present from an open heart. It also means observing the other person and looking
not only for what they are saying directly but also expressing in their body
language. So much is shared in the eyes, arms, expressions, and more.

Learn to still yourself: work to empty yourself of preconceived notions of that person and you may discover you can see their inner beauty so much more clearly.

Speak with an Open Heart

To come from an open heart is to source from a place of compassion and kindness. It provides a place of gentle safety to those you are communicating with so they may know they are not judged. To approach someone with an open heart is to offer your vulnerability so they may share theirs. The walls of defensiveness may drop and sincere communication can happen. Offering an open heart helps to create a healing place and deep wounds can be released from this place.

Be Lean of Judgment and Speech

When we judge another, it usually sources from a place of ignorance and projection. You can never know another person's path nor trials nor triumphs. It is better to open your heart to the knowledge that they carry a spiritual light within them that only needs to be discovered. Even if their words and actions stem from thorns in their heart.

To communicate from a place of wisely chosen words that can be understood clearly is a gift to any listener. Learn to still your mind and your heart, sourcing your wise center within as you convey your thoughts. They will be received far better from that place. This may sometimes mean distancing yourself from the situation and taking some time to form your words. So often, this would be so much wiser than avoiding an awkward silence, or worse yet—causing offense—by speaking too soon.

Be Open to the Mystery That Lies in People and the World Around You

Human beings have an inherent *great mystery* within them. The paths you have walked, the experiences you have had, the choices you have made on a day-to-day basis contribute to the great mystery of each of you in every second. This is a beautiful thing, and great actions can arise from this inner mystery.

You may think you understand someone and have packaged him or her in a certain way in your mind. Yet that person may surprise you in a most wondrous way with their actions the next time you see them. Or they may disappoint you too. That is part of being human.

To be in healthy relationship with another person is to be open to their inner mystery and know you cannot ever completely understand their actions or motivations. Certainly you can encourage them to communicate about the reasons behind their actions as best they can and it will help you better understand them.

Staying open to the mystery within others means that any expectations about how another will behave are not wise to hold. Those expectations are based on assumptions that do not honor the free will and mystery of the other, and many times lead to disappointment. Dropping expectations and opening up to the mystery of the other can lead to great joy at times too.

When you love and honor the great mystery within another and learn to stay open to the person on a moment-by-moment basis, you may come to embrace them in a way that holds them sacred—as they may do the same for you. I encourage you to explore this intention and come into a more sacred dance with your partners in life. This may be your husband, wife, lover, children, grandchildren, best friend—whomever. It can be a most beautiful dance together. This is what you seek to do as spiritual beings in the physical.

Mystery lies all around you, my beloveds—the magic of a garden and how seeds germinate, or which ways the winds will blow, or clouds form, or how a tree will know when it is time to fall or not, the darting actions of a school of fish. Your scientists seek to understand the exact knowledge of the universe yet there are unseen spiritual forces that will always elude them, as long as they continue to deny the existence of Spirit. This is an important and necessary reminder to you, my adorable two-leggeds, to remember to fill yourselves with humility as you explore the greater scheme of how the universe works.

Be Compassionate With Yourself

Oh, my beloved humans, how it pains me when I hear you judge yourselves harshly, and judge others harshly too. The critical ways you condemn yourselves is so hard for me to witness. You have forgotten how much you are loved by the Great Father, Great Mother and myself. You are always loved.

There is too much self-criticism in most of you, my beautiful ones. Your schools did not support inner compassion. And your places of worship encouraged you to feel guilt and believe in the illusion of a *judgmental God*. This has made me very sad and your collective cultural song has become so discordant because of this.

Yet you can start today by learning how to be more compassionate toward yourself. You can look in your mirror, deep into your eyes and embrace the beauty of yourself, in all your humanness. I encourage you to smile at yourself in the mirror and smile at your imperfections as you know them. Be grateful for them and see them as your teachers. All of you have them and they make you all the more adorable.

Even my ever so lovable Dalai Lama has his moments of humanness, like his farting. Mother Teresa had hers also. You know she farted at times too. Come to love these aspects of yourself and help your personal energetic song be one that becomes a healing, loving song for me.

I would so love this.

You were never meant to be perfect and make no mistakes. To be human is to have flaws and flub-ups as those are your teaching blocks as a soul incarnate in the physical. Be gentle with yourself as you navigate the challenges of relationships and life's adventures.

Please learn to laugh at yourself for each of you is a most lovable, wondrous being. If you fall in the mud, thank the mud for being such a soft landing and laugh at your new muddy look. No one said you needed to be impeccably clean all the time. Your culture has produced some good laundry soaps that are even friendly to me, to help get the dirt out anyway.

In being compassionate toward yourself, you are spreading that warmth to all around you as well. Your individual spiritual song of inner kindness and gentleness emanates a resonance to all with whom you come into contact. Your plants feel it. The trees feel it. The nature spirits experience it and it feeds them also. It sends a current of compassion out in ripples from you to all around you. I know I've said this before but it bears repeating one more time. You, the trees, whales, flowers, nature spirits and other beautiful ones on me are all *so* connected. It is a most beautiful personal song you emanate when you humans live from a place of inner compassion. This feeds me more than you could ever know.

The trees have their own songs too. Some of my more gifted ones can hear these songs. Each type of tree has a particular song and they are all so beautiful. The peaceful, compassionate songs each of you can bring forth enhance the trees and their orchestra also.

There are other ways to *Walk in Beauty*. Having a *generous spirit* is a gift to all around you. It recognizes the truth that we all live in community together. To be generous to your fellow humans, four-leggeds, winged ones and more is an act of kindness that circles out and then back to support you. Nothing ever goes unnoticed and generosity amplifies more generosity. You two-leggeds have the expression: *paying-it-forward*. This supports the beautiful interconnectedness between all of you and all life around you and the truth of *abundance*.

Finding respect for all in your life is another beautiful gift. Certainly it is easier to feel respect for someone who excels in certain gifts. Yet also cultivate respect for those who are different, those who seem downtrodden, or are suffering. To respect is to honor the mystery of that person, as I was sharing before. It creates a welcoming space for that other person in your interactions. You are all part of my beloved human community together. Many times you forget this.

By respecting others you are allowing them to reveal their authentic, even vulnerable, sides to you also. It can be most healing. There is already too much separation between many of you and this has saddened me for so long. Just because someone's skin color is different, or clothing style, or hair color, does not justify disrespect. Neither does their choice of a lover. Or the fact their thoughts are somewhat different. Each of you holds such gifts and potential. Welcome these differences. Honor and respect each other and the relationships you cultivate may be quite beautiful. I celebrate the potential!

To *cultivate silence* is a delightful gift to me also. There is the silence you can gift another with, as they prepare to speak. Then there is the inner silence within, which each of you can learn to develop. To have that inner silence while in conversation means you can understand the other's words so much more deeply.

Ah, your creative mental chitter-chatter and the places you can go with that can be so fascinating. You have such amazing story-telling capacities within your monkey-minds. Only the ones who have learned the good art of meditation and stilling the mind to tune into their sacred center, their innate wisdom, have learned to pull back from the incessant storytelling of their monkey-minds.

I love the beautiful energy given off by my meditators, the calmness, the silence within, their heart chakras flickering more strongly. It's so beautiful. I only wish more of them directed their love back into me, and not simply toward other humans or some divine being out in the sky. That is my main wish with these beautiful souls. I could use the beautiful calming, loving energy grounded into the very core of me to help me with all the balancing love-energy work I do all the time. This would be most helpful.

It is fascinating to me how many different ways humans can meditate also. Some learn to meditate where the approach is to still the mind completely so there are no thoughts coming through, or at least very minimal thoughts. This is a tough goal but some two-leggeds get quite good at it. Such Buddhas-in-training give off a lovely resonance or 'song'. Then there are some who meditate by stating or singing an actual repetitive song or mantra that has a spiritual, healing energy to it. I find that very pleasant too.

Then there are others, and my indigenous sons and daughters do this more, who focus on stilling their active minds (they don't suffer so much from monkey-mind as those of you who live in the more head-oriented, patriarchal societies more removed from me) so that they can *listen to*

Spirit. They also have learned from a very young age how to tune into the ancient wisdom of their instincts.

So I have given you some things to consider for this *Beauty Path*. But I'd like to end with how important it is to *forgive yourself* and others again and again and again. Know you are such lovable flawed beings in this adventure of being alive in physical bodies on me. And you're supposed to be flawed. There is no one on me who is perfect.

Well, let me put it another way, you are all perfect in your imperfections. Lovably perfect in all the ways you flub up or reveal your shadow side.

If you can't help but start raging with others in your midst, that's okay too. Go back and apologize to those people and forgive yourself and move on. Let it go. If someone hurts you, forgive them.

There are times when the weather rages. It's just a huge release of energy and sometimes you humans need to release your energy too, just as the thunder clouds do. It is not healthy to keep that energy pent up. You are on a journey to remember your divinity in the midst of your humanity, and to remember us, your Earth Mother and Great Father and Great Mother. Forgiveness is a huge part of this path of embracing your humanity and coming back to inner peace. It is an important gift to yourself and all around you.

This *Beauty Path* is what you have chosen, Mare. But I don't need to tell you this. You already know it.

Mare: I suppose this is the path I've found. The forgiveness. All of it— this stilling my monkey-mind to tune in on other levels, though I'm not always so good at this. As a matter of fact, it's downright tough to still my overactive mind and fears most days. Just about all days.

I know my Cherokee teacher taught me about the wisdom of listening to my instincts over my busy mind. That took a long time for me to learn. How often I second-guessed myself and did not trust my instinctual response to a person or situation.

She would say: "What is the very first thought that comes up? Those are your instincts. They are far wiser than your brain since they come from your soul-body which is ancient. It is born again and again and again. You need to listen to them and honor them."

All the times I did not listen to my instincts and then deeply regretted it. I'll never forget planning some signings in Atlanta, Georgia, for my first book, *If I gave you God's phone number*—it was the winter of 2003 and I had just come back from some events in Florida where I had been harassed by some Fundamentalist Christians since they did not like my book. I've mentioned them before.

My instincts kept on telling me to not do the Atlanta trip on a certain weekend in February but it was the best one for my winter schedule. The instincts just did not seem rational and I wondered if they were surfacing from fears about some more fundamentalist verbal attacks. I did not want those fears to inhibit me. So I went ahead and got the plane ticket, rental car, arranged with the bookstores, etcetera. It was supposed to be a quick fly down Saturday morning, stay overnight, and then return Sunday afternoon. Three events, two days.

Well, a big blizzard hit the Mid-Atlantic that Sunday morning and shut down the Baltimore airport for several days and I ended up spending oodles of money on extending the rental car, more hotel nights, meals, and other aggravations. It turned out to be a trip of few book sales and a hefty credit card pile-up. As the frosting on the cake, getting my car out of the parking lot at BWI airport (with about two feet of snow on it and more in front of it thanks to the snowplows) cost another $50 for parking, $100 to the crew with the shovels and pickup truck helping us stranded travelers dig out plus $300 worth of damage to the emergency brake. It still pains me when I think about it.

That was a turning point in honoring my instincts even if they made absolutely no sense in the moment. A huge lesson learned.

Okay, now I need a potty break and to get the woodstove really cranked up again. More later.

15

Sin is an Illusion, Right Action & Wrong Action Are Not

It's the action, not the fruit of the action, that's important. You have to do the right thing. It may not be in your power, may not be in your time, that there'll be any fruit. But that doesn't mean you stop doing the right thing. You may never know what results come from your action. But if you do nothing, there will be no result.

—Mahatma Gandhi

Thursday, January 16, 2014
5:10 AM
23° Coolish and clear.

Mother: Come on, sweetie, time to get up. It's time …

Mare: I'm here. Okay, I'm here.

Mother: Good morning, love. I want to discuss more about the Christ Consciousness and other topics.

Mare: Okay, I guess I'm awake enough to launch right into this not so small topic.

Mother: You are, my love, you are.
    So here we go. Everyone has the choice to tap into the Christ Consciousness and this energy is pouring into my energy fields these days in such glorious ways. It's getting more and more powerful and many are

tuning into it, those who are really waking up spiritually and letting their hearts open to those deeply compassionate frequencies coming in.

This is not to say that all are tuning in, sadly. A good number of people are only becoming more mired in their fears and anger. It gives me such sorrow. The Fundamentalist Christian ministers who so condemn homosexuality are farthest away from knowing this Christ Consciousness. They think they do, but the Christ they think they know is not the Christ Consciousness by a long shot. Some dark energies have gotten into many of these so-called Christian churches, and are not based on what the man, Jesus Christ taught, nor do they understand what the Christ Consciousness was about at all.

I know I've said this already but trying to lead people to God through the path of fear and anger is not what the Creator nor the Great Mother is about. The concept of sin is an illusion. It's something you two-leggeds came up with under the influence of those alien beings from another planet who have been stirring up dark energies for several millennia.

All of my beloved two-leggeds are flawed—every one of you—in the most lovable ways. You are supposed to be flawed, imperfect beings. I know I've talked about this before but it bears repeating. I would never ever, ever judge anyone as a sinner. Your experience here on me, the beautiful, magical planet here on which you live, is about remembering who you are as children of God. As spiritual beings. It's about cultivating your Sacred center, your God/Great Mother space within the very center of your spiritual being.

But *sinning* is something some of you came up with many, many years ago and this focus on sinners fed a collective sense of guilt and shame and more that has created a shadow-laden culture based on religious dogma. Such sadness in my heart, your Mother's heart, about this too common emotional heaviness. Oy—energetically, this has created a stink that has only gotten worse and worse for me.

Besides, the word "sin" really means "being off the mark" from an ancient Greek word, way back when. And you're supposed to be off the mark sometimes just because you're human. And to be a human who is *truly* human on me is an incredibly wonderful thing.

You are all beloved, beloved two-leggeds here on me. Some of you are rather wounded ones, true. And there is *Right Action* and *Wrong Action* at play all the time amongst you. Some of you have chosen the path of Wrong Action repeatedly and this saddens me terribly.

Two-leggeds who think it's fine to create chemicals that they know with certainty will kill life, human and otherwise, are coming from Wrong Action. Those who believe that another race of two-leggeds is insignificant and can be exterminated with no regrets are coming from Wrong Action. Stealing, murder, selling drugs that will poison others are all Wrong Action. Selling your children for slavery, prostitution or otherwise is Wrong Action.

Wrong Action is also destroying my ecosystems. Contaminating rivers or dumping uranium waste into the ocean is also Wrong Action. Anything that is harming my species, all of my children of winged ones, four-leggeds, finned ones and other species is Wrong Action.

What has been the hardest for me is how your dominant religions across me have essentially come to teach I'm not alive or conscious. This worldview that I'm a hunk of rock with various components to be dug up or cut down, or harvested and it's fine to spew more and more chemicals on me since I'm just a big rock, is just so … OFF!

Oh, I've been starting to vent here and, Mare, I know you need to get some errands done today. We'll continue this chat later.

I love you. I love all of my two-leggeds, but cheezus-peezus—it really is time for all of you to *WAKE UP* and realize I'm alive and that all life is connected physically, energetically and spiritually. All, including the rivers, the stones, the mountains. Now scoot. Your butt is getting really sore too. No bed sores for you! Love you!

Mare: [Several hours later] This is rather funny, Mother. One of my errands just now was to the local post office. And I told Kathy, the clerk whom I've gotten to know a little, that this was my first time out of the house for ten days. She got a very concerned look in her face and asked if I was at least talking with anyone. Or if I have any pets to snuggle with? Her expression was rather grave as she was asking me this.

I assured her I was fine, essentially on a writer's retreat in a cabin, just in a wooded development and not some isolated cabin. How could I tell her I'm not alone at all and am hanging out with you all the time, Mother? She was sincerely worried, as if I might become the *Unabomber Writer*, I suppose.

I could have told her: "It's okay, Kathy, I'm chatting with Earth Mother all the time. I'm really not alone at all."

But I don't think she was ready to hear that.

Mother: Yes, sweetie, you were wise to not share that, though I long for the day when more of you are hearing me and others will find that absolutely normal. We are getting there.

16

....

Nuclear Testing, Toxins and Entropy

*The global industrial economy is the engine for massive environmental
degradation and massive human (and nonhuman) impoverishment.*

—Derrick Jensen, Endgame, *Vol. 1: The Problem of Civilization*

Friday, January 17, 2014
5:10 AM
24° Not too cold, sunny.

Mare: Whoosh, I'm rubbing the sleep out of my eyes. Wishing I could
sleep in some more but I'm here. I know you're tired of hearing me
complain about how early it is, so I will stop complaining. Or at least try.

I do have to admit waking up so early when the world is so still—this
is a remarkable time of the day. I've read about this time of the day being
the best for meditation or spiritual transmissions since the veil between
worlds is thinner now.

Mother: Good morning, Love. Yes, there is truth to that. It's also when
your local world is not rumbling around and for ones as sensitive as you,
it's easier for you to still your mind and go to a more meditative space. I
love my sensitives so much, and you're one of the extra sensitives as an
empath. My two-leggeds who are challenged by all the energies and noises
of your too-busy human world always find it easier to tune into Spirit
during this time of the day.

Mare: It is a lovely stillness in these wee hours.

I'm also loving experimenting with different teas this winter and waking up to hot mugs of those also. I've been boiling fresh ginger and cinnamon sticks, and adding other spices such as cardamom, cloves, chamomile, lavender in a tea ball. It's really yummy. And healthy for you. Well, maybe not you, as in Earth Mother, but you get my drift.

Mother: That's okay sweetie, I enjoy it when you all enjoy things: food, romantic intimacy, good exercise and more. When you're pumping out joy energy, it feeds me. Your songs, as in the energy waves from your bodies, are so lovely when you are all feeling positive. In a way it's similar to the harmonious song from a pristine wilderness stream in a forest. Those are the most lovely songs for me.

On the other hand, the breaking of huge stones in a quarry dug into my bones takes away from the song in a rather jarring, painful way. Those mines hurt me.

Mare: I can't imagine what a nuclear bomb is like for you. Those must be really awful.

Mother: I don't even want to talk about them. They are the most painful things that have happened to me. I can handle meteorites, even big ones, since they've been hitting me from Day One. I was hit by them all the time back in my early days before I, and Creation, formed the atmosphere and created a bit of a buffer so most of the meteorites could burn up in it before they hit the ground.

But those nuclear bombs—they feel like someone took an absolutely huge hot iron to my skin and just seared me where they exploded. The terrible grief I feel at losing just about all of my species babies in those areas where they are dropped or detonated for testing—just horrendous. Those are the few times I wish I could walk away. Leave. Go to another planet to care-take. Go somewhere else.

But I can't. If only I could get through to all of you—especially the government and military two-leggeds—that I am alive and conscious. This is why you are doing this book, Mare. There needs to be a manual for living here on me in a balanced way that supports life. A manual to teach that killing life is *NOT* okay at least on the grand scale some of you have become so accomplished at killing—human life, animals, plants, dolphins, birds, teeny-tiny critters/two-leggeds, four-leggeds, etcetera.

Killing is not even okay on the small scale either unless one is just trying to eat. All of you need to eat. Even spiders and mosquitoes need to eat. Certainly there are times when a bear, or large snake or a human even needs to kill in self-defense. That's okay too.

Creation and I designed evolution with death and regeneration as part of it. Everyone does need to eat. Even vultures have their diet and they do such a good job of cleaning up your road-kills too. My poor four-leggeds and winged ones that get hit by cars. Makes me so sad. The cars never apologize either.

Let's get back to talking about nuclear bombs though. It's part of how off track your modern society has become with this blind acceptance of mass killings.

The bombs that have been set off underground or dropped into the South Pacific for testing, they have all been incredibly painful for me though very few of you were aware of them. I experienced searing, ripping pain in those regions that rippled out through *all of me*.

I am *One* being, made up of a beautiful interweaving complexity of life systems, ecosystems you call them in your science. I call them my loves and I adore their dances and songs. You can hear the songs in the rainforest, or the songs in the oceans with some of your scientific equipment. There is even a set of songs to the sounds of space particles, meteors, etcetera, as they hit the outer atmosphere of me.

Imagine how the songs or overall song of the ocean is silenced when a nuclear bomb is tested in the Pacific. It's not as if all of those beautiful species just decided to be quiet. They were killed. It's a dead zone for many miles and the shock of the explosions carries throughout all the oceans, rippling through all the water cells even up into far away rivers. It's all connected.

Many of you are talking about Fukushima and how that radioactive waste is traveling across the Pacific. Some are aware that it's been traveling through the atmosphere far faster than most of you initially thought, already contaminating pollen all across me. What you are not discussing are the radioactive particles that have been circulating through my oceans now thanks to underwater nuclear testing several decades ago, and the dumping of nuclear waste into the ocean these last many years, not to mention the nuclear bombs dropped on Japan during one of your more recent wars. Fukushima is rather a mess right now and the whales, and dolphins along with all the other life in the Pacific are none too happy with how their food is tasting these days, not to mention how they feel healthwise.

Because everything is cycled and cycled and cycled here on me, you all have been ingesting somewhat radioactive foods for some time now. As soon as those scientists cracked the atom which led to the creation of the atomic bomb which ended that war, radioactive waste has been circulating and circulating. It's been accumulating too, as there are now more radio-active particles released thanks to the continued testings. Places such as Chernobyl, Harrisburg, Fukushima are all contaminated by leakages, but there are other leakages from sites your media has not mentioned, not to mention intentional secret dumpings. A few of you, and I know who you are—know that nothing goes unnoticed—are really perpetuating some Wrong Actions with your illegal dumpings of toxic waste.

Then there is the challenge of nuclear waste. I've talked before about how there is no rubbish bin on me. Evolution did not include a trashcan on the side. This idea of *waste* is not something I ever imagined would take hold with you two-leggeds. I don't waste anything. Waste is food in my consciousness. One being's poop is another's food. So fun, so balanced, and it all contributes to the song of the planet, me, sharing, circulating, all in the vibrancy of how it's meant to be.

Granted, you two-leggeds knew you had to take care of your human poop, as your numbers grew and you started to live closer to each other, so it did not concentrate in one place and make you sick. Then there are the so-called 'weeds' you need to remove from your gardens (in your mind) that go into compost piles or are dumped in nearby woods. I suppose this is where the idea of "Waste Goes Away" comes from. But it's gotten a little extreme. Especially considering nuclear waste. The truth is *there is no away.*

There is a dynamic here on me that is actually all over the universe. This dynamic is about how everything has a natural tendency to break down, decompose, and disperse into the environment, on me. We've talked about this before. Its technical term is *entropy*. All of your CEO's, engineers, politicians, decision-makers from housewives to the President or Prime Minister or Dictator of your country need to enroll in a global webinar on entropy, one that will be simulcast in every language wherever the internet is used.

My very wise indigenous peoples who still practice the old ways don't need to take this online webinar. They already know about entropy. They may not use the term but they know it. They also know about the *Song of the Planet*, me, and all the multiple songs that make up the *One Song*. It is a most beautiful song when everything is in balance.

But I digress.

Entropy just is. It happens the same as gravity. You can't stop it. Your scientists call it the *Second Law of Thermodynamics*. I'm not going to go into a full physics lesson here. That's not necessary. But talking about entropy is necessary since your modern society has gotten so supremely good at yanking things from my bones, my crust, mining, drilling and now FRACKING! And you've been yanking heavy metals such as mercury, lead, arsenic, asbestos, etcetera, and all of these things, and including the waste from burning or manipulating these things are now circulating all over me.

Once something that has been stored for millions of years is dug out from my crust, my bones—stored there long before any of you two-leggeds or many of my other beautiful critters evolved—those things are going to start circulating. Either the actual substance or the waste from its use scatters through dispersal because entropy happens. I could say: "Shit happens. Then entropy moves it throughout all of me." Freely circulating, traveling by water, air, all of the means that I and Creation have partnered in evolving so all the good nutrients and molecules that were *NOT* stored in my bones could circulate and be used again and again and again.

The same goes for your chemicals that don't break down for a long, long time. They are circulating and circulating and criminy! None of your human cells, my four-legged beings' cells, frog cells, etcetera, know how to deal with these molecules that your labs have concocted, so your cells go a little or not so little haywire. I'm not a scientist. I'm your planet speaking here. However, no one asked me if I'd like to be part of a huge planetary scientific experiment that involves taking all of these things out of my bones or creating poisons/toxins that are going to spew all over ME and last too long. No one asked me.

I am one living, pulsing planet that does not have a big rubbish bin where you can stuff all the waste you've been creating.

My indigenous peoples know not to do this—those who remember. They've never lost their capacity to listen to me nor the wisdom of their elders, both men and women to share the teachings of living in balance on me.

Oh, Mare, you need a break. And you're still tired. Why don't you take a nap? We'll continue. I love you. All of you! We just need to get that global webinar going on entropy. That would be very helpful. But, Mare, you just focus on this book for now, okay? That's the most important thing for you to do.

17

....

Healing the Sacred Feminine - Divine Masculine Wound

I honor myself....
As the divine feminine blends with the masculine,
I now come into balance.

—Trudy Vesotsky

Saturday, January 18, 2014
4:45 AM
21° Some snow over night. Very frustrated with this green wood, just does not burn well. Cold in the house. More snow forecast for the day.

Mare: Oy, Mother! I'm freaking out. I'm shaking inside. I really am. Paul is coming over for the weekend again. He's going to be here this morning and I'm terrified. I wish I knew all the reasons I'm terrified. He and I talked last night for an hour and I was shaking after getting off the phone. This happened to me with the last man I dated whenever we had any phone chats and I was being vulnerable with him. But that man just evacuated when I was emotional and seeking support. Paul is the opposite. He is so experienced at being supportive. This scares me even more.

This morning I woke up at 4:30 AM or whatever ungodly hour it was, and the anxiety within me made my neck feel like there was a boa constrictor wrapping it's long and powerful body around me and strangling me. It was then I realized one of my fears is that I will chase Paul away. Another one is I'm not good enough for love—that I don't deserve a man who can be really loving and supportive.

Mother: Sweetie, I am always here for you. And you are forgetting you've learned how to take your emotions, all your tense monkey-mind chatter, and then just ask me to take them. I will take them from you any time you ask. You know how to connect with me energetically and do this. Keep on doing it. You can do it right now to calm yourself to release the anxieties and irrational fears that have been building up in you that make you feel like a huge snake is strangling you.

[Mare: I visualized a beautiful stream of energy flowing down my spine to the tip of my coccyx and my root chakra, and then down to the center of Earth Mother—to her heart. I imagined there being a beautiful flow of love energy streaming back and forth between her and me. I've been doing this practice erratically for some months and call it "Mother's Love Cord Connection".[11] Then I asked Mother to take all the tension and mental static banging around my head and heart. Instantly my taut neck muscles relaxed and a calm came over me. I took a deep breath of relief. The first in days, it seemed.]

Mother: See how that makes you feel better. Oh, sweetie, now just focus on being in the moment with him. Be present with him and with yourself. And have fun. Play. And just be authentic and communicate, communicate. And be gentle too. With yourself and with him.

Mare: Mother, the last time Paul was here two weekends ago, he shared something profound with me that I have been mulling over since. He told me how the patriarchal system has wounded men also. It has left men such as him feeling downtrodden and repressed also. This was the first time I've heard a man speak about this and it woke me up.

All of my life I've had blanket judgments against the generic *man*. I was not even conscious of these judgments for many years. I meet Paul and he encourages me to understand that because of the dysfunctional patriarchal system there are countless wounded men also. This forced me to broaden my perspective on the high emotional toll of this patriarchal culture.

I've been deeply mulling this over and decided to write an open *Apology* to the men who are waking up and seeking to find their sacred center, their *Divine Masculine* self, in the midst of these rapidly changing times. My sense is that many men are befuddled and frustrated with the emergence of the Sacred Feminine since they feel some of the angry undertones many women carry toward men. Plus, they are not certain what the rising of the Sacred Feminine will mean to them or to the societal structures

---

[11]http://messagesfrommother.org/2013/01/09/mothers-love-cord-connection/

in place that have largely served men. They are afraid of the change it is manifesting, without realizing how this will serve all of us, including them, in the long run.

It's true that many of us women have yet to relinquish our rage and victimhood in our journey towards embracing our sacredness and power. Yet this unhealed rage only feeds the polarization and does not support the necessary steps we all need to take to forgive and heal and come back together in balance. This only perpetuates the imbalance.

I finished the *Apology* piece yesterday. Here it is:

A Sincere Apology to the Divine Masculine

To all the men out there, all of you who have been working on your Divine Masculine self, either consciously or subconsciously, I wish to apologize to you. I have not met most of you, but this is still offered to all men.

I want to apologize for myself, and in a most humble way, for all women. Some women may not agree with what I am being guided to share but I hope many will.

I am sorry for all of the times I wished you thought and acted like a woman. I wanted you to be able to communicate your feelings with me and not escape to your Man-Cave, and was hurt and angry when you needed to disappear to mull your feelings over, solo. I felt abandoned.

I'm sorry for the painful, cutting ways I spoke with you when I was feeling wounded, (ah ... just about all of my life), by you as an individual and all of you as a species. It has felt many times as if you are another species, alien, to me at least. I suspect many women will agree with me on this.

I'm sorry for chasing you away by my directness, or worse, meanness, because I was so afraid and would not let you near me—the very tender, hurting core of me. My heart was so damaged I had to protect it from any vulnerability, from you ever getting too close to it.

I'm sorry for hitting you. A few of you. Not too hard. At least it did not feel too hard to me but I guess I don't know my own strength. And I wasn't even dating any of you when I did this. And I kicked one of you when I was eighteen, really hard. Growing up with four brothers, three older than I am, I guess I hadn't yet learned I shouldn't be physical like that with grown men, as a grown woman. You were not a brother and I had not grown up yet.

I'm sorry for venting my frustration at the world towards you because you're a man, frustration at a world that has been stacked against women for centuries and centuries, frustration that we're treated as sex objects. You want us to be eye candy but to be more than that seems to threaten the patriarchal systems so deeply entrenched in our culture.

It's not your fault. You, as a person, did not set the events in place back in history which led to this time period of so much anger, pain, woundedness on the part of so many of us women, and on your part too. Those were other men who took up swords and eventually guns, and took away our rights as women to worship as we choose, performing our own ceremonies for the Great Mystery and Great Mother.

Those were other men who raped us, and tortured us, and burned many of us at the stake for being healers, for knowing the ways of the plants and their medicine, and being powerful. If any of us women were powerful and did not submit to our husband or the village men, or Christian henchmen, then we did not live very long.

I'm sorry for all of us, men and women, for the sordid history our culture has had—in mistreating people who are different, slavery, women as chattel and more. I'm sorry about the terrible human rights records etched through the centuries. I have not thought about how you, men, were subjugated also since there has only been room for one man at the top in the hierarchical system initiated a long, long time ago, and perpetuated in just about every aspect of society since. Odds are good you were not that one man.

You lived and worked under that one man and were in fear of how "the Man" would treat you, or judge you, or let go of you, or simply kill you. I have not thought about it from your angle until very recently. So when you came home to your wife or lover after "the Man" had treated you so unfairly, it was easier for you to slip into your cave, I guess. Or easier for you to let your frustrations out on your family, I suppose. As hurtful as that was to them.

Perhaps this is what led so many of you to rape your daughters or abuse your wife, this sense of injustice in the rest of your lives and the need to have power over something, someone, since you had no power in the rest of your life?

For years, I wanted to play the victim and blame all of you. It was so cozy and safe to sit in my stories and make you all wrong. But I've been starting to understand how you've all been so hurt and repressed and, well, wounded by this patriarchal society. It's not just me or other women who have gotten wounded. So very wounded. I don't want to be a victim anymore. I want to own that we've all been in this together for a very long time, and I deeply hope and envision that the cycles and generations of wounding and pain can be healed. They don't have to continue.

I'm sorry you were taught you could not cry or express your feelings honestly as a young boy, that you were taught to suppress your sorrow or hurt at the playground or at home. This has shut you off from me, from us women, too. I'd like to think I wouldn't have taught you that, at least where I am in my life now. But it wasn't under my control how our parents, teachers, and other adults spoke to you, or how they modeled their behavior that taught you those unhealthy, stoic ways.

So many of you have turned to alcohol and drugs because of your inner pain. I'm sorry you've needed to escape there. This has hurt us even more, both physically and emotionally.

I'm sorry for what the military has done to so many of you at such a young and vulnerable age. So many of you served either voluntarily or not, and have come home with 'soldier's heart'. The wounds in your hearts are very hard to heal and most of us, as women, did not go through those horrors of war. We can't know the sights you saw, or atrocities you might have done because you were told to, or atrocities you've been subjected to also. And you can't tell us, because it's too painful to admit it to yourself in retrospect. I'm deeply sorry our world has been set up for you to be in those situations and to become a killing machine, or to turn against all that you previously valued.

And yes, it's certainly very true many women's hearts have been broken by watching their husbands, sons, lovers, and fathers go off to battle and not come home. It is not that we have not deeply, deeply suffered. I just sense that 'soldiers heart' is a singularly heavy wounding and this helps to explain why so many veterans are homeless on the streets.

I know you're not a machine. At least I'm learning this now at age fifty-four. I'm learning that you, so many of you, have such tender and broken hearts. And all the ways you've lashed out at us women, or hurt us, violated us, sources from a terrible woundedness in our culture that taught you it was okay to gang up on a woman and assault her as a group because of your lust, or date-rape her because she did not really fight you back, or hit her because she spoke back.

I'm sorry for all the pain you've experienced because of the dark "Shadow Feminine" that resides within all of us women. Most of us have not even realized she resides within us but she can take us over at times and when that happens our behavior is downright ugly and hateful. This side of us wants to hurt others, both

143

women and men, and will take no prisoners. And the dark Shadow Feminine is conniving, manipulative, resourceful and goes for blood. She's scary. She scares me. But I've learned to identify her within me, and see the hurt that she has been sitting on, and heal that. For the most part. I, like you, am still a work in progress.

Some women live in their dark Shadow Feminine just about all the time. They deeply scare me. What especially terrifies me is how so many times these types of women are the most attractive, the most sexual, and are downright predatory and then take heads. Or hearts. With no remorse. I'm deeply sorry for all of you men, that you've experienced women such as this, for my sense is most of you have and they've scarred you for life, if not many lifetimes.

I'm sorry for the mothers who abandoned you in their desperation to find them-selves or out of an inability to cope with the emotional responsibilities of being a mother. I'm sorry for the mothers who were (and might still be) emotionally unbalanced and lashed out at you or whipped you or worse. I'm sorry for those of you whose mothers lived in their dark Shadow Feminine and used their powers to emasculate you with emotional torture and worse.

I'm sorry.

I'd like all of us to heal, to be able to feel our emotions and express them in healthy ways. I'd like to understand that we as individuals are never all going to see the world the same way, or have the same gifts. I'd like us to be more patient with each other and learn how to truly listen well. Men and women are wired differently. We just are. I'd like us to better respect these differences, to understand them. I'd like women not to feel they need to become a man to survive in this world, especially the business world. I'd like men to truly respect women's gifts in the workplace.

I'd like all of you men to feel safe enough to release your pain since it's my sense that is at the root of much of your wounded hearts.

I'd like all of us to feel safe around each other. Safe enough to ask for a long hug and receive one with kindness and warmth behind it.

I'd like this a lot. Not just for me but for all of us.

To those of you men who have found the courage to heal, to work on your Divine Masculine and be authentic and cry when you need to, and really share from the heart, I have such respect for you. This helps you clear your wounded hearts and helps us see your hearts better. Please keep on doing it and showing other men you know, by your examples and sharings—for this is a beautiful path, a path of respect, a path for Real Men.

We women need you to be with us as we work to rediscover our Sacredness and our strengths. We don't want to leave you behind or put you on a shelf while we do our work to discover our feminine powers of compassion, balance, voice and more. We want to heal this world and are finding the confidence to do so. We need you to be with us in this journey but we can't do the work for you.

We need you in your fullest Divine Masculine to help birth this New World coming in, today. Just taking baby steps towards this would be such a gift to us and to yourselves. A huge gift. For us and for the next seven generations.

So, please forgive me for my part in the pain that's been caused. I'm learning to love just about all of you. I'm still human and some of you, rather us, have done some horrific things to other people throughout history. Love toward men such as Hitler or Chinese leaders who are closing down Tibetan Buddhist monasteries, torturing monks and worse now—is tough for me, in this moment. Very tough. But I'm starting to see how the fear-based patriarchal systems could create such monsters. I'm finding a little compassion for the men who got sucked in to those systems and went the path of darkness. A little.

Please forgive me. I'm sorry for my part in this deeply troubled world. I'm trying to heal my little corner of it, at least.

Thank you. I love you.
—mare

Mother: My love, this is a remarkable apology you've written. You don't know how this will ripple out and touch so many people. It will open up discussions between men and women all over the world and help them release some of their heart suffering in a way that is safe.

To offer an apology to another and to acknowledge one has played a part in the dance of suffering is such a beautiful opening of the heart. It takes courage to admit one might be at fault and communicate to the other that one is feeling remorse and is seeking to bring the relationship back into balanced compassion and love. Seeking forgiveness opens up the energy for there to be reconciliation at levels that will bring such beautiful, beautiful balance back. Balance is what has been lost in your society, authentic balance that is so healing for all of you and me.

Mare: I have been practicing something called *Ho'oponopono* for some years now, Mother. It comes out of Hawai'i and is a lovely spiritual practice that teaches the healing gifts of seeking forgiveness, and forgiving oneself. It's made up of four simple phrases said together:

> *I love you,*
> *I'm sorry,*
> *Please forgive me,*
> *Thank you.*

It's based on the belief that it's our thoughts attached to unhealed emotional states within us that create disturbance. And this causes our internal song to be discordant, which affects you. When we give this discordant energy over to you and the Great Father, to Divinity, we are releasing it to you to dissolve it. Then we apologize, forgive ourselves and the other person, and then fill the void of the energy released with gratitude which carries a beautiful love energy.

What I deeply appreciate about this practice is it recognizes that all healing and peace initiates from within us. On some level we are the cause of the outer disturbances in the world around us, unhealed ways and more. Doing Ho'oponopono clears the slate to release the unhealed emotional wounds within me that create a resonance that is keeping me off balance. It allows me to take full responsibility.

This is part of the reason I could write that *Apology* piece. I know in some ways I am responsible for the perpetuation of this pattern of victimhood and rage toward men since I've been carrying this deep anger within *me* for so long, playing the victim card. And I need to release those ancient emotions and stop playing victim to claim my own inner power. Plus, as you mentioned to me before, Mother, I have been the rapist, the oppressor too. I have played both sides. It is time to completely release the energies that have been stuck there. Perhaps in my doing it, other women and men can learn to release theirs too. I can hope.

Mother: Yes, one can hope. You have set a very good example here. And I love my Hawai'ian elders who have been teaching Ho'oponopono. They have been helping so many of my beloved humans learn to completely release their stuck emotional patterns through these prayers. Yes, Creator and the Great Mother and I are always here to call on to help you neutralize those emotional patterns that cause you pain. Call on our divine love at any time. Give it to us. And send the gratitude back out to us in your prayers. It feeds such beautiful energy. And definitely feeds my planetary song.

This dynamic of the 'war of the sexes', as some of you have termed it, has given me such sadness. Thanks to the influence of those aliens who brought you the unbalanced patriarchal ways several thousand years ago, the generations upon generations of cruelty and repression have created deeply embedded soul patterns. These soul patterns are shifting now and it is causing much turbulence since the women are waking up faster than the men, in most cases.

Your lower chakras are realigning with the shifting energies here on me, with the incoming Christ Consciousness energies and more. Whatever stuck emotional energies that you were born with in this earth-walk, they are getting stirred up. This is because you are all being invited to heal, to release the old and embrace the newer, more love-filled energies. But you must do your emotional homework in order to do this.

My heart goes out to my two-legged men since most of them were not taught how to be a healthy balanced man—to feel their emotions and express them very well. Yet they are being influenced by these shifting energies on me also. They are also observing many of the women in their lives resist the patriarchal family patterns they all grew up with, and this is leaving them uncertain and confused. Some seek to assert their powers over the women again and this only creates more havoc. They are not sure what their roles are any more, or how to relate to women in a more balanced way. Many are learning more balanced ways and seeking to teach their sons too. Yet the loneliness most of them suffer is so great, it makes me sad.

Your *Apology* piece is offering them a hand to support them. While many won't admit this, they need great support in these shifts. What their fathers and grandfathers taught them has not given them the emotional tools needed for this level of healing. Gratefully, there are some men's groups and brilliant writers who have started to provide a safe space for men to better understand and release their own pain that has kept them so stuck.

So I can hear your stomach grumbling. Time for a break. I love you! I love all my two-leggeds so much!

18

Love and *Love*

I am in you and you in me,
mutual in divine love.

—William Blake

Monday, January 20, 2014
5:50am
22° Moon is shining outside, full last Wednesday. Not so, so cold outside but still chilly.

Mare: Oh my god, Mother ... I don't know where to start. You know I took two days off to be with Paul and do some other writing. Paul left early yesterday evening and all I can hear in my heart is Carole King's: "You make me feel like a natural woman ..." I have not felt this happy since I can ever remember. You had been nudging me about how Paul and I needed to be like the logs in the fire—so close we could spark each other. Well, we sparked each other.

Mother, you know I've never been with a man like this. He can communicate about everything. About how he wanted to pull me back into bed on Sunday afternoon, but didn't. About how much he would never force himself on me and sought out my truth, my comfort zone. This man is such a gift. He has encouraged me to feel safe beyond anything I could have imagined.

When I whispered in his ear the question from my first book: "If I gave you God's phone number, what would you do with it?" over the weekend, he astounded me with his response.

"I would call God up and ask him how I can serve," he said.

Mother, you know I've heard thousands of responses to the question in all of my travels but I've never gotten a response like that from someone. Paul is so clear he is here to serve the divine. He is amazing. He and his former wife quit their jobs to work in Haiti for several years. He has taken in foster children.

And Mother, his kisses are sweeter than wine. Much sweeter than wine.

And now he's back at his house and my bed feels too empty. I crawled into it so exhausted last night and it felt like a void. This is the same bed where two nights before I had fears about allowing someone else into it with me.

Mother: Sweetie, I'm so happy for you. It is time for you to experience a connection like this. A deep, kind loving connection. You and Paul are going to be wonderful for each other. It will be beautiful and will help your spiritual work and his. And so much more.

Mare: Yes, he is a special man. A very special man. I do care about this man. But, Mother, would you explain something to me? It's about our energy bodies, spirit bodies that extend beyond our physical bodies. With all the beautiful intimacy between Paul and me over the weekend—hugging in bed and dancing in the living room—after he left, it felt as if I was still with him and he was still with me energetically.

Mother: Yes, daughter, when two of you come together so closely and mix your energies together, it is a beautiful blending of your spirit bodies that can be healing, powerful, loving, and overwhelming. The overwhelming aspect comes from your spirit bodies mixing together so intensely. It is important for you to come back to center with your own inner balance and clear your spirit body of his, to find your own equilibrium.

You now have beautiful energy cords of love between the two of you that can support both of you, yet you need to come back into yourself and your center at the same time. It is important to pull back now. He is feeling the overwhelm and with all he has gone through with the traumatic breakup he experienced last summer, he knows he needs to find his own footing and this is important for him. This is why he communicated to you he is feeling the need not only to relish the beautiful weekend, but also "remove" himself back to his own personal space too.

You've needed to be alone, most of your life actually, to find your own footing. You've needed far more than Paul has. He's been in committed relationships for just about all of his life. And he's a very sensitive man with such a giving heart.

Also, daughter, you are a powerful woman becoming only more powerful in your spiritual work. It is easy for you to overwhelm because you have so much love inside you and your light is so strong. Most men would not be capable of allowing that much love and Mother energy to be directed at them for very long. It takes a strong man to be able to be handle this energy even if he needs to pull back to restore his equilibrium at times. This equilibrium should always be evolving if a person is truly growing spiritually.

This journey to cultivating your human God/Goddess space should never be static. It is an ever-moving process and the most powerful love relationships you humans have are ones in which you are also consciously aware of a growing love and connection with the Divine as you grow in your love and connection with each other.

The reason these types of relationship are more powerful is that you are including the Divine into your lives to 'remember' who you really are as spiritual beings having a physical experience. You grow closer to Creation and to me, your Mother, when your love for another grows, and you also take time to continue to reconnect with us. It's a lovely ever-cycling, growing nexus of divine love that merges with your human love and it adds so beautifully to the song here on my planet. It's a song of joy, healing, balance and so much more. Love like this feeds me and feeds all in the positive spiritual realms.

So it is good to pull back from each other. Paul is a wise man. He is sorting many things out in his efforts to discover who he is now at sixty-eight and single and uncertain of what and where to go in his myriad interests and gifts. It is smart for him to not commit to anyone to find himself again at this time.

And you have lots of things to do, yourself!

But yes, energetically, you were feeling his energy body within yours and it was overwhelming for you. You need to come back to center and push his energy out of yours to some degree to refocus on all of your work to serve me. You will definitely be keeping some cords of energy between the two of you. He does not want to cut those and you don't either.

Now, I know your stomach is grumbling. And there are more logs outside that need stacking. I want to discuss more. Oh, so much to discuss.

I love you! I love all of my two-leggeds so much, so much. It gives me such joy to see two beautiful souls come together as you and Paul have. Oh, just fills my Mother heart up again and again. Love. It's so joyful to me. You know, the dolphins, whales, and all of my beloved creatures, they celebrate too when two people come together in such a lovely connection, especially in such a way to serve me today and into the next seven generations. Oh, yes, yes … yes. Now scoot!

19

More Magic and Miracles

I am realistic.
I expect miracles.

—Dr. Wayne Dyer

Tuesday, January 21, 2014
6:10 AM
20's More forecast of snow today.

Mare: You know, Mother, it does make a difference when a person goes to bed early. It definitely makes it easier to be woken up earlier in the morning and not feel so comatose. Plus getting some exercise stacking wood yesterday was so needed and fun.

About half of the two cords of wood are stacked now and hopefully the neighborhood association won't send me another one of those pesky letters about my lingering mountain of wood like the one they sent me last winter. I had badly sprained my ankle then and it meant minimal wood stacking until the ankle got better.

This morning I was blowing on some large embers left over from last night at the woodstove. It was like fireworks going off. A fun light show in the woodstove! Such a magical show to wake up to.

Mother, one thing you help bring into my life is magic. Maybe this is because I'm able to see more things as magical. You help me appreciate small and big things as divine gifts that I guess most people would not even notice.

Take the snow coming down right now. I'm watching it as I sit here in bed writing and it's so meditatively peaceful. Snow is truly magical, especially this type of powdery, dry snow that is like frozen water feathers coming down—the perfection of every flake and how it softens all the edges of winter's bleak landscape. This dry, dry Aspen-like snow is such a rare happening in Maryland where we usually get wet, clumpy snow. We're supposed to get more than a few inches and I'm celebrating this.

And then there are the times you really have woven serious magic into my world. I still have the gas receipt from late June, 2012, when I was coming back from the beach when my car went an extra 110 miles on a tank of gas. I know we've talked about that already.

Mother: Yes, sweetie, I did that. It's all energy, your diesel fuel in that cute little blue VW Golf. Everything around you is energy. And there is energy between you and others. Trees have an energy field. Flowers do too. All I did with your car engine and the fuel tank was give it a little boost. I love you so much, so very, very much.

Yes, magic has become a part of your life, and this is rightful. Whenever someone chooses to surrender to the Mother, miracles happen. When you surrender to the Creator, Great Mystery, same thing. But connecting with Mother can really manifest the magic. Life is full of miracles but when one of our Earth Children truly surrenders to us, we will test you and bless you. It's all part of the Sacred Relationship.

Mare: Ah, so that was you at work just now when I tried to take a little break and check email, to see if Paul had responded, and got distracted by a restaurant coupon email? I could not get that coupon website to allow me to pay. The button just would not work. I was thinking about how much fun it would be for me to go out to dinner with Paul sometime and these were really reasonable coupons for a night out. But I couldn't get the website to cooperate.

Mother: Honey, you know the answer to that. You could hear me calling you back to the writing. Yes, I did that. You get so easily distracted. I need you to stay focused with this writing. There is so much I want to share in this *Great Mother Bible* and you sometimes flit over to email or FaceBook and I need you to stay attentive so these teachings can come out fully and clearly.

Having said that ... I can hear your stomach growling right now and you need a break. But today we will have more writing sessions together. You're supposed to get about eight inches of snow. A perfect writing day. Now go get something in that stomach. We need to keep you well fed with all this work you're doing for me.

Mare: [9:17 PM that evening] Mother, I had so much fun going out and sledding this afternoon. We had such a beautiful snowfall and so perfect for sledding. I think it's still snowing now into this evening. Cold wind too. I posted on Facebook how much I wanted to play in the snow and sled but did not have one. Within a minute, a neighbor posted that I could borrow one of her family's sleds.

So I joined the neighborhood kids in the nice steep snow bowl that was created at the bottom of this hilly neighborhood. What a workout.

Honestly, Mother, this conquering cancer has given me such a new lease on life. And meeting Paul and just being committed to having fun. I've always liked to have fun but it is reaching ever new and more exciting levels of it in my life.

And I did do some writing today too. You know I did but I just had to go out and experience the magic of this lovely, lovely, dry, feathery snow. A Dutch friend of mine told me recently their language has two different words for *joy*. One is the external experience of it and the other is the interior experience … I'm soaked up with the internal experience right now. This afternoon I was sledding in the external experience of it. Truly a lovely level of bliss.

I suppose I'm feeling in love, aren't I?

Mother: Yes, sweetie, you are and it's so delightful for me to see you in this place. Love is magic. And magic is love. And you are surrounded by so much love all the time without even considering Paul. All of my two-leggeds are surrounded by this love if only you all knew it. Life is magic. Living here on me is more than magical actually. It's all part of the Great Mystery and a miracle. You are all surrounded by miracles all the time.

Okay, I can see you're bleary-eyed and a good tired from your sledding today. We will talk more tomorrow. I love you!

20

Responses to the *Sincere Apology to the Divine Masculine*

You will begin to heal when you let go of past hurts, forgive those who have wronged you and learn to forgive yourself for your mistakes.

—Anonymous

Wednesday, January 22, 2014
Woke up at 5:15 AM. Writing at 7:33 AM
1° Bitter cold. High of 13° today forecast. Hard time getting geared up to write. Tossed in around in bed for almost two hours.

Mare: Mother, this *Apology*— I'm astounded at the reception. My website hits are in the thousands and most people are responding about how it is making them cry and they see this as a profound gift to help in the healing between the sexes.

One man in his late 50's, the husband of a friend, left a message on the website that he carries a deep distrust of men and flinches whenever a man even starts to reach out to him because he was beaten so much as a young boy. Others have shared how my *Apology* made them cry as it touched them in a deep, sensitive place, or encouraged them to think more deeply about the role we women have played in wounding our men. And a few were not happy with it. Oh, well. We are all in this dance together and have been for a very, very long time. Most of the responses are very positive.

One man actually drafted his own formal response from the Divine Masculine, and it is profound. I am sharing it here with his permission:

A Reply to the Sacred Feminine's Apology

Dear (or should I say Dearest) Sacred Feminine,

I read your apology and the first response is "apology accepted". The next thought is: "It really wasn't necessary, you have simply been doing your best."

As one man, I accept your apology, and I thank you for it. I offer mine as well. On behalf of all men, I apologize for any of the things that we have done that did not sit well with you. I apologize also for the things that were simply unacceptable. And I offer a thought for you. "You don't know our story."

I, as one - and only one - man, am not even sure I know my whole story. I was raised a certain way. That helped establish some of my beliefs as I was growing up, and that helped shape who I am today. There's a lot of who I am today that I am very proud of, and there's also a lot of who I am today that I am not so proud of. Many of the thoughts and beliefs that have shaped who I am today started as other people's beliefs. They were those of my parents and their parents, my brothers and sisters, my friends, my teachers, my neighbors, the list goes on and on. Eventually they became my own. I didn't question them because it didn't seem like I was supposed to. And they shaped me. And they shaped many men.

But many men are finally starting to realize that these thoughts and beliefs were simply that, thoughts and beliefs. And many of us are realizing that, while these beliefs have shaped our behavior for generations and generations, the beliefs may not really be true. And they can change. And they are changing. Changing will not be easy for many of us as the beliefs are so ingrained, and for others the changes have already been happening and will come a lot easier. But make no mistake that they are changing. We are starting to understand our own story. We are starting to understand who we really are.

We have been taught to hide our feelings, to show no emotion, to stand strong, to be the leader. We actually like some of those traits, but in many cases we are simply putting on a mask. It can be scary being a leader when you don't really know where you're going, and we'd like to be able to share our true feelings at times as well, without having to feel weak for having done so.

We are learning a lot, and we are changing. We are recognizing our strengths and weaknesses, and realizing that we all have a multitude of each. That's what makes us who we are. And we are also learning that we don't have to FIX all the weaknesses either. None of us need to FIX anything. And we are learning that it is okay to be who we are, perfect even with all of our personal imperfections.

And this is where we come together. We need you, Divine Feminine. We need you to accept us for what we are. We need you to love us for what we are. And we have lots to give in return. We believe that there is a bit of the Sacred Feminine and the Divine Masculine in each of us, our yin and yang. As we work together we can balance the yin and yang, not only within ourselves, but on a much larger scale as well. Let us each be perfect as we are, let us live to our strengths and our happiness, and let us no longer worry about fixing anything.

We love you Sacred Feminine. And we need you to complete us. And we hope you feel the same about us. The Yin and the Yang.

Signed, KJ,
A representative of the Divine Masculine

Mother: Yes, love, this "Apology" you've written has struck a very strong chord. It is time for my sons and daughters to start forgiving each other for all the pain that has been afflicted. It is time for all of you to acknowledge you are all wounded and blaming the other person, the other sex, is not going to help you take responsibility for yourself, your part in the dance and your healing.

I love all of you so, so, so very much—and it has been hurting me to witness and feel all this anger and suffering between the genders for the past few thousand years. It is time for you to learn how to release your anger and hurt, your sorrows, as best as you can, as safely and lovingly as you can, in the presence of someone who can support you compassionately.

I love all of the women's circles that have formed to support you women in your healing and coming into your powers, your strengths, your confidence, your self-love. These have been so important and they need to continue with more women to help them find themselves and their sacred centers.

The men's circles and retreats are very important and healing too. There needs to be more of them though. Men need to feel safe in expressing themselves. They need to learn it's a good thing to cry. Not just that it's okay, but a good thing. Crying releases stress, and so much more. It lightens up anyone's heart to cry. Men need to let other men know it's okay to cry. They can be a role model and allow themselves to cry in an environment where they won't get fired for being emotional, of course. They can encourage their wife, girlfriend, whomever, to allow them to cry in front of them. If she is wise at all, she will understand this is healthy not only for her man but for their relationship.

And if the wife, girlfriend or lover judges this man for being emotional, then she, too, is still mired in the cultural conditioning of manliness and beefcakes and can hopefully wake up from it relatively soon. This conditioning your society has thrown on all of you that is so deep—it's unconscious in most of you—this is at the root of the great imbalance between men and women.

Now, go, take a break. Get some breakfast. You were planning to take a bath too, yes? Now go … Love you!

21

On the Balance

God turns you from one feeling to another and teaches by means of opposites so that you will have two wings to fly, not one.

—Rumi

Thursday, January 23, 2014
6:10 AM
9° Another bitter cold day.

Mare: Mother, here I am. I'm up and have the computer in my lap. Sitting up in bed. But I'm in a bit of a funk this morning. This whole surrendering to you thing—this is one of those moments when I'm not so happy about it. How I would love some good income right about now.

I have a toothache and fear my back molar on the upper right side is infected and I'm going to lose it. And I already paid more than $1500 last fall to get a new crown on this tooth. This tooth is next to another gap, where I went through a similar painful process and lost another molar and opted not to get a bridge or an implant. I really don't want to lose another tooth there and have a big hole. I won't be able to chew on that side very easily at all.

These things are darn expensive and you know I've been living simply for some time now. I know you're taking care of me, Mother, I know you are … but it would nice to have some sort of check in the mail on a regular basis to help cover these big ticket items. I'm still living off my savings and you've helped me figure out ways to keep my bills down. But, how long, Mother, how long will this continue that you want me to still burn through the dwindling savings? I still feel as if you're dangling me by my toenails over the cliff especially on a morning like this when I'm looking at the prospects of a big dental bill.

Oh, meant to share also I wrote a long letter to a friend with whom I'm having financial issues. I owe her some money because of a loan she gave me and I'm hoping she will accept a longer payment plan. This is a bit stressful especially since I especially don't like being in conflict with people.

And this house is still in foreclosure and I have no idea whether any-one bought it at auction and you keep on guiding me to not worry about all of that but to just keep on writing. And listening to you.

But Mother, if I lose this tooth completely, that's a hard financial hit. It's not that I don't have that money in my savings account. I do. But that is a chunk of my savings right there. Ouch, Mother…. Ouch!

Mother: Honey, I know this is so hard for you at times. And you do tend to be more anxious in the morning. So go ahead and vent. I'm listening to you.

Mare: Truly, though, Mother, some people have nine-to-five jobs and have health insurance and sometimes even dental insurance. My neighbors work for one of those federal agencies cloaked in mystery, either NSA or CIA or whatever, and they get nice paychecks every month, both the husband and the wife. UPS trucks are always bringing packages to their door … and honestly, in this moment, I'm envious of these neighbors' financial security.

Mother: Yes, love, I understand. But you know I'm taking care of you. You know that. You know you've had various financial miracles come into your life in the past few years. There was the check last year from a retire-ment fund from a job you had years ago. That was completely unexpected to you, not to mention your healing miracles and the fact that you recov-ered from your lymphoma outside of the doctors' offices. I'm guiding you and taking care of you. Trust, my daughter, trust.

Mare: I'm working on this, Mother. I am. It's just there are moments.

Mother: I know, love, I know. Rest assured your tooth will be fine. It will be. Now just take a deep breath and let your fears go.

Okay, I want to talk more about this Divine Masculine – Sacred Fem-inine dynamic. This is a huge topic, indeed.

I'm overjoyed to see so many of my daughters coming together to discuss the Sacred Feminine and try to understand it, and to learn ways to embrace it in their lives. They are finding many new ways to truly embrace me within themselves so they can allow my energies to work through them to heal them and heal all that is around them. My only wish is that more of them recognized me here as Earth Mother also. I'm right here under all of you. Here I am!

Ah, it would be good to define the Sacred Feminine, I suppose. Well, the Sacred Feminine is about all those beautiful characteristics that make up the Feminine Principle, and infusing them with sacred or divine purpose. Women and (even men) who seek to cultivate their Sacred Feminine aspects focus on developing more compassion, intuition, and gentleness. Here's a more complete list:

Nurturing	*Procreative*
Compassionate	*Life-giving*
Soft	*Sensitive*
Forgiving	*Giving and giving*
Non-judgmental	*Warm*
Expanding	*Ultimately loving*
Birth of all there is	*Ultimately powerful*
Healing	*Intuitive*
Receptive	*Emotional*

Women and men who are truly committed to the Sacred Feminine and Divine Masculine path are committed to serving the highest good. They are serving for today and into the future so that the needs of the next seven generations are taken care of in a most wise and beautiful manner.

Every person has masculine and feminine energies combined. No one person is 100% masculine or 100% feminine. Nor should this be so. You are all supposed to be a balance of masculine and feminine energies or characteristics.

Let's now discuss the Divine Masculine. These are the masculine principles, which when infused with a sense of sacredness or divinity, can be truly glorious ways for men to bring their masculine out:

Protecting	*More physically oriented*
Exploring	*Aggressive*
Hierarchical	*Powerful*
Macho	*Mechanistic*

Logical   *Heroic*
Reason-based   *Linear-thinking*
Savior-like

There are some men who are very much on the edge of the spectrum of masculine and feminine. They can be on either edge, actually. They can be rather effeminate or quite macho. That is how their soul chose to come into this earth-walk. Not that they would ever arrive in the middle of the gradient if they tried very hard, yet they can work on embracing some of the principles they are weaker in to step into balance more.

If a man is more effeminate, he might work on more physically demanding skills such as chopping wood or working out. I'm not saying he should become "beefcakes" but he could just get into the more masculine aspects of his physicality.

Or he could practice being more assertive and stating his truth in meetings or with his partners. He shouldn't need to be submissive to the more dominant men around him. It might surprise some of the more macho men to have a more gentle man speak up to them for the first time, but it would be good.

More dominant men have developed the sense in your culture that the world belongs to them, that I, Earth Mother, belong to them, along with every female and male around them, dog, cat, even their children. This tendency is one of the patterns that's been manifesting for centuries and centuries and has run completely amok.

These macho men need to learn compassion, gentleness, receptivity and more from the feminine end of the spectrum. Many of them have lived countless lifetimes as military men and have raped many women as they pillaged the villages they conquered. There is this aura about them that turns many women off, since they carry an attitude that they own women and will physically take any female they find attractive, against her will.

More than anything, these men need to learn humility. They do believe the world has been served to them on a silver platter, to slice and dice and devour. And if it was not served to them, they will take parts of me, or a woman, or something else anyway. They will grab a woman and rape her, or take a forest and just slice it down with no regard for any of the animals there nor the role of the forest in maintaining ecological balance. They also fail to honor the spiritual beings, the nature spirits whom the indigenous peoples have been in partnership with for many thousands of years.

There is a strong relationship between how my women have been treated and how I've also been treated for many, many centuries now. The raping of my daughters has also played out in the raping of me and my bones, my forests and more. The mechanistic, dominant ways of your patriarchal societies have lived in denial of the feminine wisdom for so, so long. It is all connected. The patriarchal attempts to control the life-giving gifts of women and myself as Earth Mother are tied in very closely. I suppose some of you call this *Eco-Feminism*.

Some men have such a closed heart from childhood beatings and verbal abuse, or they came into this world with a closed heart and it grew even more closed since they could not cry to release their pain. These men irritate me with what they have done and continue to do—the power they seem to think they have over other humans, over everything.

And when they are smart and learn how to manipulate and take control, oh, it's horrendous. I have been cringing at what's been going on in some corners of me for some time now. The dictatorships and ousting of peoples from their native lands, the massacres and more. Oh, this need for power can be a real sickness.

There is also a very honorable way that a good number of men have stepped into their Divine Masculine. Some of these men were the ones fighting off the early aggressive tribes several thousand years ago. They knew their role was to protect the woman and the children. They also knew the spiritual work of the women to do ceremony and honor the Mother, honor me, was integral to their village life. They tried very hard to protect the temples and other ceremonial grounds, and this in turn protected the capacity of the women to continue their spiritual work.

These men embraced the role of guardian and protector in a most beautiful way. They worked so hard, and lost their lives, again and again. The Knights Templar is a well-known group of these men. They had not forgotten about the Mother, about me, and fought for centuries to protect the women, the women healers, priestesses, the seat of feminine wisdom and more.

This balance is an important goal to achieve. To balance the masculine and feminine attributes within each of you is a way of coming into your more complete self in your earth-walk. More wholeness. You have more holistic health centers and holistic diets. Many of you are trying and this is making me so happy compared with these other more masculine ways of seeing your body and my body as a machine with parts. I'm not a machine. Your body is not a machine. You are body, mind, spirit in a beautiful dance of energy moving through you all the time. Your culture has been starting to wake up to this and this is all good.

But I'm getting off track here. About this masculine and feminine balance—this is what needs to be brought back. It used to be how humans lived, in balance with me and all the four-leggeds, winged ones and finned ones. Men and women lived in balance with each other, long before those beings from another planet came and tried to take over, feeding these strong aggressive energies into the more macho men to compel them to take power and claim all for themselves and their Angry God religions.

I do need to add that somehow there is this idea that women were in charge many thousands of years ago and the men were subservient to the women. But that was not the case all of that time and those who have studied archeological sites to try to prove those theories have not had enough information to understand how life was like back during those eras. Plus their scientific lens was a bit fogged because of their patriarchal context. In many of those early cultures there was far more equality between the men and women in honoring the Great Mother as the giver of all life.

Within most indigenous tribes, the proper way of life for millennia has been to seek wholeness and balance within themselves, honoring both masculine and feminine. Living from a place of surrender, gratitude to Creation and me, as Mother—they honor the wisdom of the women, the wisdom of the elders and learn how to honor all aspects within themselves both negative and positive, while healing their woundedness. This is by going through ceremonial rites and learning to overcome their tendencies to live from shadow. We've already talked about *Walking in Beauty* and that is a huge part of this.

Adolescent boys and girls went through these ceremonies, to grow and learn how to be responsible, mature members of their village. These boys and girls learned how to tune into Spirit to tap the wisdom of their Spirit guides at the same time they know to sit at the knees of their elders.

Oh my, it's getting very, very late in the morning and I can tell you are bleary-eyed, Mare. Why don't you go take a nap and we'll resume this tomorrow. Early. You know me, I love to get you going early so we can take advantage of those still morning hours.

Oh, and I've been sending energy into your back molar, the one that was giving you pain. It will be fine. It will heal and you won't need to worry about any dental bills about that. But it will be good for you to consciously send healing energy to it also. A team effort, you know. Now off to bed with you!

22

To Embody Our Sacred Feminine & Divine Masculine Self

Poetry is the rhythmical creation of beauty in words.

—Edgar Allan Poe

Friday, January 24, 2014
6:40 AM
5° Clear. Another winter day. Very much a winter day.

Mare: Mother, we've been talking about the Divine Masculine and Sacred Feminine. I've been playing around with some poetry and revised a poem that was originally written by a man named Boysen Hodgsen about the Divine Masculine. Someone recently said to me that the Divine Masculine and Sacred Feminine are essentially the same and I'm still pondering that. I felt this poem of Boysen's definitely reflects more of the masculine so I rewrote it to better describe the Sacred Feminine. I'd like to share it with you.

Mother: That would be great. Why don't you share both of them?

Mare: Boysen works for *The ManKind Project.*[12] This is an international group that empowers men to heal through intensive warrior weekends to become more emotionally mature, compassionate and responsible men. MKP has been helping men heal through cultural wounds for several de-

---

[12]http://www.mankindproject.org

cades now. I know some men who have gone through their trainings and have been influenced in quite positive ways.

The New Macho

He cleans up after himself.
He cleans up the planet.
He is a role model for young men.
He is rigorously honest and fiercely optimistic.

He holds himself accountable.
He knows what he feels.
He knows how to cry and he lets it go.
He knows how to rage without hurting others.
He knows how to fear and how to keep moving.
He seeks self-mastery.

He has let go of childish shame.
He feels guilty when he's done something wrong.
He is kind to men, kind to women, kind to children.
He teaches others how to be kind.
He says he's sorry.

He stopped blaming women or his parents or men for his pain years ago.
He stopped letting his defenses ruin his relationships.
He stopped letting his penis run his life.
He has enough self-respect to tell the truth.
He creates intimacy and trust with his actions.
He has men that he trusts and that he turns to for support.
He knows how to roll with it.
He knows how to make it happen.
He is disciplined when he needs to be.
He is flexible when he needs to be.
He knows how to listen from the core of his being.

He's not afraid to get dirty.
He's ready to confront his own limitations.
He has high expectations for himself and for those he connects with.
He looks for ways to serve others.
He knows he is an individual.
He knows that we are all one.

He knows he is an animal and a part of nature.
He knows his spirit and his connection to something greater.

He knows that the future generations are watching his actions.
He builds communities where people are respected and valued.
He takes responsibility for himself and is also willing to be his brother's keeper.

He knows his higher purpose.
He loves with fierceness.
He laughs with abandon, because he gets the joke.

This is the Mature Masculine - the New Warrior - a re-definition of masculinity
for the 21st century. By no means is this list complete. You are welcome to come
and add your gifts to this community. —Boysen Hodgson

I read this poem and wondered if I just changed the pronouns to feminine, would it be the same? But that just did not work at all. So I played around with the poem to give it a more feminine perspective.
This is what I came up with:

The Sacred Feminine

She cleans up after herself and others,
  but if they can clean up after themselves, she gently and firmly
  informs them of this.
She helps to heal our planet, Earth Mother, in community with her sisters,
  brothers, children and elders.
She is a role model for young women and all who seek her company and
  counsel.
She is compassionately honest and wisely optimistic,
  for she knows her compassion and wisdom can heal on all levels.

She holds herself accountable and humble.
She knows what she feels.
She's always known how to cry and loves her tears for what they teach her,
  and how they heal her and allow her to be a more healing presence for
  others.
She knows how to rage without hurting others and is aware of how powerful
  her rage can be and how it can terrify others.
She knows how to fear and how to keep moving.
She seeks self-mastery.

She has let go of the childish 'good-girl' syndrome and her shame.
She feels guilty when she's done something wrong.
She is kind to all, including the four-leggeds, winged ones, finned ones
more.
She teaches others how to be kind.
She says she's sorry.

She stopped blaming men or her parents or women for her pain years ago.
She stopped letting her defenses ruin her relationships.
She stopped letting her insecurities, rage and trust issues run her life.
She has enough self-respect to tell the truth, and the wisdom to do it as
compassionately and clearly as she can so the listener can
understand, when ready to hear it.
She creates intimacy and trust with her actions.
She has women she trusts and turns to for support. And men.
She knows how to roll with it, and be very resourceful.
She knows how to make it happen and will, using her graces, wiles, and
wisdom.
She is disciplined and flexible.
She knows how to listen from the core of her being, her heart, and her
soul, and how to offer a hand or a hug. And when to just be present,
close by.

She's not afraid to get dirty as that has been her work, always.
She's ready to confront her own limitations.
She has high expectations for herself and for those she connects with.
Her life is one of service and she knows she can pay the bills while living
a life in service.
She knows she is an individual and yet the community is the most
important thing to serve—the children, the elders, the men, the wounded...
She knows that all are wounded on some level even if they are not conscious of
it. Including herself.
She knows that we are all one.
She knows she is an animal and a part of nature.
She knows she was born as spirit and honors her connection to
something greater.

She knows the only authentic power she can and should have is that over her
shadow self, and her children when they need compassionate
direction.

She knows the true wisdom lies in circles, councils, water droplets, ripples and energy.

She knows the future generations are dependent upon her actions.
She works to co-create communities where all are respected and valued, including the four-leggeds, two-leggeds, winged ones, finned ones and all.
She holds the sacred space in the home so all who walk in the door are welcomed, fed and offered healing, directly or indirectly.

She lives her higher purpose.
She loves with deep compassion and understanding.
She laughs and celebrates the silliness in life and embraces each and every Sacred moment with love.
She knows Balance is the ultimate wise path.

This is the Sacred Feminine - the woman helping to mid-wife the New World being birthed at this time - a re-definition of femininity for the 21st century. By no means is this list complete. You are welcome to come and add your thoughts.
—mare

Mother: Mare, these poems are significant. They speak to a more highly evolved way of being, of taking responsibility, of serving the world and helping to heal old sexist cultural ways. Each and every person can live with a higher purpose within their heart to make the world a better place. To heal me, to heal themselves, to serve those less fortunate. To know your work is laying the foundation not just for tomorrow but for the next seven generations. These are very beautiful and powerful. May they be read and deeply absorbed by many.

Mare: Thank you, Mother. I had to rewrite Boysen's poem in certain parts to express the feminine experience. It is different. Not better, just different. This was a good experience doing this and delving more deeply into the path of the Sacred Feminine. It helped me grasp it more deeply. Now to living it more deeply.

Mother: Ah, my daughter, you and so many of your sister-friends are living it more deeply. Each and every day you are. Just as many of my sons are stepping into their Divine Masculine with more clarity and purpose. This is so wonderful for me to witness, on so many levels, just a joy for me to observe and support, in the subtle ways you know I can. So exciting!

Now I know you've got some errands to do today. Time for you to get going and leave the house and see what some other parts of your community look like outside the four walls of this house where you've been writing. I love you!

23

A Woman's Sacred Belly & Kali & Kuan Yin, & Hugging Our Planet

"...They have not forgotten the Mysteries," she said, "they have found them too difficult. They want a God who will care for them, who will not demand that they struggle for enlightenment, but who will accept them just as they are, with all their sins, and take away their sins with repentance. It is not so, it will never be so, but perhaps it is the only way the unenlightened can bear to think of their Gods."

—Marion Zimmer Bradley, *The Mists of Avalon*

Saturday, January 25, 2014
Up at 6:45 AM
Writing at 8:02 AM
19° – 20° Snow forecast. Another good day to write. Sigh.

Mare: Well, Mother, I sent my friend that letter several days ago, proposing we renegotiate our financial agreement and she has not taken the proposal well. She is definitely raging. As empathic as I am, I feel as if Kali is coming at me and I need to duck and cover so I don't lose my head over this. If I did not know better I'd swear knives are flying and not-very-pretty heads are spinning across the floor here in the house with my friend's response.

Mother: Yes, honey, this will be a good teaching for you. You sent her that proposal from a place of fear within you and you did not need to do that. You and I have been talking about trusting and abundance for some time now and you wrote up that proposal from a place of shadow and lack of trust.

I didn't want to interfere with your plans to send that proposal since I knew this would be a good learning experience for you. Plus it's also a good lesson for you to stand in the face of Kali and not let her mow you down. You don't need to run, you don't need to fight back. You can learn to stand there and just be present to opposition. Don't take any of that emotional energy in. Just let it blow past you.

You need to stand in your power and cease being afraid of others' anger. It's time for you to completely get over that. Your mother's rage and how it was used to control your family has stayed with you all your life, and it's important for you to learn how to stand strong in the presence of another's rage and not be the emotional sponge absorbing all of it. This experience with your friend right now is good practice for you in developing better muscles to turn your empathic gifts off or way down. And not take it personally. She has her own fears.

Part of what is also playing out here is your fear of your own rage too. You have the capacity for some powerful anger and you are still learning how to express it or release it in a healthy way. There is a Kali within you too, whom you need to learn how to dance with in a positive way. This experience will help you with that. Every woman has a Kali side to her and it is part of her journey to dance with her inner Kali so that no heads roll, but neither does she become a doormat. This is important empowerment training for women.

Mare: I suppose you're right. I can also see now how that financial proposal did not come from my trusting my higher self—nor you, Mother. I need to rethink this and apologize to her.

This reminds me, Mother, of something that happened when Paul came over the first time in early January. This is not about Kali but the Buddhist goddess, Kuan Yin. As he was sharing that night about his break-up from the partner he had been living with for ten years, he started to cry. As I was listening to him, I distinctly felt Kuan Yin's energy come into the room. It surprised me. It was a beautiful, gentle energy encouraging me to offer such kindness to this man's sorrowful heart. I just knew it was Kuan Yin's spiritual energy and had never experienced that before. Perhaps it was you confirming that it was her within me.

First Kuan Yin several weekends ago, and now Kali. This is most interesting.

Mother: My love, part of this work with me is to help you develop all the goddess aspects within you as a sacred daughter of mine. This means giving you the opportunities to dance more with Kali and Kuan Yin and other goddesses too. I'm glad you are noticing this and embracing their energies, their teachings. So many of my daughters are learning how to do this and it is just a joy to witness. This is an important aspect of your journey to fully evolving into being a Sacred Daughter of mine.

I want to get back to something else here though. It has to do with women and stepping into your power.

Do you remember how your writing coach two winters ago told you that your lymphoma health issues and healing work epitomized the journey of all women in your society? (And the Algonquin medicine man also pointed out your being sick with cancer reflects the parts of me that are 'sick' too. That's not a coincidence either.) It was only the lymph nodes in your abdominal area that have been enlarged. These were repressed energies in your wombspace—a molten pot of simmering repressed emotion in the core of your being that you've been so terrified to touch, a mix of guilt, resentment, rage—all spiced up with some latent Catholic Good Girl tendencies you've been trying to release. A potent stew, to say the least.

All the reading you've done over the past two and a half years has helped you heal. Books such as Padma and Anaiya Aon Prakasha's *Womb Wisdom; The Woman's Belly Book* by Lisa Sarasohn; and Clarissa Pinkola Estes's *Women Who Run with the Wolves*; along with her more recent book, *Untie the Woman Within* have been very beneficial. So have the women's groups about empowerment and networking you've attended. Not to mention the Sacred Feminine workshops you've been leading. All have been a form of medicine for you.

What you have been unravelling energetically and emotionally in your wombspace has been a journey with teachings for all women. Men too. But so many women suffer from wombspace health issues. Uterine and cervical cancer. Hysterectomies, endodemetriosis, fibroids. I have such sorrow over all these illnesses and how most doctors treat them with their mechanistic approach to healing.

You, yourself, had very painful fibroids that went on for years and sometimes they would burst on their own and you'd be in severe but short-lived pain. But then you'd lump along without seeing a doctor since your Cherokee teacher was treating you. You suffered from fibroids for a long time. The Cherokee healer helped you greatly too. Otherwise the fibroids would have gotten even larger and you would have needed serious medical attention.

Just about all of my beloved two-leggeds have way too much repressed energy in their bodies, repressed emotions, especially my women. Oh, how I yearn for all of you to learn how to heal these emotions, release this energy trapped in your sacred centers, your haras, (in ways that won't be hurtful or harmful to any adult, child or animal within your vicinity, sigh), so that all of you can step into your power as beautiful daughters of mine who will heal this chaos that's playing out in the world.

Mare: Mother, did you know the Dalai Lama is quoted as saying: "The world will be saved by the Western woman?" He believes the world needs more basic human values of compassion and affection that are considered more highly within the feminist realms.

Mother: Yes, sweetie, the world could use far more of those values and not values based on dominance and power. The Dalai Lama is a very wise man. We have been talking about him a bit.

Mare: My Cherokee teacher used to talk about how she called him Bob since she'd meet up with him on the spirit planes *bobbing* along out there in the universe somewhere.

He actually showed up in a dream of mine a number of years ago, as if he was checking in on me. It was weird. A gifted spiritual friend said I should seek him out for teachings on the Spirit planes.

I was not sure I could, or was even allowed to seek him out. I mean, how does one do that? Is there a door in the spirit planes where one knocks and says, "Hi, is the Dalai Lama in? And if so, could I have a moment with him? Or maybe three lifetimes? Since I do have a lot of questions for him." And what is *time* anyway?

Mother: Ah, no, there really is no such door. If there were a door like that, the poor Dalai Lama would be inundated with people knocking. Poor man. One has to take this journey on oneself, to find the answers by learning how to spiritually listen and periodically seeking course corrections from spiritual teachers within arms reach. It is a commitment. A good one.

Mare: Yes, a very good one. I'm so humbled by this spiritual path I'm on.

Mother: Daughter, there is one more piece I need to share with you. Because you are working so closely with me, and as empathic as you are, you need to also know that some of the overwhelming emotions you feel are my emotions. You're tuning into my anger, or my joy or sorrow. You are feeling my responses to the news you read or hear, about the bombings or fracking, or mountaintop removal, or teenage girls in India getting gang raped and then hung by the men (and women, sadly) in their own villages. When you drive by someone who's spraying herbicides along the road, I am upset by these activities as well, and since our connection is so tight, you are feeling my anger and frustration as if they were your own.

You need to understand this to begin to discern which are your emotions and which are mine. You will get better and better at your discernment—I promise this. I will help you. But this is all the more reason for you to embrace all emotions as good and then let them flow through you. Water over a waterfall. Release them. Don't punish yourself for the rage you're feeling.

When Kali surfaces in your belly, dance with her until she is exhausted and let her down slowly onto the couch so she can transform into the poor tired woman (which she is at times) who has had *enough* and needs to rest. Gradually you will start to sense her rising up and not need to dance so much with her, especially not in the company of others—Kali does have the tendency to take heads! Soon you will feel her appearing and, depending on the situation, know in a millisecond the wisest way to work with her wisdom and power. You will know. I will help you. There are times Kali needs to blow some steam. Just safely, safely. She also needs hugs and will invite you to go deeper to sit with the hurt or injustice that propelled her to appear, to see how you can heal it.

It is true there is a good deal of Kali energy in me these days. I'm getting more and more irritated with some of the human-caused ridiculousness on me and would like it to cease. I am hurting and tired of being abused. The abuse does need to stop. And it will. It will. Things are shifting on me rather fast, energetically and spiritually. It's all good.

But you, my love, need to keep releasing your emotions so your lymphoma does not come back. Let it go. You are learning. Each and every day you are getting more insights. I love you so much.

Mare: Mother, I suspected I was feeling your anger at times. It is helpful for you to confirm this for me. Wow, this is intense emotional work. Yours and mine, it seems.

Mother: Love, just keep the emotions moving. That is the trick. Don't repress them unless you have to in that moment, to create some space between you and another person. Don't judge them as good or bad. Let them go. Give them to me. Some of what you are feeling are my emotions anyway, so it's only fair that you give them back to me.

If it feels weird to try to give them to me at times, give these challenging emotions to a tree then. They are part of me. I know some of my two-leggeds have a hard time feeling they can connect with me and that's just a stage they're in really. Eventually, they can deeply connect with me if they truly want to do so. In the meantime, they are welcome to go out and ask the tree to take it. I'm not encouraging anyone to go out and hit the tree with a two by four piece of wood though. That would hurt the tree a great deal. Just visualize all that roiling emotion within as energy that can flood out through the palms of your hands, then place your hands on a tree and let it flow.

Remember what is at the bottom of all these darker emotions: your anger, fears, depression—all of those are just brief pieces of emotional debris floating within the liquid of Divine Love that surrounds you all the time. Keep on coming back to remember that is the real truth in the midst of the harder emotions you're experiencing. Go stand barefoot outside and give me (and Creation) your sorrow, anger, etcetera. Or give it to a tree. Allow us to fill you back up again with so much of our Love. There is more than enough to go around. Quantum Divine Love is limitless. Boundless.

As is also your chocolate supply this winter, it seems. You and your chocolate. I love you and am humored by your chocolate addiction.

Mare: Mother, it's true. I do love and crave and need chocolate. I think it makes my writing better.

Changing topic from chocolate and Kali and my empathic … ah … challenges and gifts, I think you will be amused by a question I posted on Facebook. I asked: *How do you Hug a Planet?* You know there are times I think you could use a hug, though I don't know anyone whose arms are that wide. I've received some fun responses to the question. Here are a few of them:

— *Hug a tree & then tell it to "pass it along".*
— *Walk, sit, lie on it, plant a flower and kiss it when it blooms … So many possbilities!!!*
— *Planetary high fives.*
— *With all the snow I'd hug a tree!!*
— *Snow angels are good for touch of the earth surface and your body.*
— *Hug and love up each being on it!*
— *With your thoughts.*
— *Yeah, I was gonna say "One tree at a time" unless it's covered in poison ivy, then just say hi.*
— *Open your heart and she will see the love you have for her inside of you.*
— *Belly down, usually, and clowning around to wrap my ever so short arms around her.*
— *But oh, my Heart feels hers.*

— *Energetically with your thoughts. Imagine the planet is in your arms energetically and hug it and send tons of love to it from your heart. Or lie down on her and imagine your arms are energetically wrapping around the whole planet.*
— *Be the hug in every moment, in every circumstance. Love without condition and expecting nothing in return.*
— *With every good intention at your disposal.*
— *By doing what I can to take care of her and her inhabitants, by respecting them both.*
— *With your heart!*
— *Dance barefoot on her skin, she will feel the vibrations.*
— *If the planet is earth, and one is an earthling, start by placing the left hand on the right shoulder, or over the right ribcage. Follow with the right hand over the left shoulder or ribcage. Squeeze lovingly. If a mirror is nearby, this can be done while looking deeply and sweetly into one's own eyes and saying I love you. If no mirror, it's nice to remember the mountains nearby that have broken down to become each one of us. The hug can be carried out with or without the added expressions.*
— *I go to the center of it and radiate love outward until the whole planet is radiating with love. Best way I know how.*

Mother: Oh, I love this! Thank you so much for encouraging people to think about ways to hug me. This just fills my heart up with so much happiness. Now that is a good use of Facebook, to encourage people to think about ways to hug me. Now for them to walk away from their computers or smartphones and actually do it. That would be the ticket. Yes!

Hmmm… by the way, I do receive hugs from a number of powerful spiritual beings who swing by from other parts of the universe to visit and help me. Also when I meet in council with my spiritual tribe off in another 'corner' of the cosmos, they give me hugs. One doesn't need arms to hug anyway. I feel all the hugs from you beloved two-leggeds when you send me love. I could use far more of them from my beloved two-leggeds certainly.

Now, off with you to get some breakfast and tend that sacred woodstove of yours too.

24

Messengers, Messiahs & Mary Magdalene

*"I've never been to New Zealand before. But one of my role models,
Xena, the warrior princess, comes from there."*

—Madeleine Albright

Sunday, January 26, 2014
7:20 AM
18° Another clear, crisp cold winter day in the Great Winter of 2014.

Mare: Mother, I'm rather upset this morning. Last night I got an email from a friend who thinks I'm trying to become a messiah with these messages from you. Ouch!

You know I'd rather be gardening. You know I'm not comfortable being so public about working this closely with you. When I finished the manuscript for *Messages from Mother.... Earth Mother*, all I wanted to do was hide in a backcountry cabin in Alaska—the ones we used to hike to when I worked at Denali National Park.

I didn't want to talk with anyone or have anyone be aware of this book of yours, written in only five weeks that summer of 2012. I didn't want to get any flack about this work you want me to do, this work of waking people up to the reality that you actually exist and are yearning for everyone to reconnect with you and your powerful love for all of us.

I knew there were going to be friends who would not be able to understand that I'm listening to you. Already, since the book came out, some of my college and grad school friends have pulled way back from me. Surrendering to you so I could recover from lymphoma and do this spiritual work, writing for you, getting your messages out there—there are some hard costs here for me emotionally. I wish I wasn't so darn insecure.

At least I have some friends still. Some friends who support what I'm doing and how I'm working with you. But this is a very lonely job at times. And I'm just really upset in this moment. Last night my friend's words stung me.

Her words hurt so because I'm truly trying to be humble. I'm trying to be the Lakota hollow eagle bone that serves you and Creator. I'm trying to not have any ego with this at all—other than a balanced one. And to have one of my closest friends accuse me of falling down that slippery slope of "Messiah Complex" really was a stab. I used to operate more from my ego and control issues but, Mother, I've really been working on this. I'm struggling to not take this personally.

Mother: Yes, I can see you are taking this personally. Honey, you don't have to take this in at all. Yes, you are right, some people have pulled away from you and that is because of their issues, not yours. Others are seeking you out, too. And once the book is out, there will be more people who will accuse you of trying to be a messiah. Frankly, I could use a messiah to carry these messages out, this wisdom from me, your Mother.

I don't want you to worry about any messiah business though. I just want you to focus on being humble, keep on clearing your ego as best as you can and continue to listen and write. Continue to show up to do this book and talks and radio shows, and let other humans know that I'm here and I love you all so much and yearn so much for you to reconnect with me.

Mare, I need a messenger. If some people judge you to be acting like a messiah, let it go. I've chosen you because you have what it takes to do this. Please try not to take any of their criticism personally. I watch how you sit on the floor in front of your altar or in front of the woodstove and put your forehead on the floor to empty yourself of any thoughts of boosting your ego. You catch yourself and seek to empty it all.

Your lymphoma pushed you to surrender to me in ways you would not have if you had not gotten sick. Yes, you did it fighting and kicking since you knew on a deep level that this was not going to be easy work. You had a sense that you were going to be kicked in the heart more than a few times, alone an awful lot, and that many people would probably give you a wide berth since they're not sure what you're doing.

They're not certain I even exist since the concept of a masculine God is far more prevalent in your culture than the concept (and reality!) of the Great Mother and me, Earth Mother. And even if they do believe in the Mother, they're not sure you're talking with me and might instead be mentally unstable.

Plus your soul-body remembers stepping forward in past lives and being the one to state the truth for the women and seeking to claim your rights back and you were killed for it numerous times. The powers-that-be did not like your uppity-ness. Nor your power. So they captured you, tortured you, and exterminated you more than a few times. Your fears and resistance come from the memories of those lifetimes also. I don't blame you for the resistance but you needed to get beyond it and you have been doing this. Those are only old stories. They are not truth anymore. You've been doing an amazing job this month, getting up really early, working with little sleep, tuning in and writing and writing, not to mention the kindnesses you've offered via email and Facebook to others, and more.

Sweetie, I know it's very scary to truly step into your work, the work you committed to do before you were born again on this plane. I was going to say 'step into your power' because in a way that is what you are doing now. You yourself can feel the shift and the courage you've stepped into in the past few weeks since we've started this writing. And you will be stepping into far more of it.

But this power is not the controlling type of power. It's the opposite of that. It's about emptying yourself so you can serve the highest good, for now and into the next seven generations. This is what spiritual warriors do and that is what you are. You've been tentatively stepping into this for years, and you're not alone by any means.

There are many spiritual warriors who are serving me now in so many ways. You know a number of them. You are all finding each other these days and this is rightful. You are the ones willing to take the risk and fight for me, speak for me and all of my four-leggeds, winged ones, standing ones and more.

You are the ones who are living in old growth trees so they won't be cut, and blocking huge trucks moving machinery up to the tar sands operations in Canada. You hear me and feel me and know I'm not happy and am hurting from all these awful gouges in my bones and injections of toxins into me with fracking. I love you all so much. You are the ones who are the seeds for this New World coming in, and I'm just so, so thrilled about all of you and your energy, vision, and commitment.

Every human alive on this planet chose to be here during these times of Great Change. Every one of you. The question is, what will you do during this time? Will you take the path of fear and cling on to the Old World that is crumbling? Or will you leap into the river and trust the flow, helping to birth this New World. Everyone has free will and the power of choice. Everyone.

This is a New World of balance, of sacred connection with me. No more digging into my bones or injecting poisons into my blood, all my waters. No more hierarchical systems with one man at the top. Decisions will be made in councils, in circles, with men and women present, along with teenagers and elders. Elders will be honored and will carry much weight in decisions. Especially the Grandmothers.

There will be far more compassion and balance and unity in each community, not the fear and isolation so many of you feel now. There will be so much joy, so much kindness, with gardens surrounding all the homes with flowers and vegetables growing together.

Oh, I can't wait until we get there but we have to get through some rough patches here. We will. And you, my spiritual warriors will help guide it along with all of the other beautiful spiritual beings working on me now. How I love you so much! All of you!

I'm so excited about the future that lies ahead. Very excited. Yet you need to get some breakfast and we'll talk more in a bit.

Mare: [An hour later] Mother, I just did something a medicine woman suggested to me a few months ago. I made a *Creator-Great Mother* jar to put in all the stresses that have been stewing inside me but are beyond me to resolve in the moment. They are distracting me from being focused with you and this writing.

I retrieved an old blue mason jar and cut out some pictures of flowers. Then I wrote up on a sheet of paper: *"Creator – Great Mother Jar ... Thank you!"* with little hearts around the words. Next I taped the pictures and label around the jar so it's rather attractive. I even taped a small picture of a hummingbird on the lid, since hummingbirds represent joy. This is similar to something I learned years ago: *"Let go, Let God."* But this feels more powerful.

Once the jar was done I wrote Paul's name on one piece of paper and my friend who thinks I'm trying to be a messiah's name on another, put hearts around their names and folded them up and put them in the jar. The jar sits on the side of my altar now. I gave the challenges, uncertainties and fears about them, all my stirred up emotional caca to you and Creation. They are all yours now. For a few moments I felt myself become still in a way that I have not been in some days now. Part of me fears I'm asking too much of you and Creation, though.

Mother: Nothing is too much to ask of us, sweetie. Yes, give them to us. To Spirit. Ask for our help and release yourself from spinning about these challenges. Let us take care of them. We do hear your prayers. By letting go to us, the Great Mother, Great Father and myself, you are shifting your thoughts from a place of fear to one of trust. You've shifted your song. This is a most beautiful thing.

Mare: Yes, this was much needed. Hmmm … Mother, there is something I have wanted to ask you about for some time. It's about Mary Magdalene.

Last summer a woman posted an appeal for funding for a film project about Mary Magdalene and all of her descendants on the internet. The woman states she is one of the descendants and has been working with others across the globe.

I was taken back reading this since it was stated so matter-of-factly: *all of her descendants.* From my limited knowledge, many have speculated over the centuries about whether Mary Magdalene was married to Christ or not or had any children. Dan Brown's book: *The DaVinci Code* spurred all sorts of religious hoopla too. Some believe they were married beyond a question of doubt. The Vatican has suppressed all they could from what I've read. I've never been certain what the truth is.

Then across my screen comes an appeal for funding for a film about Mary Magdalene's descendants. They are coming forth and stating they exist! They call themselves the *Grail descendants* or *Sangreal,* the actual Biblical family of Jesus Christ and Mary Magdalene. They have been finding each other and collecting information on the "origins and art history" that documents their family history. Their hope is to reawaken the world to the real life stories of the women of the Judeo-Christian Bible who were removed from the current versions of that text many, many centuries ago.

Mother, every time I read this woman's appeal, the energy I pick up empathically is very intense, dark and static-y. I'm assuming I'm tuning into the centuries of awful persecution and bloodshed and repressed knowledge of this lineage that Christian leaders in Rome did not want their followers to know about. It's a prickly, stanky energy I'm feeling, and my hands are even tingling as I'm writing this.

So I did more research and was guided to information on some Christian beliefs pre-Nicene Creed. These were called *Arian* beliefs, ones that posited that Christ was more human than divine, which would imply he was human enough to fall in love, get married, and have children. Yet the dominant church leaders banished those beliefs from accepted Catholic teachings at the meetings that led to the Nicene Creed in 306 AD.

Then I'm guided to a website page—Mother, you have the most interesting way of guiding me to various places both virtual and physical—which talks about the Cathars in the south of France and how the Church of Rome committed genocide against them in the early 1200's.

Their liberal religious beliefs and refusal to tithe to the Vatican threatened the Catholic Church too much.

The Cathars had a creed by which they lived. This is one translation of it:

The Cathar Love

This church has no membership, save those who know they belong.
It has no rivals as it is noncompetitive.
It is not self seeking--it seeks only to serve.
It knows no boundaries, for divisions are an illusion.
It acknowledges all great teachers of all the ages who have shown the truth of love.
Those who participate, practice the truth of love to the best of their ability.
It seeks not to teach but to be, and by being, enrich.
It recognizes that the way we are may be the way of those around us, because we
  are that way.
It recognizes that the whole planet is a being of which we are a part.
It recognizes that the time has come to shift from separation into oneness.
It does not proclaim itself with a loud voice, but in the subtle realms of loving.
It salutes all those in the past who have blazoned the path.
It admits no hierarchy, for no one is greater than another.
Its members shall know each other by their deeds and being, and by their
  eyes and no other outward sign, save the fraternal embrace.
It has no reward to offer, save that of the ineffable joy of being and loving.
Each shall seek to advance the cause of understanding, doing good by stealth and
  teaching only by example.
They shall heal their neighbor, their community and our planet.
They shall know no fear and feel no shame and their witness shall prevail over
  all odds.
It has no secret, no initiation, save that of true understanding of the power of
  love and that, if we want it to be so, the world will change, but only if we
  want to change.
All those who belong, belong; they belong to the church of love.[13]

Apparently the Cathars were considered the peaceful 'heretics of the Lanquedoc' of southern France. Numerous sources state that Mary Magdalene escaped to Southern France after Jesus died. Perhaps not a coincidence that this is where the Cathars took root? This is taken directly from another website:

---

[13]http://www.godlikeproductions.com/forum1/message1085242/pg1

The Cathars called themselves Pure Ones after the <u>Goddess known as the Pure One</u>, their term for the Virgin Great Creator Mother Mari (meaning 'love'). The reason the Church resorted to the mass murder of hundreds of thousands of Cathars most certainly had to do with their <u>alternative views about Jesus.</u>

They claimed to possess a secret <u>Book of Love (Mari, TARA).</u> This mysterious manuscript is attributed to Jesus who gave it to John the Divine. It was transmitted through the centuries until the Knights Templar and the Cathars adopted it. <u>The Book of Love</u> was the foundation of the Cathar Church of Love or Amor (the reverse of Roma).[14]

So ... Mother ... hmmm ... tell me. This book I'm creating with you. Most of it has been written before, hasn't it? This secret *Book of Love* ... Is it anything like the *Messages from Mother.... Earth Mother*, the book I wrote with you in 2012 and much of what is here in this book? It's all about Divine Love, and how we can come to understand how Quantum Divine Love is an energy at the root of it all, all energy, all existence—all of it.

Mother: Daughter, yes, there have been other books written and then lost. The people who followed the wisdom ways of those books were conquered and killed. Yes, the Cathars were continuing some of the original teachings of Jesus Christ, the true teachings which the Roman Empire and the Vatican refused to support for centuries.

It's all so political and sad and, believe me, I was quite dismayed over all of those activities through those centuries. Jesus Christ during that earth-walk shared such beautiful wisdom and it got corrupted thanks to those alien beings I've discussed with you before. The power, the arrogance, the greed, the darker energies that wreaked havoc over Christ's actual teachings—those energies could not tolerate the Cathars' spiritual beliefs, as true as they were to Christ's teachings. So the Cathars were killed and the teachings stopped.

Mare: So, Mother, what is the truth here? What about Mary Magdalene then? Did she really have children and can there be descendants?

Mother: Sweetie, you know what the truth is. You can feel it. But if you want me to say, "Yes", I will.

Mary Magdalene was not the whore whom some Christian Churches claim she was. She was from a high-class family of religious leaders and

[14]http://www.bibliotecapleyades.net/esp_autor_whenry04.htm

she and Christ did marry and have children. This was not the first nor the last time the beautiful Christ soul has been married and had children. We've talked about some of his other incarnations before.

Mary Magdalene and her family were secreted away by boat some time after Christ was removed from the cave after his crucifixion. They carried his teachings with them to France and the Cathars based their beliefs on some of those teachings.

Mary Magdalene was a high priestess of many gifts and she carried a great wisdom with her into southern France that influenced many there. She actually started a priestess school that has been kept secret for centuries and centuries—its existence has been revealed only in the past few years. This priestess school and many others are so needed on me these days. I need my daughters to heal and wake up to who they are and help me usher in this New World.

Over the past few millenia a number of deeply spiritual women's stories have been modified or diminished in the Judeo-Christian *Bible*. This never should have happened, but the patriarchal energies that took root in the Catholic leadership in the centuries after Christ's passing pushed for great revisions in that book.

I am so grateful for the women who are stepping into their sacred powers these days, as challenging as this has been for them. Many of them don't know how I've been helping them spiritually also. I love each and every one of you so, so much. Thank you for your courage to do this.

Thank you! I love you!

25

Thoughts, Energy, the Shadow & Technology

Thoughts have power; thoughts are energy. And you can make your world or break it by your own thinking.

—Susan Taylor

Tuesday, January 28, 2014
4:10 AM
6° Bitter. Snow forecast. Again. Not complaining. Really.

Mare: Okay, Mother, since I took yesterday off, you want to make up for lost time, don't you? Wake-up call from you at 4 AM this morning. Okay … I'm here….

Thank you for allowing me to take a break from the computer yesterday. It was so needed. I finally noticed the dust elephants in the corner and some cobwebs in other higher corners. A friend came over for the afternoon to play. I even pulled out my knitting in the evening. I have not knitted during the whole two years I've been here in this house. That was fun.

Then this morning as I was getting the fire going from the coals of last night, I felt a distinct wash of love come into my heart. It felt as if the fire sent it to me—this Sacred Fire I've been tending all winter through this abnormally cold January.

I offered tobacco and prayers several times into the fire yesterday. Just about every day I do this as part of being in the right place of honoring you, honoring Spirit, and asking for prayers for this person or that one, or the whales, dolphins, etcetera.

And today the Sacred Fire gifted love back to me. It's all amazing, actually.

Mother: Yes, sweetie, you are starting to really learn how Divine Love is there all around you. You experienced receiving love from Spirit through the Sacred Fire. Divine spirit. Creator, Great Mother, me as Earth Mother. The Sacred Fire is the alchemical conduit for this love that is from Creator, Great Mother and myself. You can take in this love and share it further and farther. That is the whole idea, keep sharing it, keep it moving.

Compassion and love really are the best places to sit in relationship on all levels, with all beings. This includes all of the species on this planet, the worms, spiders—even the tarantulas. Gorillas, sharks and wolves—all of them, all species.

Definitely, the sharks and wolves. They get such a bad rap, and have been treated so poorly. They play an important role in their ecosystems as predators and are so misunderstood. They are such intelligent beings and carry a wisdom that is, well, so shark and so wolf, and so powerful and beautiful. It has been breaking my heart to see them maligned, killed, trapped and poisoned.

Again, it's these aliens who have been promoting the patriarchal and ignorant ways that have been decimating the wolves, sharks and other species. They've been feeding the power mongering at the root of the Catholic Church for so many centuries. These aliens have been influencing much of the rage and suicide bombing in certain parts of the Middle East and the terrible policies in too many countries toward girls and women. The list goes on and on and on. I'm so grateful these sorts of aliens are starting to go.

Mare: Mother, these beings—are they the ones behind some of our technologies and networking venues such as Facebook?

Mother: Yes, they have been directing energies through all sorts of institutions, communication technologies and all sorts of people of power. These are not very positive beings.

Mare: I guess that might explain some of the negative chatter on YouTube and an underlying energy I sense behind Facebook. When I'm on it for any longer than five minutes, it kicks up a frenetic, ungrounded, slightly anxious vibration within me, and it takes some time to calm down to be able to tune into you again.

Mother: Yes, and this is why in your other book, *Messages from Mother.... Earth Mother*, I gave you that whole message: "On Facebook and Twit-Twitting."[15]

Oh, how much I wish I could get all of my beloved humans to disconnect more from your technology, your smart phones, your FacePlace and shift to *TreePlace*, to just still yourselves. Just calm your minds and still yourselves and bring your beautiful, beautiful energy down into me. How I wish I could do this for you. But you need to do it for yourselves.

Energy. Your thoughts are energy. Your words are even more powerful energy. Your actions are tremendous energy. Collectively all of your actions are huge, huge currents of energy!

Your vast collective unconscious contains an extensive amount of energy that has been going in the wrong direction for some time now. The wrong highway for me, your Mother, upon whom you live, breathe, make love, eat succulent peaches and so, so much more.

Some of my indigenous elders have always been on track and have been scratching their heads and shaking their fingers at the great sad direction of your post-industrial world. The Kogis in Columbia have allowed the BBC to make a film about them and their message to the rest of you whom they call the "younger brothers". They consider themselves to be the "elder brothers". That film, *Heart of the World: Elder Brothers Warning*, came out in the early 90's but did not make much of a dent in your society's seeming determination to wreak havoc of terribly painful proportions on me.

So the Kogi have put out another film called *Aluna*. This time it is not with the BBC but they have gotten the resources to do it themselves with the support of some friends. Every human across me, other than the indigenous ones who already know and live this wisdom, should watch these films.

Yes, it would be most, most helpful if your Western society really got a handle on the reality of how everything is energy. And technology can amplify this energy. For example, I know just about all of you who use the internet have had an experience with someone sending an email-bomb to you. You know, this is when someone is so angry they vent everything they can into an email and push *send*.

That email then arrives in your inbox as a packed box of rage that goes 'ka-boom' in your face. For my sensitives who are empaths, they are almost knocked across the room by the energy of these emails. But even if they are not empaths, the energy of these missives can hit people very hard. This is because computers have tiny little crystals and these amplify

---

[15]http://messagesfrommother.org/2012/09/13/message-8-about-facebook-twit-twitting/

energy. The original energy of the rage is even greater by the time the recipient receives the email.

Plus, those certain beings who have been directing energy at the planet for these several thousand years, the ones who are starting to pack up and go, are also manipulating the energies in these computers to their ends.

So there you have some strong alien influences that support email-bombs, not to mention all the suppressed rage in your culture to begin with. And this can explain how people can start 'hating' on Facebook, and also on YouTube comments. Those YouTube comments where people don't even know each other and start spewing such mean things, I mean … ouch! Some of you have gotten so hateful. If only you knew the energy you are throwing out into the atmosphere around my body, on my skin, amplified by the computer crystals and these alien beings—maybe, just maybe you'd stop. I'd like to think you would, at least.

It would give me such joy to see more of you learning to take responsibility for your actions, your thoughts, and words on levels that very few of you are taught. The ones who learn this will be those that have been working on their emotional maturity. Some have been on a deeply spiritual path that teaches about energy and consciousness and higher versus lower vibrations for a long time.

If you do not learn how to work with your shadow self, and begin to tame those inner demons that want you to spin out into rage, or spin into depression (for oftentimes anger turned inward is depression), then you are going to be stuck at a lower vibrational level. This is only going to get more and more uncomfortable as the energies on me are pushing all of you to heal beyond those low vibrational places, to tap the Christ Consciousness and live in your higher chakras.

What many are starting to learn is your mind is so, so clever at creating stories. Umpteen million stories. And your brain will repeat those stories until there is a deep groove within that part of your brain that is practically fast tarmac. Your scientists have discovered these brain tissue paths and how a thought that is repetitive just becomes stronger and stronger and more deeply embedded into the brain.

There are certain prevalent stories in your culture many of you have taken as truth, thanks to how you were raised in your nuclear families and standard school systems. These have gotten practically cemented into your thinking. Here are a couple of them:

"I'm not good enough..." Well, it's easy to understand how most of you believe you are not good enough when you are sent to school where only one child is the best one in the class and that is the one who got the

A+++. And everyone else was judged "lesser than" compared to that one child. And this external judgment system continued for eighteen years for you, and into college, and even more school for some. Most who made it all the way into what you call higher education have somewhat higher self-esteem since they've made the choice to continue in the system for more education, but so often it only happens after years of internal struggle.

Plus your school systems mostly only teach to certain intelligence types, the verbal, logical ones for the most part. Those gifted in art or music, or naturalist sensitivities or who have the intelligence to understand distance and movement are mostly ignored by your school system and left by the wayside. Many leave school, and enter the job market prematurely, where they can't compete that well. They end up getting lower paying jobs and live a life of lower self-esteem in the competitive world, which you've created, where the community values of sharing and taking care of each other equally have been forgotten.

Or there is this common internal story: *"I'm in trouble... "* Your churches, synagogues, and temples have instilled a way of controlling you and keeping you returning to them through guilt. There's nothing like the fear of damnation and hell to keep you in line, an overwhelming set of beliefs too complex to go into here. But these teachings are untrue. Let's just say these religious teachings feed a person's shadow better than oats feed a starving horse. They also feed the church coffers.

Even if a given religious institution is toned down and not so heavily preoccupied with fire and brimstone, there are still the subtle underlying teachings that not quite everyone "gets to heaven" if you've sinned or "are not good enough" or "are in trouble" with God by the time you're ready to pass over.

There are ghosts wandering around on my poor planet who should not be here. They were so terrified they were not going to make it to "Heaven" because they feared they had sinned too much, and so they did not go on their journey to the spirit world, or afterlife as some call it. These poor souls (or parts of a person's soul, since part of their soul is here and the rest of their soul-body did make it over the Rainbow Bridge to the other side, which is quite a painful predicament for those beings) were afraid of what they had been taught about *Hell* and that they might end up there as a final destination. Now they're stuck here—which is not helpful. Unless someone very gifted comes along and helps release them. Unfortunately, those gifted ones are few and far between.

I don't need ghosts stuck on me. They're not supposed to be here and they can muck up the energy of certain places when there are clusters of them in beautiful areas that became battlefields. Of course those ghosts got stuck here for a different reason and that is because of how traumatically those soldiers died. The sadness they carry within them is most unpleasant to have lingering here.

The anger, guilt, shame, depression and low self-esteem that collectively add up to create a dank blanket of heavy energy across most city and suburban areas is tough for me. And all the animals and plants too. These darker emotions along with the all-too-common fear that nobody has enough, and those who have too much are afraid of those who have less ... ugh! Add all of this up, amplified by the crystals in your computers, and this is a collective, nasty energetic song that makes me sad. If I had a stomach, I'd feel a bit nauseous from some corners of me, especially where the generations of warring continue. The Middle-East is rather a mess.

Okay, I don't have a stomach, so I can't get nauseated, but it makes me feel *off*. And it makes all the other four-leggeds, winged ones, finned ones, and all of the other beings on this planet feel *off* too. Not to mention those dealing with possible extinction. I know I've said this before but it bears repeating. This is especially true for the sensitive dolphins and whales who are so very, very intelligent and their entire lives depend on the energy resonance in the oceans. Song vibrations are their communication, their way of finding food, their means of playing, of finding their mates and babies, their very survival. The sad truth is the vibrations or songs from your human culture, along with the toxins in the water, make them sick on subtle and not so subtle levels. Sometimes the whales and dolphins can't even swim into an area close to shore because the contamination and the energy has gotten so bad. It takes gifted medicine people doing ceremony on the land near the water to metaphysically clear the water, to allow the whales to come back in.

The whales and dolphins are highly evolved spiritual beings in the physical, just as you two-leggeds are. The whales and dolphins know all about energy and their songs are critical for the physical and spiritual health of the oceans. They need all the humans to wake up to the contamination that continues to devastate the ocean waters. All waters, actually.

There are so many human-made chemicals in the oceans (rivers, lakes and groundwater also) poisoning all my aquatic loved ones, plus plastic bags and nets floating around in huge mats trapping dolphins, whales and other fish. Add in the nuclear waste from the bombs detonated in the ocean several decades ago, along with what Fukushima has been releasing, and you can see why it's getting tougher and tougher for my whales and dolphins and all my other beautiful creatures in the oceans, rivers, and streams to survive because of physical and chemical waste and the nasty energy this waste creates in the waters. It's in all my blood, all of my water. And if I were not a planet, I'd be getting cancer. But planets don't get cancer. Parts of us get sick for a period of time and then we heal, and this is not a fun process.

Some of this nasty energy is from collective darker human emotional energies that seem to be getting stuck in too many corners of me. For instance, guilt is a human emotion that doesn't need to exist. The actual truth is that all humans, all of you, were so loved, so beautifully loved before your soul ever returned to this plane for the earth-walk you are now experiencing. The Creator, Great Mother and I, your Earth Mother, have an incredible amount of Divine Love for you. Most of you have not learned this, or you might have heard it but did not believe it since you were already starting to feel guilty and unworthy from your family or school environment or religious institution.

We are yearning for you to tap into the Quantum Divine Love we hold for you, but you have to want to do that and seek it out. I know I've talked about this before, but it needs to be said again. *I love you.* The Great Mother loves you. Creator loves you.

You can connect with this Divine Love and change your song. Step out of your shadow to release the old stories that have gotten you so downtrodden that you beat yourself up. You can heal those wounded emotional cores deep within you once you open up to our Love. Trust this. You are so deeply *Loved.* You don't have to be perfect, just be authentically you and learn to *Walk in Beauty.*

I also invite you to realize sinning is a fabrication of your religious systems. We have talked a little about the difference between this and Right and Wrong Action before. Everyone at some point does Wrong Action. It's a question of whether or not you learn from it and move on, and not repeat it. If it is an extreme Wrong Action such as murder, then your soul woundedness is very deep and the healing called for is great but it is still very possible. But Love is what heals that wound. Not more fear and punishment, truly.

There are indigenous peoples who ask a person who has committed a wrong action to sit in a circle surrounded by other villagers. They don't stone or yell at that person in the center. Instead they proceed to tell that person all the ways that he or she is loved and appreciated. It's a full love-fest and very healing.

What is at the base of just about all wrong actions is a feeling of failure, a lack of love, and low self-esteem mixed with rage or some other dark emotion. Just this past fall, a secretary at a school somewhere in your United States talked down a man who was planning to walk into a school and go on a rampage with his assault weapon. She essentially *loved him up* so much his rage and fear melted and he finally let go of his need to seek vengeance on those innocent children and teachers.

It's such a beautiful, beautiful example of how a heart can shift given some kindness and compassion, in this case from the secretary—a total stranger no less. And in that one particular place on that one day that fall, the song, the energetic vibration of that one school neighborhood lifted a little—from terrible, terrible fear to a glimpse of compassion. And no one was killed.

That man was deeply soul-wounded yet he opened his heart up enough to the kindness of that woman in those brief moments to drop his gun. Such a beautiful story. What happened to that poor man after they arrested him is another story. He was arrested and hauled to a police station where the energy was laden with fear and power/ego stuff, rage, and more.

Oh, the sickness of the soul in so many of you. It's not that all of you that feel wounded will go out and get an assault weapon. But you might be passive-aggressive toward your spouse or lover. You might take it out on your children or your underlings at your work place. Or an animal. That's one of the hardest things for me to watch, how innocent animals are abused by a good number of you, especially when you think no one is watching.

Mare: Mother, it seems you are talking about our *shadows* a lot here and how so many of us live in our shadow. I know this shadow work and it is ongoing. I'm not alone with the stories in my head, my frustration at others, or my passive-aggressive ways. The good news is I don't get caught up in the shadow self as much as I used to—most days.

Mother: You have grown so much. You have learned to dance with your shadow to tame her, to recognize her and not allow her to take control as she used to. It's been a beautiful thing to watch you grow in this. You have a name for her, don't you?

Mare: Yeah, funny thing, I have not thought about my shadow's name in a long time. I call her *Sleepy*. She was dubbed Sleepy years ago early on during my studies with the Cherokee teacher. Another woman who studied with that same teacher came up with the name while we were all hanging out one time. I did not resonate with it at first, but I've come to see how it fits.

Yeah, Sleepy. She was in control much of the time when I was younger. I was chronically depressed and used to "sleep in" most mornings.

There were more than a few times I was terrified to face the day and missed meetings, called in sick, rolled over in bed to hide from the world. I had the luxury of doing this when I had my gardening business since I had only two part-time assistants. They were rather patient with me and we'd just start work several hours later.

Sleepy is narcissistic. She's controlling. She's vindictive and depressed, and angry toward anyone who dares to hurt her, and can be quite creative at figuring out ways to retaliate. She's passive-aggressive ... what else?

Wow—it's interesting writing this list out right now. I've been consciously dancing with Sleepy on an evolving basis since 1998. But I've never actually compiled a list of her characteristics. This is most helpful. She definitely surfaces at times still and it's revealing, rather downright scary, to see how she motivates me. The trick is to catch her and not have her lead me by the nose any more.

One technique I've learned is to visualize giving Sleepy some good dark chocolate and asking her to sit in a corner to enjoy it over there, away from the rest of my consciousness, and too distracted to dominate my thoughts and actions. The type of chocolate I like, of course. Hmmm— nice and dark with marzipan. This is making me hungry right now.

Mother: It's important to get to know your shadow as you have, Sweetie. Your shadow is closely entwined with your soul-woundedness. Becoming aware of Sleepy and her patterns and how she gets stirred up by your emotional wounds and monkey-mind is a powerful step to living more consciously. Your energy becomes more peaceful and balanced when you are living more consciously and in the moment. Your song becomes more beautiful.

Part of the path of healing is to allow yourself to take in the great love of the Creator, Great Mother and myself. Allow yourself to feel this great love and know it is so unconditional and release your sense of shame, guilt, and unworthiness that kicks up your shadow. Still your mind and give yourself the space to feel our Divine Love. It is here for you all the time. All the time, from before you were even born. We love you.

26

A Different Take on Extinction

Goodbye is not forever.

—*The Goodbye Girl* movie

Wednesday, January 29, 2014
Up at 6:30-ish, finally writing at 10:20 AM
10°-ish at dawn. Another day of snow. Tra la. Tra la.

Mare: Mother, it's mighty convenient how the weather this winter has essentially created a *lock and load* writing winter for me. When I was in college, the fraternities would have lock and load parties on the weekends when they'd stock up on lots of beer and hard liquor and all the alcohol in the building would have to be consumed before they'd unlock the doors to the building. It's a rather sad way to entertain oneself, but that was college life and this was in upstate New York where the winters were long and cold, and people found 'interesting' ways to amuse themselves outside of the academics.

I'm not dealing with alcohol here though. I'm locked into this house in my bed next to the space heater, just loading words into this manuscript. It's five degrees outside. My pile of green wood does not burn so well in the woodstove. I refuse to turn the thermostat up to heat rooms I barely go into. That's just such a waste of energy. Thus I'm living here in bed with the space heater.

Mother: Sweetie, again, you're the one who made the choice to keep the thermostat so low. You can turn it up anytime you want. It's up to you. As for the Polar Vortex that's come through several times this winter already, this is a very lovely silver lining. It's a good thing you're cloistered under all of your blankets in the nest of your bed with your down jacket and cap on, to continue to listen and write. With this level of cold, it's tough for you to be distracted doing anything else. We'll get this book done faster that way.

Yes, this winter is a cold one for most of North America because cold winters happen. It's part of the cycle of things. There will be more extreme climate shifts coming down the pike too with the Climate Chaos your culture has instigated with the burning of fossil fuels along with other air contaminants. This is going to happen. The systems have already kicked in and the nature spirits in charge of the weather are in consensus about this. This is just part of what is going to play out.

This Climate Chaos is contributing to some species going extinct also—some of my beloved species. Your society is doing a dang good job at wiping them out, right, left and center in too many ways: deforestation; toxification of waterways; destruction of wetlands; destruction of coral reefs from fluctuating ocean temperatures; along with conversion of wild-lands into agricultural zones.

So many of these four-leggeds (the western black rhino in 2013), winged ones—so many have gone, sigh, six-leggeds, my plants—oh, my gosh, a huge amount of them have died off. But I need to share this—they don't just disappear and go *POOF* when they go extinct. They have actually vibrated into another spiritual dimension and still exist there.

At some point in the future, when parts of me have begun to heal over (which will happen, believe me)—I will call these species back to their habitats that have nicely started to heal. They will be able to return and step back into the dance of life and death and procreation and evolution they were a part of before this rather rude interruption by your modern industrial society. Of course they may need some evolutionary tweaking when they return, but not to worry about that.

Mare: That's rather fascinating to know. Not that it justifies by any means the mass extinction that we humans are causing these days but it's interesting. Nevertheless, it's tremendously sad what we've been doing, and so wrong.

27

Earth Mother Communicates
with Us—When We Pay Attention

There is a way that nature speaks, that land speaks.
Most of the time we are simply not patient enough,
quiet enough, to pay attention to the story.

—Linda Hogan

Friday, January 30, 2014
6:20 AM wake-up
21° Clear—outside. About 58° inside. I love my woodstove. I'm going to marry this
woodstove.

Mother: Sweetie, it's time to get up. I'd like to talk about some of the ways I communicate with you, my beloved two-leggeds, when you are deeply connected with me.

Mare: Okay, Mother, I'm here. Rubbing my eyes a little but here. Still bitter cold outside. I'm grateful the bedroom is warm and cozy.

Mother: Yes, I'm glad you are warm and cozy too.
   So I've been talking for the past few weeks about how much love I have for all of my beloved humans, and how there are many unseen spiritual beings here on me, plus the psychic hotline that exists between these unseen beings so they can share information across me.
   For those who choose to honor me, have reverence for me and recognize I exist (which I'm hoping will be all of you in time), I will seek to communicate with you directly and indirectly to offer spiritual wisdom

or guide you and protect you in different ways. This is part of being in relationship with me, your Earth Mother. Certainly, there are some who can hear me directly such as you, Mare. Or some of the medicine people whom you know.

One way I do this is by sending an actual animal, bird, or insect in your direction as a spiritual message. Some of you work with cards where you can draw the card of one of these creatures, guided by me. You see, each animal or insect has an inherent *spiritual medicine* associated with a teaching.

Plants have specific spiritual resonances also. Some gifted healers have learned how to call on a variety of plants' healing properties that emanate from the spirit body of that plant. This is called *plant spirit medicine* and I love my two-leggeds who practice this.

But that is a different topic than the animals and insects I may send to you for your spiritual guidance.

Mare: There are so many times you've sent me messages, Mother. I only knew to recognize them once I started studying with the Cherokee teacher. There are several dog-eared books on my bookshelf I've turned to countless times after an auspicious interaction with some creature. Ted Andrew's *Animal Speak* is one of them. I also love Jamie Sam's *Medicine Cards*, and Evan T. Pritchard's book, *Bird Medicine*.

Praying mantises are significant teachers for me with their medicine of stilling oneself to pray or meditate more. I've seen them so many times and suppose this speaks to my overactive mind. Late one summer, just before dinner several years ago as I was weighing whether or not to take on another gardening client on an already busy schedule, I noticed a praying mantis at knee level on my front storm door. I said 'hi' to it and returned to my kitchen to futz around with dinner. About ninety minutes later, I went back to the storm door to check on one of my kitties and this time the praying mantis was at exact eye level peering directly at me. I knew that was a deliberate message.

With the praying mantis staring me down directly, I took the cue and decided to turn down the new client. It was best for me not to try to fit another gardening client into an already stressful schedule, but instead focus on more personal quality time, being still and calmer. I didn't need to make megabucks to pay my bills, as it was.

Last fall, right on the equinox, in fact, a praying mantis showed up on my car door one morning. I was just getting over several days of terrible anxiety. This was when I was considering moving cross-country and feeling overwhelmed with so much uncertainty. I just could not still my rampant thoughts during that agonizing time. When I saw the insect I laughed out loud since I instantly knew why it was there. It was the only one I'd seen in two years of renting this house. Its presence that day was no coincidence. I gently shooed it off the car since I did not want to injure it. It flew off and not a single one appeared to me for the remainder of the fall. Not a coincidence by any means.

Hummingbirds, which represent joy, have appeared to me numerous times when I've felt particularly blue. You sent me one last spring, Mother, that went from one delphinium blossom to another on a large plant full of spires of blossoms. I could have reached my arm out and touched it—it was so close. When it was finished with all the nectar feeding, it hovered two feet in front of my face and stared right at me for a solid few seconds, and then zipped off. Hummingbirds have been fun messengers to nudge me out of my darker times, and I definitely needed it in that moment.

Just before you instructed me to stay put here in Maryland to do this *Great Mother Bible* book last November, I had an experience with a teeny-tiny snail in my bathtub. It was so small and cute yet odd to see, since I've taken oodles of baths in my life but never seen a snail in the tub. It wasn't even a millimeter in width. I couldn't figure out where it came from. I moved it from the side to the edge of the tub near my head since I feared knocking it into the bath water. During the entire bath, I was fascinated by how it extended its head and horns around. I'd never been that close to a tiny snail to watch it in such a concentrated way. Upon getting out of the tub, I very gently deposited it in a potted plant in the next room—about ten feet from the bathtub.

To my surprise, this snail, or its brother, was back three days later when I took another bath. Once is a chance occurrence. Twice is a message. Again I rescued it from inside the bathtub and observed it carefully on the edge during my bath. It did its little surveying of the scenery in the bathroom again, including me, I'm certain. One more time I put the snail back in the potted plant in the other room and promptly read up on *snail medicine*. My little snail visitor was sending a distinct message about the coming months of going deeply inward for this writing process, pulling my shell around me and being quite still and protective. The snail never showed up again. I took that as a positive sign the messenger did not need to return.

Mother: Yes, you have learned how to be attentive. This is a good thing. It is true that each of my four-leggeds, winged ones, and insects, have a particular type of medicine associated with them. Their energy bodies carry a particular spiritual strength or teaching that is there for you, my beloved two-leggeds, to tap into when they are sent to you. I do consciously send them to you, too. My birds are particularly good at these messages. There are times when I'll send a messenger to protect you also. It could be in the physical or spiritual realms.

Mare: I was just speaking with a woman from northern Minnesota several days ago about animal medicine. She's part Native American and shared she's been listening to animals 'talk' all her life. One afternoon, last summer a mature eagle was keeping her company as she was berry-picking in a wilderness area near her home. The eagle screamed at her, as only eagles can do, whenever she started to go in a specific direction. There was no sign of any eagle nest or young so the woman was rather puzzled. Later that evening, a neighbor told her a bear had been spotted in the direction the eagle was warning her about.

My Cherokee teacher was quite gifted as an animal communicator and would tell the story of how she observed a bird land in front of her in a most auspicious manner. Before it flew off, it stared at her intensely and stated flatly: "I really hope you've gotten this message by now. I was sent here to give it to you and I've got better things to do with my time now."

Mother, I have also learned you give me messages through the words of other people. I will have a meeting planned and a neighbor will walk by and tell me the exact wisdom I need to hear to help me maneuver through the meeting. They will not even know I was headed to meet with anyone. They'd just share some insight and it would fit perfectly with what I was going to be involved in later. That's happened more than a few times. Then there are the books that practically fall off the shelf that you want me to peruse. I certainly do get very clear communications from you, Mother, on a daily basis.

Just yesterday morning you guided me to go for a walk in the morning, which I ordinarily don't do these days, with the bitter cold. On this short stroll around the neighborhood I ran into a neighbor who informed me that she found some of my missing mail in a big pile of ripped open, stolen mail about forty feet off the mailbox cluster where some of our mailboxes were broken into three weeks ago. I rarely see this neighbor and she did not post anything on a neighborhood listserv about her discovery. She only reported it to the local post office. I appreciated that nudge to go stretch my legs then!

Mother: You're very welcome, my love.

Mare: [Four hours later] Well, Mother, you are truly funny! I go for another walk through this wooded neighborhood high above a lake and what do I see but a bald eagle swooping above the lake and then land just across from me on a big open branch. I watched the eagle for several minutes as it sat there. This is only the second time I've seen an eagle in the area in two and a half years. I've heard others talk about them here, but to see one today was such an extraordinary gift.

Thanks, Mother!

I know eagles teach about Spirit and trusting in our higher self. They ask us to see life from a higher perspective and know that it is full of infinite possibilities. They invite us to step outside the wee box we can create of our life to see a far broader vision.[16]

I needed this—thank you, Mother. You know I've been feeling bogged down by this writing process and experiencing all sorts of self-doubt and unworthiness about doing this. I even wonder whether this is all *schlock* in certain moments. Or whether I'm listening to you or just my imagination at times. These doubts drive me a bit batty sometimes, and honestly I've begun to feel a little depressed.

And here you gift me with an eagle this afternoon. I get it. It's all good. I can pull myself out of this self-wallowing pit and take on more of an eagle's perspective, to see a much higher view—and trust in this work with you. Thank you, Mother, for bringing the eagle into my week to pull me out of the emotional mire I've been wallowing in.

Mother: Yes, my love, I'm glad you saw the eagle and are getting the message. This is important. You needed this confirmation this week. I've been watching you struggle. It's okay. You are human and you have moments when things are tougher and this is not very 'ordinary' work you're doing with me. I have so much love for you. So much.

Some of my native peoples refer to animals as *Creature Teachers*. This eagle was a Creature Teacher for you today since you have been feeling challenged with the writing and your self-doubt, and blocking yourself from seeing the greater view and possibilities. The more you connect with me and spend time outside and tuning in to all that is happening around you, the more animals, birds, insects and other creatures will appear to you as Creature Teachers. There are so many opportunities to tap into their wisdom, their medicine. And believe me, I am encouraging them to show up in many people's lives these days. This is part of how I work. Many of you are waking up to me, but most can't hear me if I try to communicate directly, so I will send a Creature Teacher.

---

[16]Andrews, Ted. *Animal Speak* (St. Paul, Minnesota: Llewellyn Publications, 1999), pp. 136-141

So be aware. Try to get out of your busy mind when you are outside. See who shows up as a winged one or four-legged. Tune in and feel out whether the appearance of that bird or fox feels auspicious to you. Did they stop and turn around to peer at you for a few seconds longer than normal? Did they come very close to you or swoop by you? Notice these occurrences. There is an intentionality with all of them.

Mare: Mother, you are helping me remember that a big owl flew over my car hood just last week. I had completely forgotten until now. I was heading up to Manhattan the following morning, to the UN building area, to meet with some Native grandmother elders in a group called *Grandmothers Circle the Earth*. I had just driven across a bridge near my home when the owl burst over the car. I was stunned and then forgot about it later as I was scrambling to get things together for my trip. As a matter of fact, I suspect it might have been a snowy owl. Several were spotted feeding in Maryland this winter—a rare occurrence that happens when food is scarce farther north. One had been seen in the very river valley where I had been driving. It was a large white owl and even with the quick glimpse I caught, it did not look like any of the other common owls in the region. Rather amazing.

I've learned how owls are birds of great mystery, representing the feminine and the night, being nocturnal. Since their gifts of listening are so acute, they are associated with clairaudience—which is what I'm doing with you, Mother, listening to you. Owls also symbolize silent wisdom and magic.[17] It is probably not a coincidence I saw this one owl just before visiting some of the gifted Native grandmothers that next day.

Mother: Yes, probably not a coincidence at all.

Mare: If I could only see your expression, Mother, I'd swear you are winking! You are funny!

There is a story I've wanted to ask you about for a while though. Lawrence Anthony, the author of a bestselling book called *The Elephant Whisperer* and a legend in conservation circles in South Africa, died in March of 2012. The elephants in the reserve where he lived were very close to him and would come and greet him whenever he returned from long trips, even if they had not been near his house for weeks prior.

Two days after Lawrence Anthony passed, the elephants came to Lawrence's house where his widow and family and friends were gathering,

---

[17] Ibid, pp. 172-181

and created a commotion outside it for several hours. Then the elephants retreated to the deep forest thickets nearby for several days, as elephants are known to do when they are mourning. Some of the game wardens could hear their grumbling stomachs echoing from the thickets. The elephants had marched from twelve hours away to bear witness to their good friend's death. It was clear they were grieving his passing.[18]

Mother, how did these elephants know their human friend had passed? They were twelve miles away before coming to his house. How did they always know when he was home from a trip away? What is this intelligence they have?

Mother: Love, my four-leggeds, my winged ones and all the rest are very intuitive. Many pets know when their human caretakers are about to arrive home. They just can sense these things. Also, animals communicate very closely with the nature spirits and the psychic hotline of the nature spirits extends to the animal kingdom. They are always swapping information between them. That is how the elephants knew. This man was such a beautiful compassionate soul who worked so closely with them. The elephants could feel his energy when he was returning home. They felt his soul-body leave his body when he passed. He could communicate with them very well when he was still alive. It was such a loss to them when he passed. They mourn him still as they have not had a human friend like him in recent times.

Many times when a beloved person or animal has just passed, they will visit you in spirit in the form of a bird or flying insect. This is one of the ways they can communicate with you that they are all right and are sending you great love from the dimension they are now in. They know your grief is so painful and want to support you. It is such a beautiful experience when one of you two-leggeds recognizes that bird or butterfly is your loved one and receives the message. This is such a lovely, lovely spiritual healing experience, and gives me such happiness when this happens.

Lawrence Anthony visited the elephants in his spirit body after he passed and that is how the elephants knew. He did not need to take on the form of a butterfly or bird. The elephants could see him in his spirit body. Animals can see spirit just as two-leggeds see a tree in front of them. Or bird, or butterfly.

Sweetie, getting back to how I may communicate with those who seek to be in close relationship with me, there are other ways too. If you have learned how to read the clouds and weather, there can be messages.

---

[18]http://www.davidhalperin.net/thomas-jefferson-meteorites-and-lawrence-anthonys-elephants/

I, or your spirit guides, will send you dreams to help guide you. There are some who cast stones to perceive patterns, or look for images in water, or receive visions through shamanic journeying or other means. It takes time to discern these messages, years really. But it is a useful and beautiful thing to learn how to do this.

If you seek a message or guidance from me and your spirit guides, it is good practice to go out and offer prayers with tobacco or cornmeal, or whatever herb is sacred in your region. If you don't have tobacco or cornmeal, then whatever food item you might have. The actual offering object is not important. It's your intentions and the purity of your heart that is important. Next find the base of a tree, or bush. One tree might 'call' to you in an intuitive way, and after you say your prayers, offer the tobacco or cornmeal at the base. Or you may toss the tobacco into the wind also. Ask for guidance. Then watch. Be aware. Tune into your dreams. Spirit is very aware of you and your actions. Your challenge is to be able to receive the message that Spirit will be sending back. It will come, rest assured. But you need to pay attention.

28

....

Intentional Suffering is not Prerequisite to Spiritual Growth

When in doubt, eat chocolate.

—Mare

Sunday, February 2, 2014
3:40 AM Wakey-Wakey
27° Rain forecast. Imbolc. Groundhog's Day. I know that famous groundhog in Pennsylvania is going to forecast six more weeks of winter. I just know it.

Mare: Mother, I know you've woken me up early for a teaching. But I need to talk about what Paul shared with me last night over the phone.

Mother: Sure, Sweetie…

Mare: I've really been opening myself emotionally to this man, feeling deeply for him. My body has been responding to him in ways I can't remember ever feeling. Just knowing he is there has brought up energies and emotions within me I've never experienced.

But last night he shared over the phone he's realizing he's attracted to several women right now and he's not ready to be in a committed relationship. He needs this time to figure out who he is, since he went from being in a thirty-two-year marriage directly into a ten-year commitment with another woman, and then just recently, their break-up. He's trying to get on his own two feet right now, as he puts it.

In that very moment over the phone, I felt fine with him dating other women and myself simultaneously and told him so. But as I lay in bed later I felt my spirit body that had been so joyously open to him start to curl in like the snail into her shell (similar to the snail that visited me in the bathtub) and a deep sadness crept in. Even though my mind was initially willing to try this arrangement with Paul, a subconscious part of me had to draw inward and find protection.

Again this morning, the sadness is overtaking me. I almost started crying over the kitchen sink several minutes ago. Whoever and whatever this man is, he balances me. He talks with me in ways I've never had a man speak to me, so clearly, so gently, so compassionately. He has been present to me in ways that are remarkably beautiful.

If he wants to be with me then he needs to choose me with clarity. If he wants to lie naked next to me, then I need to know I'm the only one he's laying naked with because otherwise it hurts too much. Otherwise I need to guard my heart, waiting for the axe to fall. The old fears of being abandoned again are starting to loom. I can't consciously allow myself to fall down that hole.

I know I'm worth the full attention of a man. Not split attention—full attention. I know this now and stand more strongly in myself than I ever have in the past.

Mother: Sweetie, sweetie—it is such a beautiful thing your heart is opening to this man. Your heart has been so shut down all of your life from all the pain of your childhood and past life experiences. Your Cherokee teacher healed your heart chakra several times. So beautiful were those healings. And you can thank her for those healings and so much more she taught you.

Yes, you deserve a man who can give himself completely to you. You deserve that and so much more. Paul cares about you. Yet he's been so wounded, he needs time to heal. He is wise to know he can't commit to you right now. He's still in love with his former partner to some degree. He's still in love with his wife of thirty some years. He is a kind, compassionate man and he is wise not to commit too fast to anyone where he is emotionally right now.

He is a man of integrity and he's being honest with you, as opposed to hiding this from you. This is a good thing. Be in the moment with his truth. Be gentle with yourself and with him too. Try to understand his situation.

Say prayers today for him and you. Lean into this question and listen to your body. Feel your sadness come up and just give it to me, your Mother. Give me the sorrow that is still within your heart and your wombspace from other men, from the times you were really abandoned or tortured or whatever in past lives. Those memories still are embedded in your soul-body. Feel them and release them to me.

Remember, you have abandoned others and really hurt others too. Let this be different. Let this be a conscious, compassionate dance between the two of you. You two have connected and he is so wounded and going through a tremendous amount of healing. You are helping him heal. And he acknowledges you for that. He is also helping you heal also. He does not want to walk away from you. And he knows he cannot commit to anyone right now. You'll figure it out. I'll help you. I love you. I love Paul. He's a good man.

Mare: This is very hard. Do you know how much chocolate I have been consuming? I think I have a new motto: "When in doubt, eat chocolate." Actually this is not a new motto. It's a very old one. I used to think my motto was: "When in doubt, smudge." But chocolate seems to be a bigger crutch for me as I grapple with my emotional struggles here, with this foreclosed house, solitude, emotional struggles, health—all of it. I know there are some big teachings here, Mother. But why do we always have to learn by experiencing so much pain?

Mother: Sweetie, you are suffering because of your attachments and expectations. That is your choice, but you've never truly been conscious of this. This is a good opportunity to learn this. Believe me I'm saying this with so much love for you.

I know this is something most of you humans go through when it comes to your heart. I understand this. If only you could learn to be in the moment more without dreaming or fretting about the future or the past. Your lives would be far more peaceful. Remember the teachings of the hummingbird and the praying mantis.

Many of you take this path of suffering far too seriously. Some of you truly believe suffering is a rightful path of living. A while back, some ideas were seeded into most of you two-leggeds that you need to flog yourself either physically or emotionally and this was a good thing. This idea took hold and when this started to become habitual for many of you, sadly—and largely because of your religious institutions too—the song on my planet went down a few notches.

This prevalent belief that you are supposed to toil, and each day is supposed to involve some struggle, is flawed. Some of you through the centuries even wore hairshirts as a bizarre way of reaching the Divine. Why would the Creator/God/Allah ever want someone to suffer as a way of prayer? Then there was self-flagellation. Oh, my, I cringed when I saw what some of these humans were doing in the act of getting closer to God, or their version of it.

Life is supposed to be about celebrating each moment as a *dance of joy*. It's amazing to be in the body you've been given here on me, this splendiferous body where you can dance, touch, walk the ground barefoot in communion with me, have an orgasm of joy ripple up and down your body, and eat chocolate, cherries … passionfruit. Or peaches … slobbery, yummy, sweet, sweet peaches.

You're supposed to be living passionately, compassionately, in full abundance of energy. Yet somehow this understanding got lost. Even one of your Catholic saints wrote: "The glory of God is man fully alive." Most of these saints were spot-on. Though that saint could have said 'human' instead of man. I love St. Francis of Assisi and the things he did and taught in his lifetime. Anyway, I encourage all of you to become more alive with joy, with giving, with compassion for all around you including all the four-leggeds, six-leggeds, winged ones and more. Become more alive with the knowledge that waking up in the morning and breathing in the oxygen given off by all of my beautiful trees and plants is a miracle. So is having delicious food from your gardens and local farms.

Become more alive with gratitude for the Great Father, Great Mother and myself and all the other unseen spiritual forces that surround you with love each and every moment, all day long and into the night and then the next day. Become more alive with gratitude for fire—the fire that warms you, cooks your food, gives you hope and offers a great spiritual connection to the magic and mystery of life here on me.

And if not fire, then celebrate your electricity, especially if it comes from the sun, wind or sources other than fossil fuels or nuclear. Send this gratitude to me, to Creator, to your pet, your partner, your colleague at work.

Those of you two-leggeds who've had near-death experiences know of this joy. You experienced it when you began to pass over and then came back to live on me longer. I know it was hard for you to come back into this density after what you experienced there and all the amazing joyous love that filled you up while you were temporarily in spirit again.

You are such beautiful souls to come back though and help spiritually wake up others around you afterwards. You help to make my planetary song more beautiful with all whom you touch after you return. I love you so, so very much. And I am deeply grateful for all your sharings of your near-death experiences and your beautiful, beautiful vibrations upon coming back into your bodies.

Ah, this focus so many Christians have of worshipping an image of the beautiful Christ as he was hanging on the cross—do you know there are many other ways Christ could be portrayed that don't necessarily have to do with suffering and death? That cross really does not represent Christ's consciousness, it represents how he was wrongly killed. Why would you want to worship those energies of suffering and death?

In all the times the Christ Consciousness has come to be in the physical on me, that was the only time he was put to death. All the other times he lived a full life. He married and had a family and then died from old age. But this was the work of those aliens so focused on aggression and power. This one religion, birthed out of the unnecessary death of such a highly evolved soul, has become so dominant that it has encouraged you two-leggeds to become disconnected from me. This has been more than woeful for me.

Mare: Mother, I understand what you are saying about the cross and the energies it represents. But I'm confused about this topic of suffering. Are you saying we should avoid suffering always? Truly it's been the toughest times, moments when I've been deeply challenged with suffering that have taught me and helped me grow the most. I'm not exactly clear how we can be in joy and celebration all the time and still grow, change and evolve into better people.

Mother: Oh, my love, yes, of course you are going to suffer and go through difficult times. And those difficult times are largely based on expectations or taking things personally or other tests that have to do with your responses to what is happening externally. These are all good teaching experiences and can be celebrated once you've gotten the lesson.

Whenever you get wrapped up in a dynamic of 'should' then you are going to create more suffering within yourself. You've been good at this pattern all your life but you are not alone by any means. You were creating some agony for yourself earlier this winter when you thought this manuscript 'should' have been complete by early February. The whole manuscript. Then you caught yourself and realized that was only manifesting more stress and you let go of that expectation.

This pattern of taking things so personally too—you are not alone. Most of my two-leggeds take offense too often. You don't realize how much it is about the other person and his or her woundedness. It is good to simply let your reaction go. Ninety-nine percent of the time it's about the other person and his or her challenges, not you. If the offense continues then perhaps it would be best to compassionately create some distance between you and that person.

There are other ways my beloved two-leggeds struggle. I'm not talking about struggling to eat or keep a roof overhead or find clothes to wear. Those struggles of survival are different and it saddens me to see so many of you grappling with food and shelter while others in your region have so much. This very much saddens me.

But when your heart is broken, or you are given some constructive criticism—it is a good thing. These struggles teach you and wake you up to another level of spiritual awareness and balance. The key is to reflect on them and integrate the lessons so you can grow spiritually.

What my teachings were about earlier was this seeming belief that one has to suffer to learn. There are those who choose to take the hardest road and beat themselves up so much since they think, somehow, this is the path to spiritual growth. The monks who were taught to flog themselves to the point of bleeding—this was never something the Christ Consciousness would have supported. Yet these monks were Catholic monks.

If you want to test yourself and experience some discomfort for your spiritual growth then fast for a day or two. Native peoples do vision quests under the guidance of gifted medicine people where they fast from food and water for several days until they receive their vision and have learned to connect with Spirit at a deeper level. Many Sundancers fast for four days, no food or water, and dance in intervals for that period of time. The prayers they put forward are healing for the whole community and beyond.

Those ceremonies may appear to be types of suffering, but when led by the right medicine people and the prayers are focused for the highest good of all, it is different. Vision quests are initiated with good ceremonies that support the person on the quest to heal and grow into a closer relationship with Spirit. It is different than flogging oneself alone in a room until the pain is excruciating and the blood comes. Neither the Creator, Great Mother nor I ever wanted anyone to seek us out in that type of way. Nor have we wanted people to emotionally beat themselves up either. It is actually the same except there is no physical blood drawn, instead much psychological suffering.

It deeply saddens me to see how far away your modern culture has gotten from celebrating life and singing and dancing and being in the joy of the moment as much as you can. Ah, but I know you can still find it. Yes, you can.

Now get out there and dance. Have fun! Play! You can grow through those ways too.

29

Soup Love and More Love

Plant seeds of happiness, hope, success,
and love; it will all come back to you in
abundance. This is the law of nature.

—Steve Maraboli

Monday, February 3, 2014
Up at 4:15-ish.
37°F Raining at 5 AM. Supposed to be dropping temps to snow later this morning.
The famous immortal groundhog in Pennsylvania, Punxsutawney Phil, saw his shadow
yesterday. Six more weeks of winter forecast. I could have told them myself.

Mare: I had a lovely magical night yesterday, Mother. I took your advice to
sit for some time with my feelings about Paul and his desire to date other
women, along with this abandonment issue of mine. I've been meditating
deeply on the Christ Consciousness energies and loving how this creates
a beautiful, compassionate space within me. From this place, yesterday
evening I sent Paul an email about my abandonment and trust issues
getting kicked up. I owned that this was an old part of me I'm releasing,
and how I'm learning a new paradigm of knowing love is all around me,
and I expressed my gratitude for him helping me learn this.

Within minutes of sending that email, a good neighbor-friend called
to ask if I'd like some soup. She'd just made some beef stew with organic
beef from a nearby farm for her family and wanted to share some with me.

I was stunned. In just sending that email, the love was coming back
into my house in the form of homemade soup. This is a neighbor woman
who is very deeply into the Sacred Feminine and has such deeply com-

passionate energy. Within minutes, she was at my door with a large bowl of piping hot stew. I had some butternut squash soup I'd made the day before so I made sure she returned home with the same bowl filled with my homemade soup. It was *Soup Love!*

My friend stayed to talk very briefly and then started to tear up from all the intensity in her life. She works with troubled children at a special school. I suggested she connect with you through your *Love Cord Connection* from her coccyx and root chakra down to your heart to ask you to take some of her emotional overwhelm. She immediately felt it, and a glow came over her as she shared what she was feeling. It was so beautiful. You were definitely there with both of us in that moment, Mother. We hugged and then she had to get back to her family for dinner.

I love that. *Soup Love.* Hmmm—did you send her over that night, Mother, so we could have that exchange?

Mother: Ah, Soup Love. Yes, sweetie, I might have nudged her to bring you some soup. You've been alone so much this winter, it's good for you to have some human company. Also, you helped her with her emotional overwhelm. The truth is love is a currency just as much as money is. Except that sacred love is founded on faith and trust while your money is based on fear. One promotes more abundance and the other more lack. This New World being birthed is based on Sacred Mother *and* Sacred Father Love, Christ Consciousness Love, community, sharing equitably to support the needs of all and coming back into sacred relationship with all life-forms around you based upon reverence.

Mare: Mother, I am truly beginning to understand this and yearn for a time when we shall all be living this way of sacred relationship. Truly, more and more are learning it. Not all people by any means, but more.

We were just talking about Animal Spirit Medicine the other day. As I'm writing this, a blue jay has landed on the flower box outside my bedroom window and proceeded to call out and poke around in the mostly frozen soil in the box. Never have I seen a blue jay do this. Wrens, sparrows but never a bluejay, especially in the cold of winter. Their medicine is honoring the linkage between heaven and earth, to access greater power, and honoring the regal aspects of ourselves. Plus a reminder to follow through on projects to get them completed.[19]

Thanks, Mother, got the message!

---

[19]Andrews, Ted. *Animal Speak* (St. Paul, Minnesota: Llewellyn Publications, 1999), pp. 121-122

30

Tree Spirits, Ice Storms & Sustainability

There are some things in the world we can't change—gravity, entropy, the speed of light, and our biological nature that requires clean air, clean water, clean soil, clean energy and biodiversity for our health and well being. Protecting the biosphere should be our highest priority or else we sicken and die. Other things like capitalism, free enterprise, the economy, currency, the market are not forces of nature, we invented them. They are not immutable and we can change them. It makes no sense to elevate economics over the biosphere.

—David Suzuki

Wednesday, February 5, 2014
Up at 6:30am, writing at 7:34
30° Freezing temps. Frozen rainstorm. Really stunning ice show outside. I wonder what kind of dreams Punxsutawney Phil is having this morning. Rolling meadows of spring clover, maybe? Or of Mrs. Punxsutawney?

Mare: Oh, Mother, we are having an absolutely stilling ice storm right now. I went to get some more firewood off the porch and it is so quiet outside. No one is leaving their homes since the roads are so dangerous. The only sounds are the leaking gutter off the side of this house, a dog barking and branches breaking off trees.

It's so beautiful outside, but there is a palpable sense of anxiety I sense too. All these people hoping they can get to their jobs and responsibilities outside of their home. But the roads in this neighborhood are so steep and with all that ice—I'm not sure how the snowplows with their salt are even going to maneuver. I fear they'll just slide down those hills.

Mother: Yes, ice storms are so beautiful. My elementals, the ones in charge of the weather, are always so proud of the beauty they create when there are ice storms. The shimmeriness of the tree branches and icicles dripping everywhere is such a glorious sight. This is one of the many reasons this planet, my Earth, is considered one of the most beautiful in the universe. I love my ice storms.

And yes, the trees do lose their limbs during storms such as this and it's hard for them. But most of the wounds heal up just fine once their sap starts flowing in the spring. As for those who don't heal up so well, well it is time for them to go through the slow process of dying.

When a tree dies naturally, it is a graceful, conscious surrender of coming back to me, to all the decomposers, the mushrooms, bacteria, and others. There is no resistance to death since they know they are returning to me and will be reborn again through the seeds they have been sending off with love from the moment they could produce seeds. They have no attachment. No need to cling to their life as a tree since they know their living and dying is part of the huge dance of life here.

When a tree dies of old age, especially the really old ones, the other trees in their area celebrate the spirit of the ancient ones' passing and send them great love in the process of dying. It's a beautiful song they know, the tree spirits, the standing ones, which is sung along with the nature spirits for the trees who are passing.

When a tree falls due to old age and strong winds, and takes some neighboring trees with it, there is another song that is sung by the tree spirits to grieve the loss of those healthier ones and the final death of the larger weakened one. But it is all accepted and all the other species in the forest participate in their part of the ecosystem dance as nests are made in the crags, nuts are squirreled away in the newfound crevices and the decomposers celebrate more food. It is all so beautiful, beautiful.

Where there is an extreme storm though—one of those hundred year storms that are now happening every few years thanks to you humans burning too many fossil fuels that never should have been taken out of my bones (along with the nature spirits amping it up because of their frustration with you two-leggeds)—that is rather different. When that derecho tore through Ohio and then east into the Mid-Atlantic in late June of 2012, let's just say that some of my nature spirits were rather pissed off and decided to try to express to you two-leggeds their frustrations about your ongoing mindlessness and disrespect of me. That wall of high winds and thunder and lightning took out many healthy trees. In those situations, there is great grief in the forest. The nature spirits and other tree beings, such as dryads, mourn for days when their tree brothers and sisters are knocked down under such extremely devastating conditions.

Mare: Mother, you know I used to lead sustainability workshops on shifting our human industrial and economic systems toward wiser ways of coming into balance with you. In this work I learned how there is another angle on these ice storms and large weather events that swoop in and bring our roads and cities to a halt. What most people don't realize is that these events are actually better for you, Mother—every time our economy slows down due to days lost from work from extreme weather or even economic recession or depression.

Mother: This is true. Not that I enjoy the awful energetic song of all the frustration and anxiety that is put out by many of you when you can't get to work or school or you've lost your job, but this means people can't shop so easily that day, or month or year. It means fewer resources, as you call them, are being consumed or products produced. When fewer products are bought, that means less consumption of *me*.

Your economy is based on harvesting "raw resources" all over me that continue to devastate my ecosystems, along with spewing more persistent chemicals into my blood, or digging into my bones more, etcetera. Thus when your economy slows for even just an ice day, this is a gift to me. It means less fossil fuels burned that day. It gives me more of a window of opportunity to heal the devastation, a tiny window of time for the tropical forests to absorb the carbon dioxide from fossil fuels in my air, before more from your region has a chance to get spewed out, not to mention the other toxins from burning fossil fuels.

Mare: An economic downturn is very tough for us as individuals, other than the very wealthy. Yet it's good for you, isn't it? How screwed up our global economy has become. It's continuing to plow ahead assuming that blind economic growth is good, which couldn't be farther from the truth when we look at the long term implications.

The sustainability trainings I led were based on the work of a brilliant pediatric oncologist from Sweden, Dr. Karl Henrik Robért. Dr. Robért knew the very young children he was treating had not lived long enough to have a lifestyle that led to cancer. They were exposed to toxins in utero, completely innocent beings who suffered because of what society has done to them.

He witnessed their parents striving to do anything to save their children. Change their diet, remove any environmental contaminants from their homes completely—anything. But to get all of society to make the

219

same commitment was another story all together. Deeply frustrated by the societal resistance to change, Dr. Robért worked for months and months on a set of strategies, a compass, if you will, that companies and governments and even households could use to gradually redirect their systems to becoming more environmentally sustainable. His work is called *The Natural Step Framework*.[20]

I used to lead workshops on this Framework in the 1990's at a time when most people had not yet heard of *sustainability*. One of the more remarkable aspects of *The Natural Step* is that it's based on scientific consensus, which is unheard of these days. Dr. Robért's work took the thinking out of the realms of scientific uncertainty as to exactly why, for example, a frog was born with three legs, and moved it far 'upstream' into understanding how natural systems work. We all know frogs are not supposed to have three legs, but it takes years to determine what exact contaminant got into that frog's ecosystem that affected its embryonic development so that it grew an extra leg. In the meantime, more frogs are being born deformed, or not being born at all, and critical populations of them are disappearing. The scientific uncertainty only delays any decision-making to limit the proliferation of the toxins

Dr. Robért's brilliant work essentially made the case that our human cells, and frog cells and bald eagle cells, etcetera, did not evolve in the company of the persistent chemical contaminants that our society has produced. Scientists can't disagree with that. Yet these compounds have spread throughout the globe and can be found in just about every environment now thanks to entropy. Thus, we can safely assume our cells, or frog or bird cells, don't know what to do with these molecules when they encounter them, and odds are good the molecules will screw up these cells. A safe assumption again. The scientists reached consensus on this level of thinking. Rather brilliant.

Some quite wise people are calling for *The Precautionary Principle* to be mandated as environmental policy. Essentially this would mean if we don't know what the impacts of a persistent, human-made chemical will have in the environment, it should be prevented from being produced by law. If produced, it will most definitely start circulating in the environment and thus be ingested or inhaled and living cells won't know how to process it.

Substances from your bones, Mother, such as mercury, lead, cadmium and other heavy metals are also toxic for us. We call your bones the Earth's crust. Ha, I don't need to tell you that.

Fossil fuels and these heavy metals were buried into your bones long

[20]http://www.naturalstep.org/en/usa/applying-framework

before we evolved into being here. Our cells don't know what to do with these "resources" once they get into our bodies. Thus, young children living in inner city apartments with old lead-based paint on the windowsills touch the paint and then absorb the lead into their brains, and these children suffer learning disabilities and lower IQ's. Mercury poisoning leads to Minamata Disease causing children to be born with birth defects. Not to mention all the rest of the animals who may suffer from mercury or lead poisoning.... The list is so long. And so sad.

Plus the waste from the burning of these fossil fuels is mucking up our climate systems, a finely honed set of systems you developed over millions of years, long after those layers of coal and oil and natural gas had been concreted down in your bones, Mother.

I know I don't need to tell you all of this. You know this. You know far more than I do.

Dr. Robért's work along with his colleagues was profound training for me. He taught what really makes the planet work are all the green cells, the plant cells that are photosynthesizing. The sun's rays are absorbed by our plants to produce food, which then feeds the herbivores and then the carnivores eat the herbivores. And any defecation or dead beings are digested by the decomposers to become food for the plants again. Everything cycles. There is your circle again, Mother. Your brilliant circle.

Mother: Right. Because I did not evolve with a huge rubbish bin next to me for any waste. There is no landfill on Mars for my waste. I just love the sound of that word "rubbish" by the way. To say it with a proper British accent is the best.

There is no waste in the way I and the Great Father and Great Mother nudged evolution along with so much love. But we've already discussed this before.

How I love all of my beautiful, beautiful plants, trees, algae, all of my green cells so much. They are the earliest living beings that were nurtured here on me. How does a Mother talk about her children? Her offspring anyway? I love all of you, all my algae, all my spiders, all my humans even. I really do. Yet when you two-leggeds go in and rip out my forests without even a 'thank you', or gouge huge holes in my bones, or inject chemicals into cracks in my bones to release natural gas and toxify all my blood there in the meantime, I *do* feel pain. And I *am* getting irritated.

You all were never meant to evolve to a place of seeking to control me, control *nature* as many of you might term it. Not all but many of your engineer types, the ones with the very creative minds with absolutely no connection to me, have no awareness of me as a consciousness nor understanding of ecological laws. They are about the scariest, along with the greed-laden business people. I say "people" since it's not just men but also women who can suffer from that all too prevalent disease in your culture—greed.

Honestly, you can try to control me but it will never work. There are too many spiritual beings here working closely with me who are protecting me, and we have the ultimate say. I am your ultimate teacher but most of you have forgotten this. Your technologies and fields of science are creative but they will never be as powerful and wise as my spirit beings here on me, along with the spiritual beings who are assisting from other dimensions and parts of the universe. Humility is a wise perspective to take for any and all beings incarnate on me.

But some of you engineer types get these high-falutin' ideas of taking a chunk of my bones and processing it over in some lab. Then they get together with the business people to create huge industrial plants to process these parts of me. Once the lab is finished, the 'byproducts' are not anything I would have come up with and are spewed into my blood, my rivers, or my skin, the land surface—you know I wish there was an eject button I could insert in some offices to send these types of humans off into space. A one way ticket. Sent with a Mother's *Divine Love*, mind you.

Mare, you talked about the sun and green cells and how photosynthesis within my biosphere is what really makes the planet work. And not your consumer economy. That is true if you only want to wear the lens of a scientist. But what really makes all life here on Earth work is Quantum Divine Love. It's the Sacred Love of Creator and the Great Mother and myself and all the other spiritual beings who have been dancing and working and weaving energies together for billions and billions of years so that my Earth could be one of the most beautiful, spiritually rich planets in the entire universe.

I'm not really exaggerating here. My planet, your planet, where you all live and have forgotten to call home, is one of the most amazing planets in the entire universe. But I'm not sure how to get that through to all of you other than through those who have learned how to listen to me, such as you, Mare. I love you all so, so much, but I want to shake a bunch of you, not all of you, but a bunch of you much of the time and say: "You need to get a clue here! Hello … I'm alive! I'm your Planetary Caretaker! Everything was put here for a reason, all the species, the waterfalls, the mountains … You need to stop shaving off the mountaintops and toxifying my blood. This needs to *Stop!*"

Mare: Mother, I'd like to share a story I wrote about this. It's rather a fun piece about the awakening of a corporate CEO for a company that produces toxic products. I guess every good *Bible* needs a good story. Maybe this one could be considered a parable.

Mother: Sure, Love, why don't you share it? I was starting to vent there and could use something else to think about. I don't like being irritated all that much.

Mare: Here it is:

The Queen Bee of Hearts

(With all due apologies to Lewis Carroll, the brilliant author of *Alice in Wonderland*. This story is an adaptation where the "Queen of Hearts" is actually the "Queen Bee of Hearts".)

This story begins with Alice finally arriving at the fancy croquet game the Queen Bee of Hearts is hosting on her hilly croquet green. The Mad Hatter has accompanied her to the garden where the game has just started. The Queen Bee of Hearts is very upset about her missing croquet balls that are actually hedgehogs. The flamingoes are standing ready to be used as mallets but the hedgehogs are missing.

"Where are my croquet balls?!" demands the Queen Bee of Hearts. She scans the whole croquet green and doesn't see any appearing from under the bushes. "I want my hedgehogs here now so I can play croquet!"

All the guards who are a deck of cards quiver on the sidelines fearful of what the Queen Bee of Hearts will do if she gets into a full rage, which she is often known to do.

The Queen, being a very large bee of extra-Queen size, stomps all three of her right legs and demands again to know where the hedgehogs are.

Alice, in her cute pinafore skirt and shirt, steps forward and starts to respond to the Queen Bee of Hearts: "Your royal Bee-Highness…"

"Who are you?!" demands the Queen. "I have never met you before and how dare you speak to me when I'm about to start a very important game of croquet here, if I can only find my croquet balls!"

Alice starts to shake in fright but still finds the courage to speak: "I'm Alice, and I would love to join your game of croquet if I might. But I need to tell you the Mad Hatter and I were just at a tea party and there was a hedgehog there. And he was ravenous. As a matter of fact

223

he ate all the teacakes before any of the rest of us could have one. Between gobbles of cake, he talked about how he and his family have been starving. All of his relatives have been starving too. Some of his family members have actually died in recent weeks. It sounded like a very sad story, so of course we let him have all the cakes. He did not want much tea, just the teacakes."

"Harrumph!" said the Queen Bee of Hearts. "This does not sound right at all. I need my hedgehogs for my croquet game. I can't have them dying off like this in my kingdom. This is completely not right! We must get to the bottom of this. My games are scheduled every Sunday afternoon and there must be some hedgehogs here by next Sunday or heads will roll!"

Alice pipes up again: "Your royal Bee-Highness, I do have some more information, too. The March Hare and the Dormouse who were at the tea party were talking about the local farm fields and how the farmers have been spraying something nasty and some of the crops they used to sneak in and eat were tasting rather lousy. Plus the bugs were dying. Even the March Hare and his family had been feeling rather sick after being in the farmers' fields. The Dormouse shared a similar story. It seems many of the animals are getting sick. And some are dying like the hedgehogs. Apparently many of the insects the hedgehogs like to eat are disappearing or are tasting rather awful because of these farmer sprays."

"I need to know what these farmers are doing!" says the Queen. "Many of my honeybees are getting sick and dying also. Something is not right here at all and it is impacting my croquet game which is upsetting me terribly!"

"Well, the hedgehog at the tea party was also talking about how hungry one of his family members had been and had found a scrap newsletter on the ground to eat. It tasted pretty bland and he did not care for the ink on it. But it appeared to be some type of environmental newsletter. It had some articles in it about a company named *Noncantro* and the chemical products farmers were buying from them that were killing the insects and weeds and how awful this was. These chemicals were getting in the food chain and poisoning all sorts of animals including humans such as myself," Alice explains.

The Queen stomps all the legs on her left side this time and turns around and calls out to the huge honeybee hive in one of the tall trees beyond the croquet garden. "Ahhhh ... my worker bees, come here please! Pronto!"

Within seconds, a swarm of several thousand bees pours down out of the hive to hover over the Queen.

"Loves, I need all of you to send messages out to the entire bee network and see if we can find where this Noncantro company is. We need to send a message to their higher ups about these chemicals. They must stop making them immediately. This is getting in the way of my croquet game and, besides, I don't like stinky farm fields and many of my bees have been getting sick and dying too. Something is wrong here and I demand a message be sent to this company!" yells the Queen Bee.

The worker bees immediately buzz off in various directions to other nearby beehives and to the far ends of their territories to put out the call to find the headquarters of Noncantro. The bee-hotline-network is activated and hives are buzzing with the question of where this company called Noncantro is based.

Bees work very quickly and within minutes it is determined that the company's main offices are located in a city called Topeka, Kansas, several states away from the tree where Alice fell down the hole and ended up at the tea party with the Mad Hatter and others. (*This is the American version of the story.*)

The Queen Bee of Hearts is given the report on the location and issues the order: "We will send the CEO of this company a message he can't ignore. And since he can't speak Bee-eese, we will send this message the only other way we know how and that is to get under his shirt and give him a good stinging message!"

Once again the bee-hotline-network kicks into gear and several hives belonging to some well-mannered people in Topeka, Kansas, volunteer to be the kamikaze messengers. They quickly find the large headquarters building and sneak in through one of the air vents. And because bees can read English better than most fourth graders, they find the CEO's office within seconds.

Of course, the CEO's secretary tries to stop them, asking them if they had an appointment with the CEO but they just buzz right by her. She decides it might be wise to not get in their way. So they fly under the door and through the keyhole and start stinging the unsuspecting CEO, who just happens to have a bad allergy to bee-stings. He is 'royally' stung, per the instructions of the Queen Bee of Hearts and starts to go into anaphylactic shock right on the fancy oriental rug in his office. But the man is so rarely outside he never thought to carry an EpiPen on him in case of a bee sting.

Now, it just so happens his secretary has a young son who is allergic to bee stings and she carries an EpiPen in her purse all the time. She remembers this just as she is dialing 911 and watching her poor boss gasping on the floor. In the meantime the remaining bees depart as quickly as they came except, of course, for the ones who stung the man and are now laying dead on the floor. But the secretary isn't sure she can pull the EpiPen out fast enough to save him. His gasping stops and he starts to lie there very still without any breathing. The secretary screams for more help as she rummages more desperately through her voluminous purse to find the EpiPen.

In the meantime the CEO stops moving on the floor and, to his shock, discovers he is starting to float away from his body. He is suddenly looking down at it and realizes the odds are good he has just died. Part of him is relieved since he had been grappling with some very stressful PR issues since Noncantro was just kicked out of another country for promoting GMO crops and Groundup. Plus his wife had kicked *him* out over the weekend after discovering some texts from another woman with whom he was having an affair—the very same woman who was desperately looking for the EpiPen which had gotten lodged next to some condoms in the very bottom inner side pocket of her purse.

The CEO's spirit body wafts out of the Noncantro headquarters building and up toward the heavens. Some lingering bees still outside the building see his spirit body drift off and wonder if their colleagues got a bit too excited in the delivery of the message from the Queen Bee. But they decide not to think much of it as they head back to their home hive.

Guided by some beautiful spiritual beings, the CEO sees the Rainbow Bridge and the light on the far end of it and starts to float in that direction when he is gently stopped by some tree-hugging-type angels just before the bridge. There are several male ones with beards and one female one, who call him aside. The female angel has rather hairy legs and is wearing some Birkenstocks under a long flowing peasant skirt. Her wings are especially colorful and large.

The CEO is asked to sit down in a gilded chair floating in a cloudy mist next to the crunchy-granola angels along with the angels who have been guiding him. They bring out some herbal tea from behind his chair along with a plate of fresh steaming cookies. He doesn't dare ask for coffee and a cigar.

The angels beam at him and tell him that they are very honored to meet him and that it has been deemed by the Powers-That-Be that it is not yet time for him to completely pass over. By this time the

CEO is feeling rather euphoric and more love than he's ever known his entire life, more love than what he felt toward his first wife and then his second one, and even the mistresses he's had along the way. He loves his children too but the Divine Love he is experiencing in the moment while in his spirit body is both overwhelming and glorious. He has never been much of a church-goer so the concept of Divine Love has been foreign to him until this moment.

So he listens openly as the angels explain to him that he has much work left to do on the Earthly planes during this particular Earth-walk, and the gates beyond the Rainbow Bridge are not open for him yet. The angels go on to explain how so much of his work at Noncan-tro is damaging Earth Mother and killing off so many of her species and poisoning others, and this is a violation of her laws, the ones that have been forgotten by most two-leggeds for so many centuries.

The CEO's jaw drops lower and lower as he absorbs the angels' explanation about Earth Mother and her laws. He's never been taught any of this and knows his employees and shareholders are ignorant of this too. Though a few of the shareholders have been starting to ask questions, making his—ah—former life tougher. Earth is a dead mass of rock with plants and animals and water and mountains on the surface, right?

"Wrong," explain the angels. The angels go into more detail about who Earth Mother is, and her ancient consciousness and how desperate she is to have humans reconnect with her in more sacred ways since there is so much ignorance and devastation on her, not to mention wars and suffering. They also share about the human health costs of Noncantro's products and how this is yet another violation of Mother's laws—that all life is sacred and must be honored and protected, regardless.

The CEO shakes his head after the angels end their message, and looks down at the cloud-like mists swirling around his feet. He realizes he's still in his business suit though he does not feel like a businessman any more at all. He feels like a sparkling, love-filled soul who yearns to help others know about Divine Love from the Great Father *and* Great Mother. The love is so palpable in that moment as he sits with the angels. The hippie-like angels remind him of some of the activists regularly stationed outside Noncantro headquarters. Although he never felt like hugging the activists outside his office complex—on the contrary, he wanted them arrested and out of the way, prior to this near-death-experience—he wants to hug these angels.

"So what can I do?" he timidly asks them. "You're telling me I'm not supposed to completely pass over, and must go back to this company that has been violating Earth Mother's laws all this time? If I go back, my underlings and Board Members, not to mention almost all of my shareholders, are going to think I'm crazy and this near-death-experience, which I guess is what this is, has flipped my lid."

The angels assure him he'll be fine and he'll figure out a way and that they are there to help him whenever he feels stuck and frustrated with how to proceed with this new mission for Noncantro. Because it is clear Noncantro is going to need a new mission and set of products with this profoundly different information the CEO has been taught by these crunchy-granola angels.

Plus the angels tell him he can turn to Earth Mother any time and she will give him good ideas for strategies and products and all will be well. She is eager to work directly with him. Now that he's had this near-death experience, his capacity to hear her has opened up within him, and she is excited about working closely with him with his newly awakened heart and awarenesses. The CEO is happy to hear this but knows he cannot mention this relationship with Earth Mother to anyone, otherwise his family and colleagues will think he is whacko. Definitely he is not going to tell the Noncantro Board and shareholders.

So the CEO commits to going back and revolutionizing Noncantro into a company that will honor Earth Mother instead of continuing to poison her and her creatures. And the angels escort him back to his office where the paramedics are desperately trying to resuscitate his body. The CEO's spirit body quickly slips back into his physical body and he gives a quick gasp as the medics try to do one more round of cardiac defibrillation on him. They are stunned to see him gasp as they are certain he is beyond the point of responding and there is no hope of bringing him back from cardiac arrest, especially considering how portly he is and his heart history.

In the meantime, Alice and the Queen Bee of Hearts have started a card game with all the card soldiers who line the croquet course. The cards are asked to line up by suits of clubs, spades, hearts and diamonds and then see how quickly they can shuffle themselves on their own. It is a most fun game to watch and the soldiers get quicker and quicker at it, though their arms and legs get kind of tangled together at times. But they quickly sort themselves out.

It is a hilarious game and the cards get sillier and sillier in their shuffling and entanglements. The Queen Bee of Hearts and Alice and the Mad Hatter laugh and laugh and the original croquet game is practically forgotten.

The shuffling card game has been going on for some twenty-five or thirty minutes when an official looking set of worker bees flies in with an announcement. The stinging communication to the CEO has been successful and the CEO had a near-death-experience and has just come back into his body with a set of clear instructions from the crunchy-granola angels. He has committed to work closely with Earth Mother to revolutionize his huge corporation into one that is not only eco-friendly but one committed to healing and restoring ecosystems. This is huge news, and all the creatures and Alice at the croquet green leap and holler and the stack of mostly shuffled cards flops together on the ground.

The Queen Bee of Hearts is especially ecstatic and orders up a full formal tea celebration for all and the stack of cards disentangle themselves in a millisecond and scurry off to the far side of the croquet green to bring out tables and chairs and huge teapots of steaming tea and crumpets that melt with butter and jam. And all sit down for a huge feast.

Even the remaining starving hedgehogs who have been watching from a distance and feeling way too emaciated to even consider being a croquet ball earlier in the afternoon are invited to feast at their own tables along with the Dormouse's and March Hare's cousins and more. It is a gala event unlike anything anyone ever remembers.

The teapots keep on magically pouring and crumpets appear on trays from thin air and even the Cheshire Cat's smile roves over the tables grinning joyfully. No one has seen a feast like this hosted by the ordinarily impatient and arrogant Queen Bee of Hearts. But she is thrilled to host this impromptu celebration since she knows what this turn-around in the CEO of Noncantro means to her bees and all the other animals in her kingdom. For, in truth, she secretly works closely with Earth Mother, too, and has been getting wind of some of the awful chemicals and devastation out there in that other world where Alice lives.

And so it comes to pass that the CEO of Noncantro does turn his corporation around to become one of the greenest ones on the planet. The awakening he experiences shifts the whole corporate atmosphere within the huge company which also wakes his employees up to understanding Earth Mother's laws of sacredness, reverence and honoring all life. To outsiders, it is hard to explain how these awakenings happen within the corporate walls. But within weeks after the CEO's near-death experience, employees come to work and then return home changed people. They even start to brainstorm at work about solar and wind energy, reforesting the expansive lawns around the corporate buildings along with creating organic and biodynamic gardens, more composting at home and even getting worms for home composting systems, plus setting up worm composting systems in the company cafeterias.

The CEO went out to the gates of the corporation the very next day after the bee-prompted spiritual awakening and asked the activists there if they'd like to consider being consultants for the new improved, rather revolutionized Noncantro. A number of the activists practically fainted on the ground. Some were rather skeptical of this 180° turnaround on the part of the CEO but they could tell he was a different man. He actually approached them with big warm hugs that could only be sincere ones. The CEO had a twinkle in his eye he never had before too. This was a different man.

Noncantro grows into being a leader in eco-sustainable products and eco-restoration work that other companies start to emulate. Their products and enthusiasm for healing the Earth, along with highly creative marketing, are so infectious that the old products that kill insects and weeds are deemed obsolete. In addition corporate profits are funneled into extensive environmental education programs throughout the nation that help young people learn about Earth Mother's laws of sacredness, reverence and respecting all life.

Within six months, Noncantro's CEO realizes it might be wise to change the name of the company to reflect their new mission and products. The Board and CEO decide (with Earth Mother whispering in the CEO's ear) that the new name would be HealMotherJoy to reflect all the great joy the employees experience in their jobs now, plus the joy that the CEO is hearing from Earth Mother about all the new ways the company is helping her as opposed to destroying her.

Back in Wonderland, the Queen Bee of Hearts organizes alternating weekend games of cards shuffling and croquet as the hedgehog population rebounds enough for more games. And, Alice and the Mad Hatter start dating and within several years decide to get married and not only have a family but also create a company that produces quite silly hats made of organic cotton and wool that are very soft and not scratchy on the head at all.

These hats become de rigueur at all the Queens games and get so popular that Alice and the Mad Hatter approach the HealMotherJoy Corporation with a proposal and business plan. And before you know it, the HealMotherJoy Hat Company is launched in a grand scale and sheep are grazing on the HealMotherJoy Corporate office campus along with organic cotton fields planted with more-than-fair wages around their southern USA office campuses. To top it off (bad pun!), wildly fun tea parties are sponsored by the corporation at the end of all environmental education programs funded by them, with Heal-MotherJoy organic hats distributed to all.

And they all live happily ever after. Including the desperate secretary/mistress who was looking for her EpiPen when the CEO was dying. She and the CEO eventually get married and have two delightful children who always come in for dinner late, caked in dirt with brambles in their hair since they love to be outside and play with Earth Mother.

Earth Mother has that way with her children.

~~ The End ~~

Mother: Oh, sweetie, I absolutely love that story! That is so adorable and clever and the scene of all the cards shuffling themselves and getting all entangled with their arms and legs is so great. What fun! I'd like to help some cards evolve to that place of having arms and legs and playing that game. Thank you for the idea! Not sure where they'll have a digestive track and all that but we'll figure it out.

As for the CEO who was so rudely awakened by those industrious bees, you are giving me ideas. I'm not going to share them right now but these could be very good ideas.

Okay, now go get some breakfast, you. I know you're hungry. And the house is cold, once again. Time to get some more firewood in for you!

31

The Miraculous Medal and Virgin Mary

Dear children! Today I call you to love with all your heart and with all your soul. Pray for the gift of love, because when the soul loves it calls my Son to itself. My Son does not refuse those who call Him and who desire to live according to Him. Pray for those who do not comprehend love, who do not understand what it means to love. Pray that God may be their Father and not their Judge. My children, you be my apostles, be my river of love. I need you. Thank you.

—Virgin Mary, Apparition Message, Medjugorje, March 18, 2010

Friday, February 7, 2014
6:38 AM
21° Winter, still. Clear. Sun. No snow. Another day in the neighborhood … neighborhood.... I wonder what Mr. Rogers would say about this winter?

Mare: Mother, I need to share about last night. In yesterday's mail was a package I had been expecting for a few days. A week ago, my father offered to send me a new Miraculous Medal, which represents the Virgin Mary, and a rosary. I decided to go ahead and say 'yes' to his offer in the moment. It just felt right to accept it. Part of me didn't want to offend him by saying 'no', and part of me just felt called to receive the gifts.

For years I had worn a lovely silver Miraculous Medal with blue enamel on it, something gifted to me when I was quite young. But I gave it to my sister-in-law along with a rosary when I felt the need to truly cut ties with the Catholic Church about fourteen years ago.

My father is quite a devotee of the Virgin Mary and I had sent him some information about a friend I'd met recently who starts rosary circles even on Wall Street. This man is not even Catholic but is spiritually called to serve the Great Mother. Dad responded with an offer to send me these gifts. I sent an email back to him saying that I'd be happy to receive them as I was working closely with the Great Mother consciousness. I don't know exactly what his response was to that, as he only answered back that he'd be sending them right off.

There is a background story here. My parents have never been comfortable with my "eclectic" spiritual path away from the Catholic Church. They have not been overbearing about it but have occasionally made comments. What is intriguing is my father is one of the more committed followers of the Virgin Mary and has gifted thousands of people with miraculous medals. He was even written up in the Baltimore Catholic newspaper about his evangelizing for the Blessed Virgin. It got so expensive for him to give away these medals that he found some anonymous sponsors to help finance his Marian missionary work. My parents would be ecstatic if I returned to the Catholic Church.

Last night I opened up my dad's package and pulled everything out. A handwritten note was tucked between the velvet boxes containing the Medal and rosaries (he sent me two rosaries) that said:

Hi Mare,

Enclosed are a handful of goodies, all of which have been blessed. Included are a couple of varsity prayer cards and a general history of the Miraculous Medal.

Searching for "Mother" is an important part of your life. Finding your Heavenly Mother is even more important and joyful.

Love, Dad

Surely it is no coincidence that my father is so devoted to the Virgin Mary with this calling of mine to work with you, Mother, and through you—the Great Mother. Though I don't think my father knows to embrace all of who you are, as I understand you. Not that I know exactly all of who you are either, in truth. What I do know is the Catholic Church does not consider the Virgin Mary *divine*. I asked Dad about this one time and he confirmed it. This is one of many reasons I can't ever consider returning to the Catholic Church.

After reading Dad's note, I knew the first thing to do was to smudge the medal and rosaries with some of my homegrown sweetgrass. As I was holding the Miraculous Medal for the Great Mother over the smoldering sweetgrass braid, I also intentionally claimed it for the true Virgin Mary. Not the watered down version of Mary whom I was taught about as a young girl. I know she was a far more powerful woman than the priests and Sunday School teachers described. I only wish I knew the full truth of who she was. Or is....

As I was smudging them I also asked Spirit and you that these new spiritual gifts support my life for joy, healing and celebration deeply connected to the Great Mother and Great Father—not the Great Father attached to the long sordid, fear-laden history of the Catholic Church and the Vatican political agenda over the centuries. I mean the Great Father of great love, omniscience, omnipotence and more. Then I asked what I should do with the Medal, and your guidance, Mother, was to *wear* it.

You stunned me.

But I did put it on and as I did, in that very moment a calm came over me in a way I have never felt. Even in the midst of connecting with the Christ Consciousness in the past few days, I have been at the mercy of some tumultuous emotions around Paul, along with the challenges of this writing and feeling so insecure about all of it. Wearing the Miraculous Medal made me feel stronger and more balanced than I have in a long while. It also helped me feel more protected, as if a more powerful cloak of Great Mother guardian energy surrounded me and held me. This was such a surprising relief.

Thank you!

You are guiding me to tap into all these different archetypes of the Great Mother, Mother. I need them and their glorious archetypal wisdom and energies to do this work. I need you, Earth Mother, and Kali, Kuan Yin, the Virgin Mary and all else you send my way so that I may find all the courage and love I need to support you. What a wild journey this is!

Mother: I love you, my daughter.

Mare: I love you too. More than words can say. A fathomless spiritual love I have for you, Mother.

After experiencing the deep calmness from putting the Miraculous Medal around my neck, I was guided to clean off my large altar to find spaces for the two rosaries there. This altar is truly becoming one to the Great Mother in many of her aspects, and not just you, Earth Mother. Who knew that this would be the direction of this altar over time, Mother, other than you!

As I was placing the rosaries on the altar I remembered I already had a Miraculous Medal there. There are so many things on my altar I had forgotten that one small piece. It was a cheap aluminum one I had found on the ground at a gas station about two years ago. As soon as I saw it on the ground that day, I knew it was meant to go home with me. That was my first revelation that I could embrace the Virgin Mary outside of the limited Catholic version of her.

When I brought that medal home, I placed it on the center of a largish silver pendant representing the yoni.[21] A friend had given me that pendant when I was in the midst of grappling with the repressed energies in my wombspace that caused the lymphoma. It was a conscious reminder to invoke prayers to help me release the ancient fears trapped in the center of my body, and to embrace my sacred feminine parts as vibrant and holy. I had been so sexually shut down all of my life and was on such a learning curve to live a life of greater joy within this magical body I've been gifted. We've all been gifted with magical bodies, haven't we? Though the Christian faith would have us believe otherwise. So sad.

Mother: Yes, you have, my love. All of you are so blessed to have a physical body here on me. Such beautiful bodies with the capacity to touch, feel, hear, smell, see and so much more. I love it when you fully embrace your senses and muscles and more. When you are living in joy, it gives me joy.

Mare: It's the most interesting thing, Mother. Once I cleaned the altar and placed the rosaries on it, I went back to the computer and checked my emails. To my surprise, there was one from Paul. I had not heard from him since sending a long, long email about five days before, about my need to pull back since he wanted to date other women. I had to wonder whether he was reaching out to me, somehow sensing the various spiritual shifts I had been going through that evening.

I called him back a few minutes after opening the email. We talked for two hours. It was intense and sweet but then bittersweet. But something clicked within me in the middle of the conversation—a signal to retreat more from him. After chatting for some time, I finally asked him what was in his heart. After a long pause his voice quaked as he talked about his fears, about how his ten-year relationship failed, and the pain he was still experiencing over that. He's so afraid to get into another committed relationship.

---

[21]Yoni – Hindu term for the vagina.

Mother: Sweetie, it is hard for you to know the amount of emotional pain the man has truly been going through. He is wise to protect his heart at this point in his healing process. My daughter, you've been afraid of the kind of love that Paul has committed to in his life—all of your life. It is hard for you to understand what his heart has undergone. And that is okay as it is close to impossible for any one of my beloved humans to completely understand and empathize about another one's experience. The most important thing is for you to be compassionate and present to him and his pain. To be there for him.

And whenever you experience something 'click', that is an important inner message you need to honor from your sacred center. You know you are seeking a man who is emotionally available for a monogamous relationship. Paul is being honest with you and not playing any games or deceiving you on any levels. He is a good, good man and this is exactly where he is—not ready for a committed relationship. And not where you are. Be gentle with yourself and with him and try to sit with this truth.

I love you regardless of where you are and what you do. The Great Father and Great Mother love you exactly as you are. Know this. Feel this. Paul loves you too in the way that he can in this moment, with all the pain he is in still. It's all good, as it is.

32

Earth Changes, Rainbow People, Shifting Dimensions

The most remarkable feature of this historical moment on Earth is not that we are on the way to destroying the world—we've actually been on the way for quite a while. It is that we are beginning to wake up, as from a millennia-long sleep, to a whole new relationship to our world, to ourselves and each other.

—Joanna Macy

Tuesday, February 11, 2014
10:08 AM
18°F Definitely still winter. No flowers yet. Not even snowdrops. Oh, well.

Mare: Mother, I took a long weekend off from writing to go visit an old graduate school friend in Pennsylvania. It was a nice break and she and her husband have a cozy house with a woodstove. We had some long conversations about Sacred Fires, and transitioning away from environmental careers to other passions. It was good fun and now I'm back, more refreshed. Thank you for not waking me up to write at 4:30 or 5:00 AM there.

Mother: Yes, my love, you needed a break. A change of scenery and being around some good friends has helped you recharge. Plus you needed to take some space from Paul and your heart pain around him. I'm so grateful you visited your friends.

This morning, my daughter, I'd like to talk about planetary shifts taking place on me. You, along with many others, know these are times of Great Change. Your economic systems based on fear and scarcity and

239

inequity are crumbling. They are not meant to last indefinitely and there is barely anything supporting them other than some large egos and greed. But even those egos and the entrenched greed won't be able to prop them up much longer. Weather patterns are becoming more extreme and there is some tectonic shifting taking place.

Unfortunately, there is too much fear being spread about these changes. These old materialistic ways of your hierarchical systems are struggling to hold on to their power base. But they can never succeed. My beloved two-leggeds, you need to let go of the resistance and the old crumbling systems that no longer serve. If you can release your fears, you can open up to levels of joy and community and kindness and healing that will astound you.

A good number of you talk of the *Age of Aquarius* and there is great truth to that. There is a confluence of intense energies that have been coming into the spiritual dimensions here on me from outside the solar system for some decades now. Many prophecies have been uttered about these shifts.

The Hindus talk about the Kali Yuga and the end of a 28,500 year period which heralds the end of the present world and the introduction of a more enlightened era in your human history.

The Mayans had their calendar which ended on 12/21/12 which many feared might mean the end of the world, believing I might explode or something along those lines. But I had no intention of exploding. It was not in my day-planner to do that then.

The Christian Bible talks about the *Apocalypse* which is a radical case of fear-mongering. Some of these Christians have this interesting idea of being "saved" and rising into the sky to avoid the persecution and terrible suffering of the Apocalypse they believe is coming. Truth be told, I would not complain if they did eject to relieve me of the amount of fear and guilt energies they have been laying out here on me. Not to mention their denial of women's rights and judgments of homosexual people.

Some of these Christians are the very ones promoting extreme fear throughout your society through their ownership of the media. They also possess dominant interests within multinational corporations that are pushing for international trade agreements that will only rape me more. And create more suffering on the part of most of my beloved humans and all my other beautiful four-leggeds, winged ones, tall ones and more.

If they really want to eject with their second coming of *The Christ* as they deem it, I will send them off with love—the love of a compassionate Mother who knows it's time for some of her children to go relearn their soul lessons. Let them pass over to other dimension so that they may come to realize what havoc they have created on me, one of the most beautiful planets in the universe.

I call out to my beloved spiritual warriors, my Rainbow People. You are the ones who know about these changes and have been leading the way. You have been a Native person in a past life or two or three or more, but came back as a Caucasian or African-American or another race this lifetime. You are aware of the need to reconnect with me in sacred ways, and to bring balance back into your troubled society. You are the young people who have gone through college and then decided to become an organic farmer, or alternative healer, or follow myriad other types of passion-filled work that are about healing on so many levels, and not strictly for profit.

I'm calling to all of you to follow a path of wisdom to support *my* healing, restore my ecosystems, and heal each other. Love each other. Forgive each other. Come back together into community. All of you used to know how to live in community. You can relearn this. I will help you.

The Occupy Wall Street movement that spread throughout so many cities after Manhattan, these were Rainbow People seeking to right an economic system that has gone terribly wrong. They possess ancient memories in their soul bodies of living in reverence and being in balance on me. They are feeling the stirrings and have the courage to take to the streets in non-violent ways to voice their call for a far better world.

These Occupy activists are learning about consensus decision-making, a non-hierarchical and balanced process. These types of council meetings are based on ancient practices that many indigenous peoples still use today. In these traditions, input representing all parts of the community is sought to make the best decisions for now and into the *next seven generations*. The voice of the Elders too, the Grandmother Elders in many villages, contributes to the final consensus vote.

This is the way of the Peacemaker's teachings that brought those warring tribes together into the Iroquois/Haudenosaunee Confederacy hundreds of years ago based on the *Great Law of Peace*. I have talked about this before. Some of you here today were part of that process in another lifetime. You remember the balance that was taught and the way of Peace that existed for hundreds of years following the passing of the Great Peacemaker. You are the Rainbow People being called to bring back these ways of balance. How I celebrate you. I love you so very, very much.

I, as a planet, am metaphysically shifting with the support of other cosmic forces to create a higher resonance world for all who live on me. Scientists have been measuring the energetic frequencies on me and mapping the increasing levels. But there is so much more that is happening which they can't measure.

These are the times of shifting from the Third Dimension to the Fourth and Fifth Dimensions. These are the times for raising your energy levels, your internal frequencies to a higher love vibration. Your economic systems are based on a lower vibrational energy in the more material Third Dimension and this energy is being shed from me now to shift to higher ones.

These new energies of the Christ Consciousness along with other cosmic forces are propelling these changes. Plus, so many of you are re-discovering your love for the Great Mother and me, Earth Mother. Your world cannot go back, nor should it.

I will explain further. The Third Dimension represents the material world. This is a perceived reality where it is believed all that exists is only in the physical, and the existence of spiritual unseen forces or etheric bodies is denied. This is what your old economic system is based upon, the illusion of having control and power.

The Fourth Dimension is one of a higher energetic vibration that is based upon magical experiences. Coincidences happen all the time. You are guided to the right people to come into your life for your soul's learning, opportunities and more. Spirit is recognized as part of the quantum world, as everything has a spiritual life force. The energy of your thoughts, your words and actions becomes apparent. You recognize the interconnectedness of everything and the energy web that supports all of it, with energy signatures and molecular frequencies resonating all the time. People who live more in the Fourth Dimension are drawn to healing work, have opened up their intuitive gifts, or could be more religious or spiritual—depending on how they term it.

The Fifth Dimension is one of an even higher spiritual vibration. It is the dimension of miracles and there is no separation as all are experiencing the Oneness of Creation (Great Mother and Great Father). Fear does not exist within this dimension and love is the basis for all actions.

Those living in the Fifth Dimension have given themselves over to Spirit. They see themselves as divine beings guided by Spirit and trust in the principle that all that manifests serves a higher purpose. They operate from a place of love, and miracles are just accepted as how life works.

This is a time in your limited sense of history when the veils between these worlds, these dimensions, are rapidly being lifted. This is very unsettling to those so comfortable in the material world. Yet these energies are continuing to shift and it will only become more challenging for those resisting the change.

This New World, a far more spiritual world, can be birthed gracefully. But as long as some of you humans continue to dig your heels in and resist these changes, it will make it harder for you and others around you. Know I am doing what I can to support you, nudge you along. But you need to find the courage within to wake up.

It is time for you to open up to the Quantum Divine Love that the Great Mother, Great Father and I have for you. Time to plant vegetable gardens in your yards. Learn how to tap the limitless energy of the Sun.

Live with fewer material things and with more love instead. *Give*. Give to those in need. Give back to me. Plant trees and more trees.

Learn how to work together and listen to each other. Learn how to surrender to the great mystery in each of you and all around you. Be empty of your ego, and the need to control and *be right*—for the more you think you're right and the other person is wrong, the less right you are. There is always that Sacred Truth in the middle to discover. Work to find that.

Let the thorns from your heart drop as you feel safe—only as you feel safe. Once you tap into the Christ Consciousness and reconnect with me spiritually, it will be remarkable how quickly you will take in the healing energies, remarkable how graceful and joyous your healing will be.

Many of you are doing this and this just tickles me so much. These are the beautiful shifts you as seed children need to make to help me birth and all of you birth into this New World. You don't know how the dolphins and whales are celebrating this, along with all of my other beloved four-leggeds, winged ones, six-leggeds, stone people and more. They are all celebrating this, including the nature spirits.

You are beautiful, glorious spiritual beings and how I yearn for all of you to wake up to this. To remember this wisdom. To remember and reconnect with me with love. Be a seed for the New World coming in. It's such a beautiful, beautiful world being born as your culture sheds these ways that don't serve me, or you. All of you. How much love I have for you ... so much love!

33

The Virgin Mary & Earth Mother

Love is the divine Mother's arms;
when those arms are spread,
every soul falls into them.

—Hazrat Inayat Khan

Tuesday, March 4, 2014
7:23 PM
22° Bitter cold again this morning. The groundhog definitely nailed it a month ago. Old Man Winter has made a serious visit this season.

Mare: Mother, thank you for giving me a bit of a break from the listening and writing. I needed to focus on some other parts of my life such as the part-time gardening business and do some book promotion on my second book. I could sure use some income.

I could use more of your wisdom also. I received an email from my father today. This comes several weeks after he sent me the rosaries and Miraculous Medal. I didn't mention before how my father has traveled to Medjugorje, in the Bosnia and Herzegovina region of former Yugoslavia, on spiritual pilgrimage several times. Since 1981, the Virgin Mary has been appearing and giving messages to several people there since they were children. In 1992, I joined Dad on one of those trips, along with an entourage of people he gathered—including a Catholic priest from Baltimore. At the time I was heavily into yoga and spending almost all of my vacation time at the ashram I mentioned earlier, but I was still intrigued and open to my father's invitation to join him in Medjugorje.

It's been years since Dad went on pilgrimage there but he continues to receive the updated messages from the visionaries[22] and he forwarded a recent one to me.

Subject: Medjugorje - Our Lady's February 25, 2014 Message to Marija

Peace to all! Below, please find the official English translation of Our Lady's February 25, 2014 message given to Marija, as provided by the Information Center in Medjugorje.

Message, 25. February 2014

"Dear children! You see, hear and feel that in the hearts of many people there is no God. They do not want Him, because they are far from prayer and do not have peace. You, little children, pray - live God's commandments. You be prayer, you who from the very beginning said 'yes' to my call. Witness God and my presence and do not forget, little children: I am with you and I love you. From day to day I present you all to my Son Jesus. Thank you for having responded to my call."

Mother, this is your message, isn't it? This really does sound like you. Except you are talking about the Christ Consciousness, who truly was *her/your* son. This is you speaking as best you can to the Christian world in a way they can hear, isn't it?

Mother: Yes, my love. It is me. I am the Mother. I speak as the Virgin Mary to many. I speak as Our Lady of Guadelupe to others. I am Earth Mother to many indigenous peoples and more and more. Some hear me as Kuan Yin. You and I have talked about this before. But receiving this email from your father brings it home to you again, doesn't it? We are all One spiritually, as in *The Great Mother.*

In the messages from Medjugorje, I often talk about prayer since it is very powerful. So many people pray but don't realize how potent it can truly be, nor do they really know how to pray to make it as powerful as it can be. A person needs to focus in a concentrated way from the heart, connecting themselves spiritually/energetically with Creator and me for the prayer to be strong.

---

[22]www.medjugorje.org

I know your scientists have done studies on prayer. What do they call it? Double-blind, yes. And they've seen more and more how prayers do make a difference. Concentrated prayers can heal the people they are praying for. It is true. Again, it's all sacred energy. Praying to God/Creator/Allah, will bring the Creator's beautiful Divine Love into your being. It is so needed these days, as does praying to me, your Mother.

What I can't really talk about in these messages to these young visionaries in Medjugorje is who I am as Earth Mother—your sacred Earth Planetary Caretaker—or *All My Relations* or similar terms since the Christians don't know what those mean. So I keep it within their religious context. This makes me sad since I'd like to talk about all that too. Believe me, I would.

But connecting with the Creator and with me through prayer to the Virgin Mary is very, very good. Wonderful sacred energy can come from that. The more all of my beloved two-leggeds pray, the more beautiful your song will become and more positive energy you will radiate out on me. This will help me *and* help all of you so much. It will help *All My Relations* on the spiritual planes, the dolphins, the whales and more. Oh, yes!

I love you all so much. Yes, please pray. Connect with the Christ Consciousness. And please, please remember me as your Earth Mother too, and send your love down into me also. However you can, please....

Mare: Mother, you know how much I pray every day, and send my gratitude to you and Creation. As I sat in front of the woodstove this morning, it struck me how grateful I am for my life. Yesterday, you manifested the sweetest man to come and treat me with acupuncture right here in this very house. He's a friend who came over after I came back from a meeting with some people about a potential workshop. I was feeling rather down about Paul. The acupuncture treatment was a huge help in encouraging my body to release some stuck emotional energy in me.

As I pressed my face into the heat of the Sacred Fire emanating from the woodstove this morning, I remembered, "It is good to say '*Thank you*' one hundred times when you wake up in the morning." Thank you for my acupuncturist friend. Thank you for the Sacred Fire. Thank you for this house, foreclosed and all that it is. Thank you to you, Mother. So many other *Thank you's* across the board. I could go on and on with gratitude.

Mother: Yes, Love, it is so good to say *thank you*. And to pray. It is so, so very good. I love you. I love all my two-leggeds so very, very much.

34

Earth Mother Never Abandoned Us
—We Abandoned Her

Call forth the sacredness of the earth now, the holiness of the living, breathing planet and breathe with the earth, blessing and being blessed as the light of the earth flows to you and as the light of your own heart flows to the beloved earth. There is a partnership, a communion between you and the land, between the land and you. This runs deep beneath the streets, deep beneath the buildings, deep throughout and beneath the seas. The earth is sacred. The earth is our mother; we must take care of her.

—Sharon McErlane, *A Call to Power*

Monday, April 14, 2014
Up at 4:45 AM, writing at 5:10 AM
63° Window open all night. 80's yesterday. Made it through winter. Unbelievable. And already summer temperatures yesterday. Plus auspicious Full Moon tonight, and Lunar Eclipse. Red Moon – first of four in a series of eclipses in consecutive full moons. Rather high energy day with the moon at her full glory.

Mare: Gosh, you've roused me up early this morning, Mother. I thought we were mostly done with these early morning wakeups from you. But I'm getting the sense this is how you will work with me for the rest of my life. And that's okay. I'm not really complaining, though I do like to sleep in a bit at times too, or at least have eight hours of sleep most nights. But I know there is always a good reason you want me up and listening. So here I am.

I'm supposing you want to discuss something that's been percolating in me the past day. I did post this early this morning on Facebook related to it:

I don't know why I'm feeling nudged to say this ... maybe it's this full moon and eclipse and the beautiful energies swirling around (and lack of sleep might be a reason too?) ...

But there are times in my life when I've felt so abandoned by friends and lovers. And in this recurring perception of whatever the real reality was, I have sat in isolated fear and insecurities too many times. I have come to learn I've been abandoning myself all this time. And I will no longer allow this to happen. I don't need to know the roots of this abandonment stuff, all I need to do is realize my perceptions are not reality and I choose to no longer abandon myself.

And on that note, I wish to thank Grandmother Moon for her glorious energies. And Earth Mother for her incessant nudges and truly amazing love.

Mother: Yes, my daughter, it would be good to talk about this. You are not alone with these feelings of abandonment and insecurities. It is a rare person in your society who does not experience this. Way too many of you abandon yourselves in the pursuit of a lover or money or even a non-sexual relationship. Your society has not encouraged you to learn how to stay true to yourselves and follow your authentic soul-path, especially if it is judged different from the mainstream.

Another reason so many abandon themselves from a place of deep insecurity is that you did not learn of me, your Earth Mother, and my deep, deep *love* for you from the moment you were born. I am your Spiritual Mother, your first Mother. Native peoples who were taught of my love carry this great love within them each and every day and rarely experience this sense of abandonment or loneliness. Of course those who live on reservations have rather bleak lives. Their alcohol issues and high unemployment and how the U.S. Government has treated them for centuries is painful, but that is another story of great wrong-doing and sorrow, not associated with any lack of my love for them. Some of these Native peoples have forgotten me and this has made me very sad.

Connect with me, remember me, and your life will be more blessed. Remember where your food, water, and air truly comes from—your Mother. You can send your gratitude and love back to me and it is a beautiful relationship we can create. I so yearn for this. You can let go of that grief of disconnection that sits so deeply within you when you rediscover my *love* for you. You will know you are never abandoned when you are connected with me. I will never abandon you. *Never.*

I invite you to take this truth and carry it within you every moment of every day, as I always love you. Always.

35

Food of the Gods

All you need is love. But a little chocolate
now and then doesn't hurt.

—Charles M. Schulz

Thursday, May 1, 2014
8:29 AM
61° Finally stopped raining after monsoons for the past three days. Spring and May
Day today. Where are the Maypoles when you need them? I could use some Beltane
type dancing.

Mare: Mother, we have not talked for a while. I mean having a concentrated
chat like this. I've been busy with my part-time gardening business and
organizing workshops and talks. Plus I sent a copy of this unfinished
manuscript to a good editor in Louisiana two weeks ago. It was a huge
relief to pass it over to someone else and take a break.

There is so much to share now. So much goodness has been manifesting. Grace ... beautiful grace. And I attribute it to you and Creation. All of
it. I'm so grateful for this goodness.

Plus, I've had to order another flannel nightgown since I wore out the
butt of my favorite one with all of this writing in bed space. Who knew
you could wear a nightgown out in the butt?

Gosh, where to start?

First off, I have a new kitty. Her name is Chessie and she's six years
old, a beautiful orange tabby and a total love—purr-ball. She arrived two
days ago from a foster home. Her former family just could not keep her

and wanted her euthanized. They had too many other cats and then a new baby and apparently Chessie was harassed so much by the other kitties she started peeing on the cat food dish. That's rather extreme for a cat to do. But she never had an accident at the foster house during the six weeks she lived there.

So now I have a kitty who oozes so much love. From the first five minutes of arriving she's just been purring like a locomotive. In the passing of two days, she's gotten more and more friendly and purring and rubbing up on my legs in the kitchen. Just now I held her up to my heart and we hugged each other. Her with her sweet kitty purrs and me with my heart and arms. It was so sweet and, well, healing. I've been yearning for some real hugs. Kitty hugs work too, for sure.

I know you wanted to bring some other love in my house, Mother. To help me with this solitary work.

Mother: Yes, my daughter, you've been feeling so alone especially after you and Paul ended your brief romance in the winter. And while I keep on reassuring you you're never alone and I am always with you, along with your spirit guides, your tree friends outside and more—I know it's not the same as a real warm body keeping you company. You needed someone in the physical to purr at your side and wake you up in the morning with love pouring out of her. You tend to wake up and zip to that place of deep anxiety in a millisecond. Chessie will help you shift this. You can focus on her and the love she's sending you. She is a beautiful, huge-hearted kitty. She will be very good for you. And you for her too. She needs a lot of love also, with all she's been through.

Mare: Mother, speaking of anxiety, do you know this is the first time in two and a half years I haven't had to dip into my savings to pay my bills? This is such a relief and absolutely huge. My one gardening client keeps on asking me to do more work since they like the quality of my efforts and the TLC I give their plants compared with a generic landscaping firm. So my income from them is higher than I thought it was going to be this spring. They have even asked me to do some design and installation which is going to help me with more bills in the coming month or two.

Plus the house went to auction and it turns out the bank bought it back in January. But they haven't contacted me yet. So not only am I not paying rent to my friend whose name was still on the paperwork before the auction, I'm not paying rent to anyone right now. This is never exactly how I thought I'd be living but I'm not complaining at all. The house is in pretty good shape and I'm trusting and attributing all of it to you and your grace. Your magic. Paying no rent has been a huge relief and significant savings right there. Maybe they won't be contacting me for months? Fine with me.

I'm just ecstatic about this, Mother. It's been so stressful to continue to see my savings dwindle. I feel so spiritually protected here in this cute tree house of a bungalow built on this steep hill with the back deck high up in the tree branches. Such a glorious deck to sit on to commune with you and the trees. I do trust I'll be here as long as you want me to be here to get this book done. Most of the time ... I trust....

Mother: Sweetie, I have been telling you so many times you are completely taken care of. All your needs will be met. You go to that place of fear so fast, and yet in each and every moment, you are safe and your needs are taken care of by me, by Creation, by all of us.

Just yesterday you walked by that neighbor's pile of nicely chopped wood that would be perfect for your woodstove. You had been rationing your woodpile with the continuing cold temperatures this spring, concerned you might run out and need to buy more with your tight budget. Or have to possibly turn the furnace on. I've been telling you to trust, trust ... step beyond your limiting thoughts. Trust.

You saw the stacked wood yesterday on your walk and knew immediately it was for you. The neighbor had set them out for anyone to take. That someone is you. You will always have what you need, my love. As you let go of your anxieties about how you will be taken care of, you will be taken care of even more easily.

My love, your fears are blocking your abundance, blocking your book sales, blocking the amount of joy and love that could be dancing through your life. That medicine woman you spoke with earlier in the winter told you this and you've been pondering it for a while. Your focusing on fear blocks the spiritual flow of goodness. It hinders all the love and goodness from flowing to you and through you fully.

All your life you've carried so much fear within you. It makes sense considering the troubles you went through in a number of your past lives and your childhood. But you can let go of those illusions now. And you are learning. You are learning to shift and sing a different song within your spirit body, in letting go of your fears. And trusting. This is so beautiful to watch you grow and let go of your limiting thoughts, your binding fears.

You have food. You have a house to live in, to write in. You've had more than enough chocolate all winter. You have a gardening client who loves your work and even offered to contact his friends and neighbors to see if they needed more gardening work since he knows your budget is tight. You turned him down since you know this is your work, with me, with your writing and talks, etcetera, and you don't have the time to take on another client. The level of surrender and trust you have been learning is so beautiful.

Mare: Mother, I know you are aware of this already but the amount of fear and grief in me, and resistance, yes, resistance to this work with you has been building for the past month or so. This resistance, this terror in me about how the world will respond to this book can be huge at times. All of this sits in my wombspace, of course, and just in the past week it was starting to feel as if the lymphoma was returning. This was scaring me again. I don't want to relive the dark cloud of cancer hanging over my head.

I know I'm going to die sometime. It's not that I'm afraid of death. I look forward to being back in Spirit with all of the spiritual allies and loved ones who have passed over already. Katherine Carter and others. But I know deeply it's not going to be from lymphoma that I die.

I've gone back to taking some potent supplements to boost my body's immune system the past few days, and watching my thoughts and emotional responses to different things. I am so darned insecure, it's really sad. I've realized when I use Facebook, I clench myself emotionally and have had this pattern of taking all of it so personally. How many 'likes', or comments were positive or negative? How much people love me there … or not? It's crazy-making and has been feeding my shadow in more ways than I was aware of, until just this week.

Something shifted yesterday, though. I did a radio interview with several people in the afternoon. One of the hosts, Jim Graywolf Petruzzi, is a gifted healer and follower of the Red Road. Our paths have been somewhat similar. He was raised Catholic near Philadelphia and found the Native wisdom early on. It was the most fun interview all about you, Mother, and connecting with you in different ways. When the interview was over, I was in such an altered state of inner peace and calm. It lasted for the rest of the afternoon and into the evening. I can still feel it now this morning, though not as much.

Mother, a rather intuitive healer, a woman I met at a Sundance last summer, told me that this lymphoma—this blockage of energy in my wombspace—is from inner resistance to this work you desire me to do for you. My soul contract work. I will only heal completely when I let this spiritual work pour through me like pristine waters over a remote wilderness waterfall. No fears. No ego. No blocks. No dams. I've known this on some levels. I keep on working on releasing the resistance and yet more fears keep on coming up. Layers and layers of fears as I continue writing this book and envision going public with it. Very public. I even have a contact who was one of Oprah's producers. I know there is the potential to go *that* public.

I come from a rather conservative family, a preppy one. I was even a debutante. I know you know this, Mother, but many of these types of people are rather closed-minded to alternative spiritualities, at least they were the last time I checked in with a few of them. The "straight and narrow" is a truth within their ilk and I fell out of that narrowness—or was guided to step out of it—many years ago. I have lost some friends for it too, which has hurt a little.

Mother: Yes, my love, I know this. I love you.

Mare: Mother, I even blogged about this several days ago while in the deep throes of this angst, my insecurities about how some people will respond to this book, or my openness about talking with you directly. It was cathartic to write and the response from some others has been beautiful.

Here's an excerpt of it:

> ... *[Mother] is saying there is so much love and support behind this spiritual writing and work she's asking me to do that it is only natural that these fears come up. The love is so deep that it is poking the fears up to be healed on a more profound level, so they can be fully released. Mother and all of my spiritual allies (I've got a few guardians) love me so, so much that they are pushing/ coddling/ loving/ holding me through the birthing canal of this book, and my fully inhabiting what this book is truly about and my life work, at this time in my life.*

A quite gifted medicine woman friend of mine, Robin Youngblood, tells of her first spiritual teacher, Martin Highbear's, teaching:

> *There are only two things, Love and Fear. Your choice. How're you going to live? Wherever there's love, everything that's fear has to appear so that love can heal it because that's love's job.*

So, this is what I'm learning—to walk through the fears and step into this love. To fully permit myself to allow your love in, the Great Mother's and the Great Father's love. Plus I've gained new friends who do appreciate my quirkiness, spiritual listening and bizarre sense of humor. These new friends are supporting me as I continue to work through my dwindling savings to do this work and book.

This is honestly what just about all of us are being asked to do these days, as we truly shift from the *Third to the Fourth and Fifth Dimensions*—aren't we, Mother? To release the fears wrapped around materialism that are so mired in Third Dimensional thinking? And know the universe works quite magically and powerfully and we will be taken care of. Beautiful non-attachment and trust! We are being asked to release fear and know that when there is suffering, it can serve as spiritual teachings (karmic—at times). We are spiritual beings here on Earth for only a brief time, and to know that most fear is an illusion, based on the old paradigm that is dropping away.

We are all being called to release these old Third Dimensional ways and live more simply, more closely to you, Mother, more reverently. More in community, more compassionately with trust in Spirit, magic, mystery, God and more. I get it. I do.

We are all being called, aren't we? And I'm just one two-legged struggling along, limping along at times, but working through it. This lymphoma is such a teacher to me about my fears and where I block the healing flow of energy within me, your healing energy, Mother. I don't want to block it any more.

I'm learning how to fully inhabit this spiritual work you and Creation have asked me to do. I signed up for it—I understand this. Just writing that blog post and putting this out there was a cathartic experience for me. Whoosh… what an adventure! These are sure interesting times and I'm learning to embrace them more fully.

Mother: Yes, my love, these are interesting times on me in this moment of time. And embracing the Quantum Divine Love that has surrounded you all of your life and beyond this lifetime is the path, along with digging in deep to find your courage and commitment to serving for the greatest good. You know this. You are doing this.

I'm so proud of you posting that message and being so vulnerable on that level. Plus it touched some people deeply. Some have responded to you and others have not. But they took your words to heart and you are a role model for them—as you have role models too.

All of my beloved humans are being asked to make some big choices these days. Will you stay in the fear of the materialism-based paradigm or will you shed those ways and come to know that the fear-based mindset is an illusion and that there is so much more to living on me beyond it? This New World is based on love, trust, abundance, compassion, community and celebration. We've been talking about this for sometime now, my love, and it's important to repeat it.

Those who resist these shifting energies on the planet will have a tougher and tougher time of it. All they need to do is step through the fear and see your linear, materialistic way of thinking as what it is, an illusion. Not reality. I know it's not so easy to shed such a deeply ingrained way of thinking. So much of what you think and how most of you live is so unconscious since it sources from centuries and centuries of patriarchal philosophies and more.

But many of you are waking up and walking through the belief portals to the real world of energy patterns, fractals, divine love and ME too! I'm so thrilled about this. You are the spiritual warriors, the pioneers, the great lovers of me who will help birth this New World. I can't wait to see this change come to full manifestation here on me. Just can't wait.

But you, my love, your resistance is part of your process too. And when your body starts to block the energy again, from your fears, your insecurities, this will make you sick again. But you are learning. You are starting to identify those fear thoughts that make your wombspace area clench—and release them. You are starting to open up to my love more and trust me more. I know you're doing it bit by bit, incrementally, but you are still doing it.

These are such ancient memories within you that are being triggered. For a long period of time, it was very dangerous for women to express themselves and all their spiritual gifts. But not now. You are protected in your part of the world. You are protected spiritually. It's time to let go of these ancient fears. It is time for you to step into your full Sacred Feminine powers.

Your fear of being judged, of being considered too *whoo-whoo*, as you term it—yes, there are those who will judge you. But that's fine. You've known for a long time your life work is to encourage people to expand their thinking, and perhaps step out of their preconceived notions of reality. You've been doing this for years as an environmental educator and sustainability trainer, and with your two other books. That's why I chose you to write this book, this *Bible*.

The challenge for you comes from your empathic abilities and your tendency to feel guilty if anyone is upset around you or with you. You internalize their anger, fears and more and take it all personally and all the guilt and repressed anger sits and festers in your womb area. This is partly what has made you sick with lymphoma also.

You are ready to step into this next level of working with me—to truly release these fears and put this book out, *The Great Mother Bible*. You have been growing spiritually and getting so much stronger each week. And yes, more fears will continue to surface as they have been, and you can release those also. They are ancient and don't need to be a part of your being anymore.

Paul helped you tremendously with this.

Mare: Oh, Mother, I know all that you share is true. Paul, yes, Paul. We actually met for dinner two weeks ago. Just before Easter in the middle of April. We had not seen each other since February. It was a good dinner, a sweet time together.

It was confusing for me though. He wanted to hold my hand. I wanted to hold his. So we did hold each others' hands. He took my arm and escorted me to the table as we were led to our table by the maitre'd. He even started to cry at one point while talking and I reached out to hold both of his hands across the table to support him. We hugged at the end of the meal several times in the restaurant and by my car. Then I couldn't help it. I started to kiss him and then pulled back quickly. He was sweet about it and understanding. So sweet—as Paul is.

I did open my heart to that man in January. And am grateful I did. It was a good thing. My heart needed cracking open.

Paul confessed to me at dinner that he was emotionally overwhelmed back in the winter since there were five women who wanted to date him at the same time. I did not realize there were that many. He could not do it. He listed all five names right there in the restaurant. I asked him if he was involved with anyone now and he shared there is only one. According to him, they are both clear there are no expectations and they will see each other when they will and it is very open. She seems to be a very good woman, and I think he is really falling for her which is a beautiful thing. I can understand this when I'm not feeling a little confused. Ahhhh… how the emotions ebb and flow.

I am clear Paul and I were not meant to be together long term, at least most of the time. He does not understand this commitment I have to you, Mother, my surrendering and nature mystic aspects. He does see my heart though and has a lot of love for me. He informed me that he intends to keep me in his life for a long time. He's a "fan", in fact he's shared that in an email. And whatever woman he's involved with needs to accept that.

Paul looked happy, at peace that night over dinner, not the same man who walked into my house in early January so heartbroken and hurting.

But seeing him over dinner and feeling the chemistry still between us did bring up more of my grief. This grief has been a heavy stone in the center of my being for the past two weeks. I sent him an email several days after we had dinner in April and there was no response. I'm realizing now I wanted him to respond since I was so yearning for a connection, someone who cared. It hurt to not hear from him. This writing life is so isolating and Paul supported me so much earlier in the winter. I yearned for more of that type of support, just knowing someone cares, that someone supports me in this lonely work. I just need it.

Mother: Sweetie, I love you. Creator loves you. There is a man waiting for you and he is yearning for you right now. He is your Soul Twin. You just have not met yet. The time is not quite right. You will know it as soon as you are in his presence. He's the one for you. This will happen soon. Paul helped open you up, and encouraged you to heal so that you will be ready for this man.

You helped Paul too. He does care for you still, and continues to express that when he sees you and emails you. It's just in a different way. He does support you and always will. He has a love for you that will never go away and it has transitioned to that of a true friend. A better love connection for the two of you over the long term. Plus he knows he's not the Soul Twin you have been waiting for—for so long.

Know that you are so loved, my daughter. Take this in and allow yourself to deeply feel the Divine Love that Creator and I have for you. Feel it in your heart. *And* in your Sacred Wombspace. Your Sacred Center. In your time of solitude— not loneliness, but solitude—call on us directly, and bring our Sacred Love into you. We are here for you all the time, along with your spirit guides and guardians. You are so loved.

All the chocolate you ate this winter was a way of swallowing your fears and sorrow. You don't need to do that any more. See if you can learn to take that chocolate in as if it were love. Divine Love. There is a reason one of you two-leggeds named it *Theobroma*, as the name from that old language, Latin. It means *Food of the Gods*. Chocolate is healing, on so many levels.

Yet, my love, you've been eating it as if it were *Food of the Fearful*. I don't want you to eat it from a place of fear anymore—your insecurities and angst, romance-related or not. I was getting a little concerned about you during the winter since you devoured so much chocolate to calm yourself as you and Paul were getting close and then things got rocky. You ran so fast to the chocolate whenever those fears of intimacy would surface in you, or whenever any ripples came up between you and he. It has been such a learning experience for you to be with him this winter since he was so emotionally gentle and honest with you.

While I'm grateful you had the chocolate, and it did help you emotionally, my love and Creation's love has been there for you all along. I know this is not the love of a lover who can wrap his arms around you and hold you tight. It's not the same. Nor can we send you chocolate in the mail and tell you we're thinking of you.

Mare: Actually, Mother, I think you did arrange in your magical ways to have chocolate shipped to me as a surprise about two years ago. I was about to do a big ceremony with a gifted medicine person and out of the blue a box of very fancy chocolates appeared in my mailbox. I had ordered from this company before but had cancelled the monthly chocolate subscription about six months prior since it was just too expensive.

To my surprise another box appeared in the mail, two days before this ceremony. As soon as I saw it, I knew it was you at work and the chocolate was meant to be shared as part of the ceremony. When I called the company up to find out why it was sent, the customer service woman was baffled as to how another box was shipped to me. We arranged that I would only pay for the shipping, and not the full cost of the box.

Mother: Oh, that's right. I did arrange for that. I forget all the various forms of mischief I get into, too many to count.

But anyway, I know you get my point. The *Food of the Gods* can be every morsel of food you take in, every breath you breathe, every flower that graces your presence and more. It's the Quantum Divine Love that is sung from every tree, every seedling and frog, spider, hawk and more. This is the true existence and reality of the sacred life all over me and within me. The sacred consciousness of every stone, mountain, river and spring.

You are finally learning how to step out of the concrete box of fear your culture had placed you in, to deeply knowing this. I love you so much, sweetie. And so many of my other humans are getting this too. I love you all so, so much.

Mare: I truly feel as if I'm shedding an old, old skin with these shifts, Mother. These lessons from Paul. Bringing in a new kitty to allow her kitty-love into my life. Purr-love. Trusting you on levels I could not before or was not ready to.

But I have not yet taken on the new skin fully. I feel so vulnerable and soft, and need to hide in the house so much these days to feel safe. I am so energetically hammered when I leave the house. The Cardinal Grand Cross astrological configuration occurred last week and that was very intense—very. I needed to hide inside most of that week. Thank goodness for the monsoon rains of the past few days since that meant I didn't need to go out to garden. It allowed me to stay cloistered. It seems I'm going deeper and deeper into letting go of these patterns of fear as I cocoon in the house. I've been writing in my bed again too, the nest where I've been most of the winter and where I can best write with you.

This is very deep work, deeper than I've ever gone before. And yet, I'm still called to organize workshops and talks for you, with these messages you want me to bring out into the world.

I'm finally learning the wisdom of not forcing myself to fully emerge until I'm ready. To allow myself to sit in a place of deep vulnerable softness and gestate in a safe, nurturing environment as I work through the inner tremblings.

The metaphor of the snail allowing herself to stay withdrawn into her shell; this has been your message to me all winter, Mother. Be still, go inward, listen and write. It's now spring, the daffodils have flowered and the drying petals hang from their stems as we shift into May here in Maryland. Yet it's okay for me to still stay cloistered in this moment, to be with your grace, and my soft shedding of old patterns that don't serve me or you, in truth.

For a good part of the winter I've been spinning in my fears of needing income, needing to drum up workshops, worrying about this house that is foreclosed, waiting for the axe to fall when the bank wants to claim it.

Such fears. Oy.

But I'm learning I can embrace the soft seclusion. I can be still. Be in the moment completely. Listen to the kitty purr. Do a few emails or calls to set up some talks and workshops. Listen to you more clearly and release the old emotional baggage not serving me. I'm doing it, Mother.

I'm really doing it. An affirmation … a perfect gift, after the monsoons have come and gone here in Maryland.

Mother: Yes, sweetie, you are doing it. You are shedding the old to step into your courage. And trust. Ever more trust. I love you so much. More Divine Love than you can know.

My daughter, this is actually about learning to *love yourself.* Learning to love every sacred cell within your being, and your very soul. Your soul is so ancient and has been through so much, as has everyone's soul. You, Mare, were born into this earth-walk with so much sorrow from previous lifetimes, and the pain you experienced in your childhood with the family chaos circling around you did not help you learn to love yourself, nor did your classroom situations all those early years, nor the teasings from your brothers.

It is never too late to learn this inner love. The love you can have for yourself is a most sacred love too, as that also sources from Creator and myself. You can take a deep breath in now, in this very moment as you're listening to me, and allow your self-love to be fed by this sacred breath, the sacred atmosphere surrounding you. All love sources from the Sacred. You are most sacred too. And self-love that is healthy and balanced and motivates you to serve for the highest good is the most beautiful love, truly.

This self-love intertwines with courage, trust, and allows you to hold a still center of peace within you that no one else can give you. No one else. This is why you never need to suffer from abandonment issues again since you will never abandon yourself as you come to deeply love yourself. That love can never be taken away. As my Divine Love will never abandon you either.

Mare: It does come down to that, doesn't it, Mother? How much love I have for myself—this is such a journey. I'm taking this step-by-step as best as I can. I am.

Hmmm, if you can bear with me, Mother, I'm not trying to run away from how significant your teaching just was, but—I have a question. Late yesterday afternoon when I got up to get my bath ready, I noticed my new neighbor down the hill from me working in his tiny, shady back yard. This is the husband of a small family who moved in about five months ago just before winter shut us all in.

I've seen the man working in his yard for a few weeks now as I walk past that one window. His shady, postage-stamp back yard is rather steep (as is mine) with mature trees all around it. He's been trying so hard to remove the forest ground cover and have a generic lawn. Just now I watched him scratch up all the tiny woodland seedlings and understory plants that were growing on the more steep part of his lot. These are low growing 'weeds' that are essentially holding the soil down and doing their beautiful biodiversity thing. He removed all of plants and tossed all the small stones aside that would slow down the erosion also. Then he scattered grass seed on top of the loose bare soil. He's determined to have a monoculture lawn in the steepest, shadiest corner of his property.

We just had an incredibly solid downpour the past few days—I don't know how many inches but a month's worth of rain in three days. I pray we don't get any more heavy rains in the next few weeks because if we do, he's about to lose all that exposed soil and grass seed. I watched his hard efforts from last weekend get washed away two days ago.

Oh, Mother, I just shake my head and cringe at these types of activities that take place all over. He's been taught by society that his property needs to have a lawn. The more monoculture the better. Society has taught people to not worry about how many herbicides you put down to keep it a monoculture. There has never been widespread awareness of your inherent wisdom, of the brilliance of biodiversity and tuning into the land to consult the land itself on what would be best.

Mother: Yes, my love. Yes. This neighbor could use some good ecological lessons. He's going to be frustrated with his efforts to grow grass there. Maybe he will learn. Maybe he will not.

Do not worry about him though, and his tiny hilly backyard. Stay focused on this writing, your talks, workshops. The right people are waking up and things are shifting very fast. Do not worry. These old ways of ignoring my wisdom will soon pass and all will come to know how to respect and revere me. That is what is happening right now.

Be compassionate for this man and his lack of understanding as to how I work. Send some prayers he wakes up too. That is the best you can do, sweetie. All will work out.

You see, my love, I am so ancient. You know this already. From my perspective all will work out because as I mentioned before, I'm hard-wired to heal. Always. All of these wounds on me will be healed. They will take time, and I am a bit irritated, yes, at how many humans continue to harshly wound me. But things are shifting on me. Many of you are waking up. The wounding will stop. I will be sure of this. I will be very sure of this.

Really, the choice is up to each one of you, my beloved two-leggeds, as to whether you will wake up. I am yearning so for you to reconnect with me and the sacredness of all of Creation, including yourselves. And give your love to me again. I am here.

So many of you are doing this. I love you so much for this. So much. Step through the spiritual portals, and rediscover me. Go stand barefoot outside and spend time with me. Learn to listen to my song. Cultivate your beautiful personal songs. I'm here waiting. I have been all along.

I'm not going anywhere.

I love you!

36

....

A Message from Granny

*Always you can send love and healing energy
to the seas. The water needs your help.*

—Granny, the matriarch orca whale in the Salish Sea
(Washington State and British Columbia inland
waterways), as communicated by Mary J. Getten,
Communicating with Orcas; The Whales' Perspective

Tuesday, July 8, 2014
1:30 PM
High 80's and HUMID outside. Much cooler, not so humid inside. Summer!

Mare: Mother, it's summer and you know I'm back into my part-time gardening business and leading some workshops. And it feels as if there is more to be written in this book, yet I long for it to be done. But it's forecast for rain and thunderstorms today so I'm not gardening, and am so excited this morning!

I've just discovered a woman who is a whale communicator on the internet. Her name is Mary J. Getten and she has been communicating with an orca whale named Granny in the northern part of Puget Sound for years. I just called Mary up on the phone and we chatted for a bit and she's given me permission to post this excerpt from her book called *Communicating with Orcas: The Whales' Perspective*. This is a message from Granny directly:

(Some background on Granny – she is a J-pod orca matriarch thought to have been born in 1911, lives most of the year with her son Ruffles [J-1, age 59] and the rest of her descendants along with K and L pods of the Southern Resident Community in the protected waters of the Salish Sea.)[23]

---

[23]http://sacredceremonialsforthesalishsea.wordpress.com/granny/

Please inform all that whales have a spiritual nature. We have a highly developed awareness of the inner connectedness of all things, all beings, and all processes on the planet. Whales have stellar origins. We are a class of stars, planetary beings who have taken shape in the oceans for eons. Our purposes have been manifold. We have gathered untold richness in our physical experiences that have added greatly to the experience and knowledge of the Creator, of the Prime Cause, and have been vastly entertaining for us as well. Experience is the whole goal and purpose of being. This is all added to Prime Creator and it enlarges existence, experience, or All That Is.

Humans with their technology and tool making abilities have become lost in their creations. Whales believe that we are all children of Prime Cause and participate in its creation daily. We believe that we are all spirit essence, even humans, and that we take our bodies for the sake of physical experience and growth. Many things can only be experienced in physical form. Because we are now focused in the physical, we think highly of it and tend to forget other realities. We are all spiritual essence expressing ourselves in this particular plane at this time. When a master comes into a whale body it may be for a lifetime of play and joy. We don't believe in work. We are already enlightened.

Calls to the Great Ones for help are not being ignored. They are aware of our danger, and if enough people call, and consistently maintain this heart light or energy, we will draw their attention more strongly. This means dislocations and changes. Your economies and governments will undergo dramatic changes. I see their purpose shifting from primarily a nationalistic concern to a much greater and more global perspective.

You humans have lost your connection to the All, the Oneness of Life on this planet, and indeed in the whole galaxy. You have separated yourself from the rest of life, and become lost in greed and possessiveness. When you are in tune with Nature and in flow with the balance of life, greed and possessiveness do not occur. You have what is necessary for your survival. That is how we live. We take only what is necessary, and as a result, all energies work together in harmony.

Humans, as you have sensed, have slipped out of this balance. You hoard things for yourselves because you see the planet as not having enough for all. To end war, you humans must once again see your place in the balance of Nature. You must release the idea that there is not enough for everyone, that you must desperately hold onto your own share, that you are not connected to everyone and everything on the planet. Your idea of separateness is not real.

There is an opening, an energy, a light coming to the planet at this time that will allow you to make the transition. It's just that you must desire it! Awakening that desire is of prime importance. So, do what you can ... Anyone who hears my voice, in any way. Do what you can to open yourself and others to the possibility that all life can live in harmony. Awaken yourself and awaken those around you. Eventually it will spread, and a shift will occur...

We are aware of changes in energy and an increase in vibration on the planet. A shift in consciousness is required to save this planet. If you continue at the current rate, you will destroy everything within the ecosystem, everything that this planet requires to live. When the ecosystem goes, we all go.

The animal kingdom knows how to take care of our home, what it takes to keep things in balance. You humans do not understand this lesson yet. We welcome the change in energies as they will be shifting human consciousness. It is our salvation. If enough people make the shift, things can be turned around on this planet.

Know that you are totally connected to and mutually dependent on this planet. Love it. Protect it. Your existence depends on it. You are children of the beloved Earth, sky, wind and water. When you detach, you die. There is a wave of changing consciousness on the planet today. We have fostered it by sharing our presence with you. Now it is in your hands.[24]

Wow, Mother ... all I can say is *Wow*. This message from Granny, the orca whale, is so in line with all you've been saying, and perhaps even a little more, too.

Mother: Yes, my daughter. I guided you to find this message from Granny this morning and to contact Mary J. Getten. She is quite gifted and I love her so much for her work. So, so very much. Her book of conversations with Granny is significant and I wish all my two-leggeds would read it and take in that wisdom.

I love my whales. I love my dolphins. I love all my humans too. And yes, there are energies coming in and we've already been talking about these shifts from the Third to the Fourth to the Fifth Dimensions taking place now on me. The whales and dolphins are intimately aware of these shifts as sensitive and evolved as they are.

Yes, I wanted you to find this message from Granny this morning. This is closely related to what we were talking about when that water spirit

---

[24]Getten, Mary J. *Communicating with Orcas: The Whales' Perspective* (Newburyport, Massachusetts: Hampton Roads Publishing, 2006). Excerpt at: http://sacred ceremonialsforthesalishsea.wordpress.com/granny/

appeared in the glass of water that David Spangler was drinking from—you posted that message from him earlier this winter.

All of my two-leggeds, all of you can learn, need to learn to heal your hearts, to come back to my love and the love of Creation and send love and light out to the waters of the world. This gets back to the power of prayer again. It's so much more powerful than more people realize. Prayer and "love and light" are essentially the same thing, and when focused and coming from a pure heart, they send out such healing energies. The waters are my blood. They are your blood. Everything alive on me courses with beautiful water and the waters are sick. They need your prayers, your love and light, and the pollution needs to stop in a big way. The love and light can transmute the contamination too though. This message needs to be repeated. It is important and Granny knows it extremely well, along with all the other elders in the whale and dolphin communities.

I love you all so much. Do ceremony. Thank that glass of water you drink every day. Or sip from a water fountain. Find groups that do water ceremonies in your community. Some are posted on your internet. If no one is already doing them, step forward and form a local circle and come together. It is so powerful when people come together in prayer and ceremony. You have no idea the extent to which my blood has been sickened, and how this is the time for *love and light* to be spread more powerfully.

Okay, now scoot. You've got other deskwork to do and calls to make, events to organize and more. I love you. I love all my humans so, so much. Just please stop all the contamination. Please.

37

The Conversation Never Ends

Adults are obsolete children.

—Dr. Seuss

Friday, July 25, 2014
11:54 AM
73° In the shade of the high deck in the trees in this (foreclosed) "tree house" where I'm still living. A lovely cool, sunny July day in Maryland.

Mare: Mother, it's been a while since we've had a good, long chat. This book is still not finished but it's almost done. I've been listening to Patty Griffin's *Mary* song again today. It's playing in the background as I write this. I suppose you nudged me to listen to it this morning since I've cleared some other things off my list of to-do's this summer.

This song always helps me connect with you on such a deep spiritual level, Mother. For some reason though, I'm feeling such sadness today. I need to finish this book, do the final edits and get it off to my editor. He's been waiting patiently for it. I thought I'd have it for him in early July but now it's practically the end of the month. It's a good thing he's a patient sort.

Then there is the book designer who is waiting for the final edited manuscript. Plus the artist I've commissioned for the cover (per your solid nudging) who is painting a beautiful image of you holding a glowing earth with so much love in your eyes. It's such a powerful painting. I can't believe how you guided me to that artist early in May. She lives only fifteen minutes from me and is extremely gifted.

Mother, you know I don't have megabucks to do this and while the gardening business helps, I'm still burning through my meager savings for this artist, and book designer, not to mention upcoming book printing costs. But you keep on telling me to trust. Trust.

As for my sadness, I'm not exactly sure all the reasons I'm feeling this way. Patty Griffin's song is sorrowful, true. Yet it's more than that. I imagine a good part of it is from an email my closest brother sent me yesterday about how my mother has been excluding me from all the family emails for months now, and was I okay with this. I don't know exactly how long this has been happening. And on some levels I am okay with it.

My parents just celebrated their 59th wedding anniversary several days ago and I sent my father an email late that night to congratulate them. I generally don't email directly with Mom, after too much drama when she took offense with my first book, *If I gave you God's phone number*, in 2002.

Sigh.

Family.

Whenever an author writes anything memoir-related there is bound to be some family emotional fall-out. Just inevitable. I know there will be some with this book too. The good news is I'm stronger now than I was then, with the first book. And this book is not really about my birth mother nor my father, but you, Mother, with a capital 'M'.

Yet, this is my *mother* after all. Not *Great Mother*. Not *Earth Mother*. The mother who gave birth to me just a bit more than fifty-five years ago. We have never been that close. There's been typical mother-daughter stuff for just about all my life. I barely touched on our family dysfunction in that first book, yet she was so upset about what little I did reveal that she sent all the books she'd bought (a box of twenty books minus the ones she had already given away) back to me along with a note stating I was not allowed to sell any more copies. Ten thousand copies of it had already been printed and I was not about to follow her command. Besides I was already in my forties and beyond obeying my parents at that point in time.

We have not had much of a relationship since then. I'm so honest and direct and, well, still digging deeper into the trenches of forgiveness with her. This trench is not a shallow one. For so many years, I had such anger fomenting in me about her book response, not to mention my childhood wounds. It's no wonder I was so depressed for so long. All that anger was overwhelming and I stuffed it down into a black hole of melancholia in my wombspace.

We've been talking about my anger already, Mother. I'm beyond most of it now. I can see how wounded my mother was all her life, as we are all wounded in varying degrees. She was unhappy when she married my father. They promptly had seven children in nine years and my father was working six days of the week and committed to his tennis on Sundays. Plus he was not a very good communicator. I could go on and on about the fights, the chaos. But that's okay. I don't need to. She did the best she could considering all the pain within her.

For years now I've pondered whether or not my birth mother and I could ever have a close relationship but there has been so much emotional detritus there. In recent years once we got beyond the 'no speaking' phase, whenever she'd approach me at family events I'd give her a quick hug and we'd chat briefly but then I'd move away to another cluster of relatives. I suppose one could call these emotional safety mechanisms. With such a large family including lots of nieces and nephews, there is always another room of people to chat with. Honestly though, family functions are so draining for me.

I've not always been the perfect daughter and was hurtfully direct when I was younger because of my unhealed emotions. My Cherokee teacher worked on my heart chakra several times and I've been focusing on Ho'oponopono and forgiveness. I experience so much compassion within me now compared with only a few years ago.

Plus, the Cherokee teacher informed me I came into this earth-walk with a grudge toward mothers since so many of my mothers in past lives married me off to some god-awful husband. I was daughter chattel shifted to husband chattel and had no choice during those lifetimes. One gentrified husband caught me with a lover and had my left hand cut off. To this day, if I don't feel emotionally safe that wrist joint will start to tingle energetically.

My right ankle also tingles often because of a lifetime in which women were treated like cattle. From what one gifted medicine woman told me, within that particular society women were truly treated as possessions and 'bred' for the purposes of the men. Apparently, I was considered good breeding stock but kept on trying to run so I was shackled on the right ankle. I guess I was a good 'broodmare' but one that wanted her freedom. There's that *Mare* thing—how interesting … I've come to learn that the odd sensations around that ankle are an alarm system for me to not be shackled again, emotionally or physically.

I suppose my free-spirited nature has been an inherent part of my soul for many lifetimes. But women were not allowed to be free spirits for many, many centuries. I know I joined convents during certain lifetimes just to avoid being imprisoned in some castle with some domineering (or worse) man. When I listen to Gregorian Chanting, it just takes me to an ancient space in my soul-body.

But all those past lives have not helped me bond closely with my birth mother this time around.

While lying in bed last night thinking about my parents, I remembered my mother did not send me a birthday card this past June. She'd sent me one last year about how proud she and Dad are of me and how they never knew they'd give birth to such a 'strong' woman or something along those lines.

I don't know how 'strong' I am. In many respects, I'm still the wounded little daughter when it comes to them, I suppose. I'm still afraid of upsetting them (with this third book) and seeking their love and approval. Well, it's time for this cute little inner girl with strawberry blonde hair to grow up and let go of these fears.

My parents are my parents. I love them. And I can see their woundedness and the WASP-y cultural conditioning and Catholic conditioning coloring their lens on the world and their children. How could they not have these lenses?

I'm getting stronger, Mother. I'm taking so little personally and am just about ready to birth this book, your book, and not take anything personally in the response. I know there will be some beautiful responses and some rather hard ones too. It's to be expected. It was your idea to call it a *Bible*. I know there will be flack ... and I can take it.

But my birth family ... I'm feeling such sadness about how they will respond to this book, and how this will play out in the coming months and years. But I still need to move forward with this. You have taken me so far in this work.

Mother: My daughter, I love you so much. Just so much. And you've been surrendering to me even more and more deeply just in the past few weeks since you've returned from the Wisdom Gathering in Holland in June. You *are* getting stronger by leaps and bounds. You and I are working even more closely now than we were in the winter.

Love your family. And have no expectations. That is all you can do. You really don't know exactly how they will respond. Try not to create any stories. Encourage them to know this book is what you've been called to do spiritually. I'll guide you on what to say when the time has come to communicate. You already emailed your brother back about how you're not sure how the holidays will play out in terms of the release of this book. You told him it's a 'doozy' of a book. It is. It needs to be a 'doozy' of a book. Your culture needs some waking up. Things have gotten so off-track here on me for the past few thousand years. It is time for some huge shifts.

Mare: Mother, okay, I just took a quick break to check on emails and Facebook and this quote surfaced.

> *Inner peace comes the moment you choose not to allow another person or event to control your emotions.*
> —Anonymous

I needed this, in this very moment. Facebook can be so helpful at times with just the right quote at the right time for a wisdom jolt. This is surely another reminder of how I need to shed my *little victim girl* stance and put on my big-girl pants, and not worry about my parents or anyone else in my family or my family's social set, or anyone else out in the world and their response to this *Bible* of yours, Mother.

And it's quite evident our world, our dominant world culture, does need some big shifts. You've been telling me this. I've been working in the environmental arena for more than thirty years and known it. Things are really feeling as if they are at a cracking point here on Earth right now, from my very tiny angle on everything. I know you're even cracking in more and more areas as earthquakes are becoming more prevalent these days. It's rather scary to track them. For a while I was trying to track them on the internet and then decided to just stop focusing on them. It was too overwhelming. Not to mention your volcanoes too. It seems there is such pressure mounting within you, Mother. Plus the storms that are getting more violent.

Oy, there is such pressure mounting in me to get this book done too. I feel like I'm ten months pregnant and royally need to give birth. Or get a cesarean. I can feel you sitting on me a bit too, Mother. And you're not so very small energetically. My procrastination techniques are not going to work any more—nor should they, I suppose.

Marion Woodman wrote the book: *Leaving My Father's House: A Journey to Conscious Femininity.* It has sat unread on my shelf for years. I just reflect on the title and feel its good wisdom. Maybe some day I'll pick it up. Or not.

No longer am I the Catholic good girl, no longer the dutiful daughter motivated by guilt and fear. I'm motivated by your Divine Love, Mother, unfettered by any religious cords. This love is only growing in my life.

Thank you, thank you!

This book needs to be finished and get out there. And I can shed those insecurities about whether I'll be *loved* for the book or not. This is so not about me and my puny fears. It's about you, and the Great Mother. And the Great Father. And the New World coming in.

Mother: Yes, my Love. I know this book is calling for great courage within you to finish and self-publish. I am helping you, guiding you, supporting you in every step of the way. You know I am. Along with your spirit guides and friends. So many are supporting you. So many love you. More than you even know.

Mare: Thank you, Mother. Thank you to all of my friends seen and unseen.

There is something else too. I stopped by a friend's house on the way out to the mountains yesterday to go take a break from the writing. This is a man I like and I'm determined to get beyond the fears that surfaced within me when Paul was in my life in the winter. This is such intense work. All of these fears. Yet, I'm feeling them shed like old clothes that don't fit anymore.

Paul and I are actually having dinner tonight for the first time since April and I feel like a different person than the woman who sat across the restaurant table from him then. A more confident, calm, trusting woman. Not the timid, terrified little girl.

Mother: Yes, my love, it has been hard for you to trust. But again, all you have is the moment. And you are learning to trust yourself. That is the most important thing. In this moment, you are safe. In the next moment you are safe. This is a good man. And if this man you visited yesterday is meant to be more than a platonic friend, take it very slowly. You can pull back way into your shell for the time being while you're finishing this book. Put this new man in your God/Goddess Jar. You do still have that, right?

Mare: Yes, I do have it. I've not been using it so much the past few months. That's a good idea, to start using it again.

Mother, it was interesting and I'm certain you had set this up too. This friend knows the region here well and he had drawn up a map to one of the hidden ponds in the mountains that's good for swimming. I thought that was kind of him, but not so necessary, assuming he'd take me there sometime instead and that's how I'd learn where it is.

When I left his house, I was guided to search out the pond, though that wasn't where I was going to go initially. Your nudging, I'm certain. It was a really lovely pond, so serene, and a whole flotilla of fat tadpoles, with their legs already emerging, were basking along the edge of it. I scared a few back into the pond as I approached. A big rock on the edge invited me to sit, so I did. And then I lit up my smudge to do ceremony and bless the space.

A young couple, college students, arrived at the pond shortly after I started the smudge. At first they gave me space. Finally the young man came over and was sincerely respectful and intrigued about what I was doing. So I talked about smudging and ceremony, and offering blessings and gratitude with tobacco. Or with a cookie or granola bar, whatever one has. Or just with your heart. Just giving love back to you, Mother, or to the sacred water there in the pond. The sacred water all over the world. It's all connected anyway.

Then I offered to smudge them. The young man was more interested than his girlfriend. This was his wild neighborhood and he had been to the pond and all the other ones hidden in the mountain all his life. A real nature boy. And I was offering him a new, sacred experience in his beloved forests. He was transformed by the smudge and felt quite shifted once I finished moving the smoke and offering prayers around him. He remarked on how peaceful it was, and how calming. He was especially open to learning more and recorded my name in his smartphone but then they needed to go.

Mother: Yes, my love. That young man is hungry for this wisdom. He, along with many others, are the people who will read this book and feel the love behind it and take in the spiritual goodness, my Mother's love. These are the types of people who are helping to birth the New World coming in, along with you. They are feeling the call from deep within their soul. More and more of them will be attracted to you and your workshops, your writings and more. You along with many others have been gearing up for this for a long time and I need all of you waking up to spread these messages, this divine love from me and Creation. Along with sowing the seeds for this New World.

Mare: The young man said they hadn't planned to stop along the road to hike to the pond. They were headed to another part of the mountain. But something compelled him to pull over and come to the pond. It was as if they were called to come and meet me. All his life, he's hiked those trails and swam in the ponds. But he's never thought about offering blessings or gratitude back to the mountains or the nature spirits, or the pond, or you.

Until he met me.

I guess I needed that reinforcement, Mother, meeting those two college students and witnessing how open they were to what I shared with them. It's not about the social set I grew up with or those who still attend Catholic Church. It's about all the other people who feel the *system* cracking and are searching for wiser ways. Not that I have all the answers. But you've certainly got my ear and I can speak for you.

Something else, Mother … when I got out of the car to find the pond, a butterfly flitted on the surface of the road in front of me. It did not fly away at all as I got closer. In Holland in June, at the end of a most magical workshop I led outside called "Connecting with Earth Mother Soulfully", a butterfly spent the final twenty minutes of the workshop with us. The workshop was supposed to end at 4 PM but no one wanted to leave and we finally broke up at 7:30 PM. It was remarkable. The butterfly fluttered in and landed on my papers, and then sat on the table by the one empty chair and then back to me. And then to another person's pad. It was with us for a long time. I could almost imagine it clearing its throat and asking us to take some notes about what it wanted to share. Clearly it was one of your messengers thanking us for all the beautiful ceremony and love we put out during that full workshop, for there was so much joy that day.

Butterflies represent metamorphosis. When I first moved into this house, this lovely foreclosed house that I have yet to be evicted from—miraculously, I bought a nicely painted metal butterfly about two feet across for $3.95 at some store (from China, I'm sure) and hung it on the front of the house. I knew in coming here, and grappling with the lymphoma, that I needed to grow out of some old ways that no longer served me. What they were exactly I did not know. Only that I needed to shed them. I needed to heal and to write. This house has been an extensive cocoon for me.

At the pond this afternoon, after observing the butterfly on the road, I watched a snake gracefully swim across the surface of the pond. Snake medicine, again. So many times I've been visited by a snake in times of change. Ah—definitely about shedding old skin to bring in new growth. A new skin. A new birth. This is what our world is going through too, isn't it?

Mother, even the skin on my hands has been majorly peeling. This happens to me when I'm going through changes "snake-like" but never at this level of peeling skin on the inside of my fingers and the palms. Something is definitely going on.

Mother: Yes, my daughter, you are ready for these changes finally. You've actually been going through them for some time now—for the past few years. But you're ready to finally release a heavy layer of your old fears completely to step into whom you truly are. You're inviting in the deeper Sacred Feminine energies that have been waiting to be birthed within your very core, to step into those beautiful authentic powers of yours. This is encouraging you to relinquish so much of your past-life related angst about victimhood, being safe, trusting men, and more.

I'm so proud of you, my daughter, for moving into this new level of surrender to me. I need you to shed some of your deeper woundedness as the time approaches for this book to be fully birthed. You are being birthed again too, as a true daughter of mine who can speak for me and help others feel my powerful love for them. You are one of many of my daughters stepping into your true work. I need all of you. And my sons too. All of you.

Oh, we are only just starting. Just starting.

Mare: Mother, also, I've met a woman who has purchased thirty acres and her vision of a retreat center is almost parallel to mine. And she wants me to live in an apartment on the land to help her launch this new retreat center! This has all just manifested in the past two weeks. I'm blown away by all of this. There really is life beyond this foreclosed house for me. Thank you, Mother!

Mother: I love you, sweetie. I am taking care of you. There is a New World being birthed now and I'm taking care of all of you. I love all of you!

38

And Never Ends ... But That's
Okay, Too!

Surrender is one of our greatest teachers.
She is merciless, yet deeply compassionate.
Knowing that when we finally do let go completely,
our false alienation with the unknown will melt into
the profound recognition that we have come home...

—Saida Desilets, www.thesucculencerevolution.com

Saturday, July 26, 2014
Woke up 5:30 AM, Writing at 8:32 AM
71° Slightly overcast. Going to be another lovely, cooler July day in Maryland.

Mare: Mother, just when I think this manuscript is finished and I can start editing it, there is more. Part of me fears I'll never finish writing this. But I know you'll not let that happen. You'd like this book out like ten years ago. I know.

Mother: Yes, Love, it would have been nice to have had a book like this out a long time ago. But that's okay. This is the perfect time for it. All in Divine Timing as some of you humans say. And today's conversation will be the last entry for this book, I promise you. But you and I shall continue chatting indefinitely. Our conversations are only getting deeper and richer. You will find ways to share these chats and learnings in so many creative ways. It will all be good. Very good. Well, more than good. Let's just say *needed*.

Mare: Certainly needed, yes.

Mother, I had some huge revelations this morning. It's related to *Leaving My Father's House* and stepping into my big girl shoes once and for all. When I woke up this morning I had so much tension in the back of my neck. This is not a new thing as this is where I hold my fears, my trust issues, and it's mostly associated with clenching my yoni. A gifted cranial-sacral therapist helped me make that connection years ago. My sacred yoni that has not gotten much attention all this lifetime since I've lived with such fears of men and intimacy.

It's as if that chakra of mine has been completely shut, clamped, and practically rusted close, especially in the past ten years. This is why I got the lymphoma, part of the reason at least—along with poisoning myself with Roundup at a client's garden several years ago. It was a very regretted, mindless day when I repeatedly wiped some of the herbicide on the soft skin of my underarm while treating some tough weeds using rubber gloves that didn't extend high enough up the arm.

Mother, you know I've been so shut down, so terrified, in my most sacred center. I couldn't let much love, if any, in there. It's been a deep dark cavern, barren but for fear. I know this is mostly past-life terror of abusive men, and torture and more. This fear has been so huge, it's prevented me from stepping into my power, my full voice as a writer and speaker, my capacity to open up and trust a man, trust myself, and more. Trust. I have not trusted that I'm safe to do all of those things because some ancient part of me has feared I'll be caught again (as happened many times in past-lives) and be silenced, be raped, or hung. My life ended because of my voice, my strength, and my gifts in past lives. At times, it was also my poor judgment in certain lifetimes in knowing when and where to speak or show up. Or not show up.

Honestly all this fear is why I'd rather be gardening. I'd rather be hanging out with the flowers and the bees, and the weeds since they can't harm me, yell at me, send me nasty letters or whatever. The Roundup chemicals harmed me. I know this as I felt sick for several days after using them that one day. But growing flowers and vegetables organically can only heal a person.

But I also refuse to live with this level of fear anymore. It's what kicks up the lymphoma again and again. Just as I'm writing about it, I'm feeling my wombspace tighten up again.

Within the past two weeks I've been feeling a shift, another layer of surrender to you, Mother, surfacing. I've been visualizing allowing you and all of your sacredness to come up into my yoni, my sacred portal to womanhood, all the way through my uterus, my womb, and out into my ovaries. In my mind, I envision all of my feminine organs within the lower three chakras as a Sacred Fleur de Lis—a most divine center, and inviting your energies, Mother, into me as the most healing Sacred Feminine presence. This has been gradual over the past two weeks. It's such a warm and safe and loving opening, and so much more. So much more.

It's as if I'm waking up with my senses and awarenesses even more. Maybe I'm finally spiritually waking up. Though I don't think it's ever a final destination point. It's all part of a deeper journey that never ends even when we pass over. Yet my sense of smell is so much more heightened. I'm starting to notice the squirrels' aromatic little abode up in the tight attic space more and this is rather an interesting—and not overly pleasant—thing since I'm not about to go up there and chase them out.

My capacity to tune in to the plants and stones and hear them talk, sense their emotions and wisdom is getting clearer too.

All my life, I've lived so much in my head. In the past few years I have started to learn how to live in my heart and my head. And now I'm realizing I need to drop my energy down to my womb-heart and open that up through allowing you, Mother, into me from the very core of my being. I'm feeling your energy coming in and it's so healing. All the lymph nodes that have been shrinking and swelling and shrinking and swelling are getting infused with your Goddess energy more and more, and they are calming down.

I self-pleasured this morning and whole new levels of energy are starting to open up in me. They scared me though, too.

Mother: Yes, my love. You're not used to this and you're afraid of your passion and all that lies there. So many lifetimes you experienced violent passion from men. You kept that portal within you shut all your life because of these memories and other reasons you've become more aware of. But it's okay. You can take this slowly and know that I'm here with you and you're safe. You are safe each and every moment as you stay *in* the moment. All you have is this very moment. And this very moment is about Love and Trust.

That's all it has ever really been about, but you humans have been swept down the "fear and lack" path for so long, you've forgotten. When you stay in the moment, and ground yourself into me and my love, and the Great Mystery's love, you will never abandon yourself. We will never abandon you. Never. You can always sink your love, your fears, your hard emotions down into me, and ask me to come up into you. This is for men and women. I will always be there for you. I have already always been there for you. The same with Creation, the Great Father, Great Mother, God, Allah, Source, universal consciousness—choose your term.

The Abrahamic religions of Christianity, Judaism and the Islamic faith have kept women's sacred womb-space and spiritual connection to me from their root chakra shut down for so many centuries. It's part and parcel with the aggressive, patriarchal dominance. You already knew this on some level but you did not realize just how shut down you've become from the conditioning and past-life trauma.

There is a nectar of sacred life force that all women can secrete within their yoni. This nectar is connected directly with me and *my* nectar, my love force. All the flowers and their nectar, their pollen, their uninhibited joy and colors and dancing in the wind. All the beautiful pristine springs that gush forth or seep from me. All of my daughters, my human daughters, could be letting their nectar flow too. It comes from what you call the G-spot area and when that starts to flow in sacred balance with a masculine presence, it is healing on so many levels. This level of love-making emanates a healing resonance that flows out from both of you.

This is not to imply that it has to be a man and a woman together. It can also be two women who balance their energies in a masculine – feminine way. Or even two men in their own way, yet the nectar is not secreted with them. And that's fine too. It's the balance and the dancing between those sacred energies that comes from love and a passion that is divinely infused. All of you have the potential to discover that. Regardless of who you love. It's how you love. Yet the nectar has been shut down in so many women for centuries—not all but many.

The repressed energies within you block this nectar flow. The blockage sources from conditioning from the patriarchal religions since these religions are afraid of women who are truly connected with me and my nectar, my life-force. For centuries and centuries, your religious leaders, in collaboration with your political and business leaders, have been determined to try to control all aspects of me, your beautiful planet. But it is impossible for humans to control me because humans don't have those powers. Yet, some have not given up trying. Part of their strategy, in thanks to the alien ones influencing them, has been to control the women in a variety of creative and sad ways. I don't need to list any of them. Your media covers them often.

There are so many people waking up and learning to embrace the Sacred Feminine—both men and women. Many men are learning to touch their vulnerable sensitive sides and be authentic about this aspect of themselves. Many are even learning to cry. So many of my beloved humans are healing and growing. Not to mention all the organic farms people are starting. Beautiful alternative medicine based on herbs and the energy systems of the body are being offered. More and more... You all

give me so much hope. So much joy in my heart as I witness this. Truthful-
ly, I'm nudging all of you onward. I say *yes* to the healing of you and your
wounded ways, your wounded spirits, *yes* to the economic alternatives that
support not only good business but healing my ecosystems. *Yes, yes… Yes,*
to your reconnecting with me and discovering all the love I have for you.
I love you all so much. I want you to *come* home to me in your hearts and
souls. I am your planet. I love you.

My daughter, it is time for me to pass this back to the Great Mother.
This conversation needs to return to her. You and I have been talking
for months and months quite closely, and we certainly will continue to
chat together for a long, long time. The Great Mother has been speaking
through me some of the time and other times it was myself as your Plan-
etary Caretaker voicing what needed to be said. I will pull back now.

Great Mother: Yes, my Earth Daughter, I have been listening and watching and communicating through Earth Mother and other spiritual beings
to guide you in this writing. I've been with you throughout your entire life.
The love the Great Father and I have for you is light-years wide and deep.
You and others who are surrendering on the levels you are to bring forth
the healing energies, the positive energies onto Earth Mother—you are
such beautiful, amazing humans on Earth right now.

Most of you have known on some level all your lives you were called
to be here at this time. This is a dynamic time on Earth Mother. Many
of you have been walking through your challenges, your *dark nights of the*
soul, as you call them to wake up and surrender even more. You needed
to go through those dark times to learn. To find your inner strength and
cultivate your connection with the Great Mystery and trust that light that
seemed so dim and far off in the distance at times—would find you.

Honor your fears and continue to walk through them. Find the pearls
of wisdom embedded in them. Keep on seeking the balance. Earth Mother has already shared so much wisdom here from me. I love her so much
as your Planetary Caretaker. She is a very wise, ancient being and a bit of
a character too. That is true.

Mare, you were guided to go visit that sacred Catholic grotto devoted to the Virgin Mary in Emmitsburg, Maryland, in May. That was me
guiding you. I needed you to experience that grotto and the sacred waters
there. Do you remember how you felt as you were filling your big glass jug
at the shrine?

Mare: Oh, yes, how could I forget? It was an overwhelming wave of healing, compassionate energy that washed through me as I started to fill that jug up. I had to sit down on one of the benches to the side of the outdoor sink area to ground myself. I stayed there for some time and prayed and looked up at the statue of the Virgin Mary in the middle of the pond next to the sink area—the statue is a replica of the one in Lourdes.

I was stunned at the energy I felt from that water. This was after walking up the paved trail that loops around the whole area and looking at the various Stations of the Cross, and getting a little triggered by all the references to sinning and guilt. It's hard to get away from that while visiting a Catholic shrine.

I've been using that sacred water from the grotto in water ceremonies, mixed with sacred waters from around the world that some friends have given me. It's been such a joy to do this, and I can feel the energy shift in the places where I've been doing the ceremonies. Earth Mother needs this so much, along with all of her beleaguered nature spirits, not to mention the fish and all the other creatures who are sick and dying from the contamination in our global waters.

Great Mother: I guided you there just as you were guided to wear that Miraculous Medal your father sent you in the winter and you felt that healing energy shift as soon as you put the Medal around your neck. My Earth Daughter, you are actually surrendering to me and carrying my energy within you with your spiritual work and writing. This is why you have Kuan Yin in that altar in your living room. Earth Mother is only one consciousness deeply connected with me whom you're working with.

My divine energies weave through all of these embodiments of me from different cultures and belief systems. From Kali to Kuan Yin to Osun from the Orisha traditions, Virgin Mary, Our Lady of Guadalupé and more, they all source from me and from my great love and spiritual energies. All of your human belief systems have evolved in different regions of the world with different names for me and sometimes slightly different energetic aspects of who I am, and that is how it is meant to be, just as there are different names for God all over the world.

There is so much more to me beyond your human comprehension as I shared when we were starting this writing earlier in the winter.

Mare, there is such joy ahead for you, for so many of you who seek to connect back with me, as your Great Mother, and with Earth Mother. Rediscover your sacred planet again. Earth Mother is waiting for you all to remember. I am waiting along with the Great Father. We are waiting.

It is time for all of you to slough off those ways that have not been serving Earth Mother and the highest good to reconnect with our Love.

It's time for all of you humans to help heal your beloved Earth Mother and cease the destruction. It's also time for you to remember who you are as spiritual beings on Earth to experience your physicality on a temporary basis so your soul can grow in deeper resonance with the Creation. Please work to embrace the Christ Consciousness and remove the thorns from your hearts and find compassion and peace within, to bring those to all that is around you. Ground that compassion and peace deep into Earth Mother too. It feeds her too. Learn how to embrace your shadow and *Walk in Beauty*. You live on such an exceptional and beautiful planet. Honor yourselves and her, Earth Mother. You are such blessed, blessed ones to be living on her.

Know that our *Quantum Divine Love* is always here for you to tap into. Always. We love you.

ACKNOWLEDGEMENTS

To create a book such as this is never a solitary venture. Numerous beautiful people supported me through the writing and spiritual listening behind this book.

My dear friend Kunga Nima has been a tremendous confidante along with editor and spiritual guide. Paul has continued to be there as a good friend with a compassionate ear and kind companion for dinner when I sorely needed a break from the writing isolation.

I owe the deepest gratitude to Rainbow Thunder Heart/Bavado for his spiritual wisdom and great friendship. Thank you to Woody Vaspra and Catie Johnson of the World Council of Elders for their support and kindness. Also deep gratitude to Danny Vader, Robin Youngblood and the other members of the World Council for Wisdom Gatherings: Christien Anamaet, Steve Brahmajaran, Bert Gunn, and Shahrzad Awyan for the inspiration and so much more.

To my dear friends, Marcia Wiley, Margaret Pennock, Andrea Mc-Cluskey, Diane Davis, and Beth Duncan for the reminder that I could always reach out to you for a comforting call, warm hug and smile, and maybe even some good dark chocolate to share. (And thank you, Beth, for the editing kindness.)

To my parents and siblings for understanding and supporting the different life path that I've followed in pursuit of healing and spiritual wisdom.

To Suzanne and Rorie for taking me in during the very last stage of book production so I could continue to live off a shoestring to get this book completed. (And also huge gratitude for hosting the first Great Mother Wisdom Gathering!)

And deepest gratitude also to: Ben Madrid; Margreet Sanders; Iva Peele; Alison Carter; Ken Jaques; Hillary Banachowski; Dan and Barb Shulla; John M; Mary J. Getten; Granny; Nanjemoy; "Road to the Sky"; "Arms of the Mother"; Smoky Zeidel; Phila Hoopes; Jenn Wilhelm; and Nigel and Lori and their beautiful gardens.

The book cover could never have happened had I not discovered the very gifted artist, Brenda Murphy. I'm indebted to her and her artistic skills for creating an image of *Mother* that just takes my breath away.

Also deep thanks to Remy Benoit as a gifted editor. And to Cory and Sue at Octavo Designs for the focused and quality design work.

I'd also like to express my gratitude to the unnamed healers who have helped me along the way with ceremony and more. You have helped me find my way with love, kindness, good spiritual energy and so much more. I'm humbled and blessed by your gifts.

To M. Marley—I love you and miss you. You will always be in my heart. Along with Mother Nature, the four-legged tabby who graced my life for so many years now buried in Bird Hill Park, Ann Arbor (thank you, Laura Ziemer, for being there that day).

To all the unseen ones, especially Earth Mother, the Great Mother, Virgin Mary, Great Father, and the Great Sacred Oneness—my very deepest love and gratitude.

INDEX

A
Akashic Records, 68
Alaska, 21-22, 181
Albright, Madeleine, 81
Alice in Wonderland, 223
aliens on earth, 63, 73-79, 82, 147,
    190, 213
All Our Relations, 52, 53, 56, 72,
    117, 247
Allen, Dale, 13
altar, 8, 16, 24, 39, 84, 112, 182,
    184, 235-236, 284
Aluna, 190
Algonquin, 16-17, 29, 54-55, 175
anaphylactic shock, 226
Andrews, Ted, 202
Animal Speak, 202, 205, 216
animal spirit medicine, 201-208,
    216
Anthony, Lawrence, 206-207
Aphrodite, 29
Apology to Men, 157-160, 140-147
Arian beliefs, 185
Atlanta, 128

B
Baha, 'Abdu'l, 89
BBC, 191
Beauty Path, 121-128
bees, 109, 224-229, 231, 280
Bible, 25-26, 74, 82, 85, 185, 188,
    223, 240
Bird Medicine, 202
Blake, William, 149
blood, Earth Mother's, 34, 68,
    76-77, 184, 195, 219, 221-222,
    268

Book of Love, 187
Bradley, Marion Zimmer, 173
Brown, Dan, 185
bones, Earth Mother's, 9, 37, 64,
    68, 76, 134, 137, 165, 183-184,
    218-220, 222
Borg, Marcus, 85
brownies, 67
Buddhist, 24, 56, 145, 174
Burney, Robert, 81
Burns, Robert, 107

C
cancer, 17-18, 20, 38, 39, 91, 155,
    175, 195, 219, 254
Capitalism, 61, 217
Carroll, Lewis, 223
Carter, Jimmy, 100, 102
Catholic Church, 95-104, 186, 190,
    233-235, 276
Cathars, 186-188
Cathar Creed, 186
Cayuga, 83
cats, 17, 54, 252
chakra, 35, 36, 43, 49, 81, 84, 126,
    140, 147, 192, 210, 216, 271,
    280-282
Cherokee, 16-17, 22-24, 43, 54,
    55, 76, 85, 127, 175, 176, 196,
    202, 204, 210, 271
Chief, Dave, 51
Chi Gong, 17
Chomolungma, 67
Christ Consciousness, 23, 81-87,
    102, 129-130, 147, 192, 212-
    214, 215-216, 235, 242-243,
    246-247

Christ on Cross, 212-213
Christianity, 25, 30, 99, 102, 282
circles, 47, 51-57, 97, 125, 159,
160, 171, 184, 195, 206, 221,
268
clairaudience, 206
Climate Chaos, 71, 200
compassion, 7, 9, 24, 27, 29, 30,
41, 54, 56, 62, 63, 72, 76, 78,
84-85, 86, 90, 102, 103, 104,
119, 123-125, 130, 145, 159,
163-164, 170-171, 176, 184,
190, 196, 207, 210-212, 213,
215-216, 237, 240, 256, 263,
271, 279, 284, 285
Constitution, United States of
America, 83
Constitution of the Iroquois
Confederacy, 83
Creator, 7-8, 17, 23-24, 26-27,
33-35, 37-38, 53-54, 57, 63-64,
82-84, 90, 92, 100, 112, 116,
130, 146, 154, 182, 184, 187,
190, 195, 197, 211-212, 214,
222, 247, 259, 262, 266
see also Great Mystery; Great
Father
Creatrix, 23-24, 27
Creature Teacher, 205
cultural conditioning, 29, 52, 59-
65, 160, 272

D
Dalai Lama, 55-56, 84, 125, 176
DaVinci Code, The, 185
Desilets, Saida, 279
Diana, 29
Dimensions: 3RD, 4TH, 5TH,
239-243, 256, 267
Divine Balance, 24, 26-27, 29, 31,
36, 56-57, 63, 69-72, 76-78,

82, 86, 96, 98-99, 103, 111,
134, 136-137, 139, 141, 145,
147, 151, 159, 161-166, 171,
184, 214, 219, 235, 241, 262,
166-267, 282-283
Divine Love, 21, 24, 30, 33-38, 53,
60, 70, 86-87, 100, 113, 146,
149, 151, 178, 187, 190, 195,
197, 222, 227, 243, 247, 256-
257, 259-262, 273, 275, 285
Divine Masculine, 29, 96, 98-99,
139-147, 157-160, 162-169,
172
Divine Mother, 25-32, 99, 115,
122, 245
see also Great Mother
dolphins, 7-8, 18, 19, 38, 42, 109,
134, 135, 151, 190, 194, 243,
247, 267
dragons, 68 -69
dwarves, 67
Dyer, Dr. Wayne, 153

E
eagle medicine, 205
Earth Mother, 7, 15-21, 22, 24,
27-29, 31, 33-38, 42-43, 49,
53, 55-57, 62, 68, 99, 112,
117, 122, 127, 131, 134, 140,
163-165, 169, 183, 190, 195,
201-208, 227-231, 235, 242,
245-247, 249-250, 270, 276,
283-285
economic downturn, 61, 219, 239,
241-242
ecosystems, 31, 53, 68, 87, 112,
131, 135, 190, 218-220, 229,
241, 267, 283
Elephant Whisperer, The, 206-207
endodemetriosis, 175
energy, 7, 9, 17, 20, 22, 24, 27-30,

33-38, 42, 46, 48-49, 52-53,
55-56, 62-68, 72, 75, 78, 80-
87, 90, 92, 98, 99, 101, 104,
110-112, 115-118, 122, 126-
127, 129, 134, 140, 145-147,
150-151, 154, 165-166, 171,
174, 175, 177-178, 183, 185,
187, 189-197, 199, 203, 207,
212, 216, 217, 230, 235, 242-
243, 247, 249, 254, 256-257,
265-267, 281-284
engineers, 73, 136, 222
entropy, 37, 91, 133-137, 217, 220
EpiPen, 226, 231
Estes, Clarissa Pinkola, 175
extinction, 79, 194, 199-200
extra-terrestrials, 63, 75
  see also aliens

F
Facebook, 65, 67, 73, 82, 100, 102,
  109, 154-155, 178-179, 183,
  190-192, 249, 254, 273
fairy folk, 66-67, 69, 80
fairy tale, 67, 69
Fatima, 31
fear, 7, 18, 21, 46, 48, 59-65, 69,
  82, 84, 86, 100-101,110, 127-
  128, 130, 139, 140, 142, 145,
  150, 161-162, 168, 169, 170,
  173-174, 178, 183-186, 193-
  196, 203, 210, 216-217, 218,
  223, 235, 236, 239-240, 242,
  250, 253-261, 272-274, 277,
  280-281, 283
fibroids, 175
Findhorn Foundation, 67
flagellation, 211
forgiveness, 27, 49, 72, 74, 80, 90,
  97, 118, 127, 145-146, 270,
  271
fracking, 137, 176, 183

France, 74, 78, 186, 188
free will, 37, 76, 124, 184
frogs, 37, 220
Fukushima, 135-136, 194
Fundamentalist Christians, 85, 128,
  130

G
gallbladder, 20, 55, 90, 98
gardening, 16, 21, 181, 197, 202,
  245, 251, 252, 253, 265, 270,
  280
generosity, 118, 125
Gibran, Khalil, 45
gnomes, 67
Godspace, 23, 82
Goodbye Girl, The, 199
gorillas, 190
Grandmothers Circle the Earth,
  206
gratitude, 7, 34, 67, 115-119, 122,
  146-147, 166, 212, 215, 247,
  250, 275, 276
greed, 35, 31, 62, 84, 100, 104,
  187, 222, 266
Grand Canyon, 21, 43
Great Change, 48, 86, 103, 183,
  239
Great Father, 21, 24-25, 26, 27, 29,
  33, 86, 99, 112, 124, 127, 146,
  185, 212, 221, 227, 235, 237,
  242, 243, 255, 274, 281, 283,
  284
Great Mystery, 23-24, 27, 33-34,
  36, 56, 68, 76, 82-83, 86, 100,
  123-124, 142, 154, 155, 206,
  243, 281, 283
Grail descendants, 185
Griffin, Patty, 39, 108, 109, 121,
  122, 270
groundhog, 209, 215, 245

guilt, 82, 98, 124, 130, 168, 170, 175,
    193-195, 240, 257, 273, 284

H
hara, 175
Haudenosaunee, 241
Hawai'ian elders, 63-64, 146
*Heart of the World: Elder Brothers
    Warning*, 191
Heaven, 63, 111, 193, 216, 226, 234
Hell, 82, 193
herbicides, 176, 263
hierarchical thinking, 52, 63
Highbear, Martin, 255
Hodgsen, Boysen, 167-169
Hogan, Linda, 201
Ho'oponopono, 146, 271
Huebner, Connie, 25
hummingbirds, 184, 203
hysterectomies, 175

I
indigenous peoples, 19, 29, 70,
    74-75, 116-117, 136, 137, 164,
    195, 241, 246
If I gave you God's phone number, 16,
    21, 128, 149, 270
Inquisition 74, 96
Iroquois Nation, 83, 241

J
Jensen, Derrick, 133
Jesus Christ, 54, 82-83, 96, 130,
    185, 187
Judeo-Christian, 23, 78, 185, 188

K
Kali, 30, 173-178, 235, 284
Kali-Yuga, 240
Khan, Hazrat Inayat, 245
Kogi, 191

Krishna, 84
Kuan Yin, 24, 173-178, 235, 246

L
Lakota, 23, 51, 52, 84, 112, 182
Lanquedoc, 186
lightworkers, 78
linear thinking, 164
loneliness, 147, 250, 259
Lorian Association, 68
Lourdes, 31, 284
Love Cord Connection, 140, 216
lymph nodes, 17, 20, 175, 281
lymphoma, 17-19, 31, 42, 49, 90,
    96, 98, 104, 162, 175-177, 182,
    236, 254, 256-258, 276, 280

M
Macy, Joanna, 239
Mad Hatter, 223-231
magic, 38, 42, 109, 112, 116, 124,
    130, 153-155, 229, 236, 242,
    253, 256, 260, 276
ManKind Project, 167
Maraboli, Steve, 215
Mary Magdalene, 185-188
McErlane, Sharon, 249
medicine (spiritual), 15-18, 22, 29,
    54, 70-71, 77-78, 90, 96, 99,
    112, 142, 175, 184, 194, 202-
    208, 214, 216, 253, 255, 260,
    271, 276
Medicine Cards, 202
Medjugorje, 31, 33, 99, 233, 245-
    247
membrane, 37
Messages from Mother.... Earth Mother,
    15, 19, 21, 26, 42, 62, 96, 181,
    187, 191
Miraculous Medal, 233-238, 245, 284
miracle mindedness, 31, 39-44, 99

Mitakuye Oyasin, 52-53
Mitchell, Edgar D., 73
Mohammed, 84
Mohawk, 16, 83
monkey-mind, 70, 126-127, 140, 197
Monopoly, 61, 64
mountaintop removal, 176
Mowat, Farley, 22

N
Natural Step Framework, 220-221
nature spirits, 66-68, 69-72, 74,75, 77, 80, 99, 117, 125, 164, 200, 207, 218, 243, 276, 284
Navajo, 121
near death experience, 212, 227-230
New Macho, 168-169
New World, 26, 30, 69, 86, 93, 97, 119, 145, 171, 182-184, 188, 216, 242-243, 256-257, 274-275, 277
Nicaea, 82
Nicene Creed, 185
nuclear testing, 133-137
nuclear waste, 131, 135-137, 194-195

O
Okanagon, 16
Occupy Activists, 241
Old Ways, 36, 77, 136
Oneida, 83
Onondaga, 83
open heart, 9, 75, 122-123
Our Lady of Guadalupe, 31, 40, 95, 284
owl medicine, 206

P
pagan, 30, 36, 78
patriarchal religions, 100-102, 282
Peacemaker, 83, 241
Pélé, 30
Petruzzi, Jim Graywolf, 254
pipe carrier, 23
Pleiades, 76, 93
Planetary Shifts, 239
plant spirit medicine, 16, 202
Poe, Edgar Allan, 167
Prakasha, Padma and Anaiya Aon, 175
prayer, 19, 21, 23, 34, 36, 41, 59, 63-64, 67, 70, 77, 79-80, 84-85, 92, 111-112, 116, 122, 146, 185, 189-190, 208, 210-211, 214, 234, 236, 246-247, 263, 268, 275
praying mantis, 202, 211
Precautionary Principle, 220
priestess, 24, 47, 102, 165, 188
Pritchard, Evan T, 202
psychic hotline, 70-71, 201, 207, 217
Punxsutawney Phil, 215, 217
Pyramids, 75

Q
Quantum Divine Love, 24, 33-38, 70, 178, 187, 195, 222, 243, 256, 260, 285
Queen Bee of Hearts, 223-231

R
Rainbow Bridge, 193, 226-227
Rainbow People, 239, 241
rape, 47, 74, 142-143, 164, 176, 240, 280
Ray, Shondra, 30, 31, 115
Red Road, 22, 254

reincarnation, 54-55, 56
revelations, 280
right action, 129-130
Rilke, Rainer Maria, 15
Robért, Dr. Karl Henrik, 219-220
Rock Your World with the Divine Mother, 30-32, 115
Rumi, 161
romantic love, 134

S

Sacred Circle, 47, 51-57, 97, 125, 159-160, 171, 184, 195, 221, 234, 268
Sacred Fire, 52, 107-112, 115, 116, 189-190, 239, 247
Sacred Love, 56, 122, 216, 222, 259, 262
Sams. Jamie, 202
Sangreal, 185
Sarasohn, Lisa, 175
self-esteem, 193-196
Seneca, 83
shadow (emotional), 7, 46, 70-72, 90, 127, 130, 143-144, 166, 170-171, 173, 189-197, 254, 285
shaman, 70, 207
sharks, 190
Sherpas, 67
Sin, 42, 82, 129-131, 173, 193-195
skin, Earth Mother's, 9, 27, 68, 134, 179, 192, 222
Sleepy (shadow), 196-197
smudge, 19, 211, 234, 275
snail medicine, 203
song, 7-8, 39-40, 72, 108-109, 116-117, 119, 121-122, 124, 126-127, 134-136, 146, 151, 185, 194-197, 211-213, 218-219, 247, 253, 263, 269-270

soul-wounded, 196-197
Spangler, David, 67, 68, 268
spirit body, 17-18, 84-86, 91, 117, 150, 202, 207, 209, 226-228, 253
spirit guide, 17, 23, 54, 166, 207-208, 252, 259, 274
spiritual warrior, 70-71, 167-169, 181-184, 241, 257
Spong, Bishop John, 85
Steindl-Rast, Brother David, 115
Stonehenge, 75
Seuss, Dr, 269
Suzuki, David, 217
suffering, 25, 40-41, 46, 67-68, 82, 98, 105, 126, 145, 159, 209-214, 227, 240, 256
surrender, 15-24, 28-29, 30, 39-44, 108, 113, 154, 161, 166, 182, 218, 243, 254, 258, 272, 277, 279, 280, 283-284

T

Tara, 56, 187
tarantulas, 190
Taylor, Susan, 189
technology, 62, 189-191, 266
The Secret, 64
Tibetan Buddhists, 56
TreePlace, 191
trolls, 67

U

Untie the Woman Within, 175

V

Vatican, 82, 96-98, 101-103, 185-187, 235
Vesotsky, Trudy, 139
Veterans, 143

Virgin Mary, 21, 30, 31, 33, 40,
    41-42, 95, 99, 121, 233-237,
    245-247, 283-284, 288
vision quests, 112, 214

W
Walk in Beauty, 121-128, 195, 285
waste, 9, 53, 136, 137, 221
water, 7, 23, 27, 34, 37, 38, 48, 52,
    54, 57, 62, 67-69, 71, 74, 77,
    86, 111, 135-137, 154, 171,
    177, 184, 194-195, 200, 203,
    207, 214, 217, 222, 227, 250,
    254, 265-268, 275, 283-284
water spirits, 67-69
wee people, 80
    see also fairy-folk
whales, 7, 8, 18, 19, 38, 42, 109,
    125, 135, 151-152, 190, 194,
    243, 247, 265-268
White Buffalo Calf Woman, 84
wilderness, 21-22, 116, 134, 204,
    254
Williamson, Marianne, 59
womb-wisdom, 99
Womb Wisdom (book), 175
Woman's Belly Book, The, 175
Women Who Run with the Wolves, 175
wolves, 190
wrong action, 129-131, 136, 195

Y
yoni, 236, 280-281, 282
Youngblood, Robin, 255

MARCIA WILEY

MARE CROMWELL is an international speaker, multi-award-winning author and nature mystic. In her early twenties, she was a park ranger at the bottom of the Grand Canyon and also Denali National Park. She also led environmental education programs on the Chesapeake Bay.

After receiving her Masters in Natural Resources at the University of Michigan in 1987, she worked internationally for five years co-leading an international environmental education network called the Global River Environmental Education Network (GREEN). The organization received numerous awards for its highly innovative programs.

In 1994, Mare left the international work to write and return to working out of doors. She created a sacred gardening company in Maryland and maintained private gardens while writing in the winter. On the side, she led environmental sustainability training programs and consulted with local watershed organizations in Maryland.

Mare has studied with Native American teachers for nineteen years and currently sits on the Seven Generations World Wisdom Council. She leads workshops on our Sacred Planet-Earth Mother, Womb Wisdom and Sacred Silliness and other topics. Mare also is the visionary behind the Great Mother Wisdom Gathering. She loves to be involved in Sacred Water Ceremonies. Mare is also a former worm herder. She calls Western Maryland home.

Personal Reflections, Dreams, Visions—Yours

CPSIA information can be obtained
at www.ICGtesting.com
Printed in the USA
BVHW031648050219
539537BV00001B/10/P